Women in the United States Armed Forces

Women in the United States Armed Forces

A Guide to the Issues

Darlene M. Iskra, CDR, USN (ret), PhD

Foreword by Vincent W. Patton III, MCPOCG (ret), EdD

Contemporary Military, Strategic, and Security Issues

PRAEGER

AN IMPRINT OF ABC-CLIO, LLC
Santa Barbara, California • Denver, Colorado • Oxford, England

2/3/11
Lan
 # 44.95

Library of Congress Cataloging-in-Publication Data
Iskra, Darlene M.
    Women in the United States armed forces : a guide to the issues / Darlene M. Iskra ;
foreword by Vincent W. Patton.
        p. cm. — (Contemporary military, strategic, and security issues)
    Includes bibliographical references and index.
    ISBN 978-0-313-37495-1 (print : alk. paper) — ISBN 978-0-313-37496-8 (ebook)
1. United States—Armed Forces—Women.   2. Women and the military—
United States.   I. Title.
    UB418.W65I85   2010
    355.0082'0973—dc22   2009046664

ISBN: 978-0-313-37495-1
EISBN: 978-0-313-37496-8

14   13   12   11   10   3   4   5

This book is also available on the World Wide Web as an eBook.
Visit www.abc-clio.com for details.

Praeger
An Imprint of ABC-CLIO, LLC

ABC-CLIO, LLC
130 Cremona Drive, P.O. Box 1911
Santa Barbara, California 93116-1911

This book is printed on acid-free paper ∞

Manufactured in the United States of America

To
my mom,
my most ardent supporter

Contents

Foreword

For 30 years I have had the privilege of serving in uniform in our nation's smallest military service, the U.S. Coast Guard. When I enlisted in 1972, there were only a handful of women serving as reservists on active duty; at the time, the Coast Guard did not allow women to serve in the regular Coast Guard. Over the span of my years of service I witnessed quite an evolution—women were fully admitted into the active duty segment in 1974. In 1977 women were authorized to serve in all capacities in the Coast Guard, and in 1979 LtJG Beverly Kelley was the first woman to command a Coast Guard cutter. She continued on to successfully command two other vessels throughout her illustrious 30-year career.

This evolution also included seeing my tiny service promote not just one but seven women to the rank of flag officer. One of them, my dear friend and mentor Vice Admiral Vivien Crea, became the first woman to attain the position as the senior-most flag officer in all five branches of the military when she was appointed the vice commandant of the Coast Guard.

The women I have met, known, and served with throughout my career in addition to VADM Crea and Captain Kelley are too numerous to mention, but I am proud to have among my mentors a significant number of women who, through their inspirational leadership and devotion to duty, have played a significant role in my own successful military career.

These significant and positive changes with women that occurred during my Coast Guard career are why I am excited and honored to introduce this book by my friend and colleague Commander Darlene Iskra, USN, (ret), PhD. A pioneer in her own right—her outstanding naval career includes being the first woman to command a U.S. Navy vessel—she is uniquely qualified to analyze the successes, challenges, and obstacles involved in making the acceptance of women in the military a norm rather than an anomaly. Changes in our military were made for the better—not just because of the acceptance of women into the ranks, but also to address the changes within the American culture and workforce that are dissolving the barriers of gender-specific occupations.

We are now reaching an era where it is not out of the ordinary to see senior-ranking and non-commissioned officers who just happen to be women. A review of how we got to this point is noteworthy and is well articulated through the six chapters of this book. When the terms soldiers, sailors, airmen, marines, and coast guardsmen are used, the visual image is no longer of five men smartly dressed in their uniforms. The valuable contributions of women in the military are indeed noteworthy. Women have not only earned a place of honor and respect among all Americans, but they are no longer a footnote in the history of women's service. They are exceptional, not the exception to the rule.

Vincent W. Patton III, EdD
The Eighth Master Chief Petty Officer
of the Coast Guard, Retired

Preface

Many books have been written about women in the military over the past 30-plus years, since the evolution of the All-Volunteer Force (AVF). So how is this one different? In agreeing to write this volume for the Contemporary Military, Strategic, and Security Issues series for Praeger Security International, I had to seriously consider the implications because I do not consider women in the military to be a problem issue. Women are in the military, and there they will remain. The main concern, from my standpoint, is that the full integration of women into the military has not yet been completed. There are policies and legislation that prohibit women from pursuing equivalent careers, and there are social issues that affect women more broadly than men. These combine to maintain the perception that women cannot perform their military duties to the same standard as men, and these policies and perceptions continue to hold women back from complete integration. It is a vicious circle.

My purpose in writing this book is to consolidate the discussion of the "issue of women in the military" into a concise, yet thorough, review of the history, policies, and current concerns about and for military women. My perspective may be considered biased, as I am a retired Navy officer who has advocated for women in the military from the beginning of my career. My voice had more credibility as I grew more senior and during my career peaked when I took command of a naval ship, the first woman in the U.S. Navy to do so. After my retirement in 2000, I started a graduate program in military sociology at the University of Maryland. I completed my PhD in December 2007, and the research and work I have done on the subject of women and the military provide me with a fuller understanding of the arguments both for and against the pursuit of women's full integration. By full integration, I mean the rescinding of policies that forbid women from serving in all areas of the military—including ground combat and submarines—and the acceptance of those expanded roles by all military leaders in the chain of command. It is generally thought that these two things must occur before women are fully integrated.

Women are not a homogeneous group, and neither are women in the military. Aside from the different cultures in the different service branches—the seagoing services of the Navy and the Coast Guard, the aviation focus of the Air Force, and the land-warfare missions of the Army and Marine Corps—women who join the military are distinct as a group, as members of one of the service branches, and as individuals. What they have in common with each other is their sense of adventure, their sense of duty, and their desire to perform to the best of their abilities. In these ways they are not unlike their male peers. What is different is their inability to reach the same pinnacles of power and success as the men. This occurs only because they are women.

This volume provides the reader with a historical overview and current policies and practices concerning women in the military. The first chapter provides the history of women's service from the American Revolution to 1990. It gives an overview of legislation and policies that authorized women to enter the military and the changes that occurred over most of the 20th century to expand their roles.[1]

The second chapter discusses the changes in policy and practice that have taken place since 1990. This chapter takes the reader through the Congressional hearings and legislative changes that allowed women to fly combat aircraft and be assigned as permanent ship's company on surface combatant ships. Current Department of Defense policy prohibits women from serving in direct ground combat units. We will see that this policy is based on an outdated concept of war and ground combat.

Chapter 3 discusses the issue of citizenship rights and responsibilities and the current restrictions on women's roles, specifically the ground combat exclusion policies, which affect the careers of women in the Army and Marine Corps. It also explores the arguments for women's registration for selective service and the expansion of their roles into ground combat positions. Although there is no desire to draft young people for military service, the inclusion of women in such a policy shift will become salient if a draft is enacted in the future.

Chapter 4 provides a look into the lives of many of our "sheros"—women who have, through their courage and commitment, made a difference in the wars and conflicts they have been involved in since the American Revolution. This chapter also includes a complete list of all women prisoner's of war (POWs), in addition to honoring the women who have earned combat awards for bravery and saving other's lives. These are stories we hear little about, and these women certainly have not been honored with monuments or ships named after them like so many of their male contemporaries.

Starting with Chapter 5, the book changes focus to discuss quality-of-life concerns that primarily affect women. Chapter 5 discusses gender discrimination, sexual harassment, and sexual assault. They continue to be experienced by many military women who have endured such treatment because they are minorities in a majority male environment, and to complain invites unfair repercussions. Although military leadership is starting to take a hard look at the fallout of ignoring this problem for so long, it will remain an issue as long as unit leaders are not held accountable for their inaction. Chapter 6 discusses the requirements of the military workplace and the conflict women (and to a growing extent men) face with regard to marriage and family formation. The arduous requirements of military service are sometimes seen as incompatible with marriage and family for women.

The Epilogue reiterates several issues that should be addressed for the future of women in the military. These include increasing family friendly policies, ending sexual harassment, and assigning qualified women to submarines and ground combat. With the ongoing conflicts in the Middle East, not assigning women to ground combat units precludes their full utilization; does not protect them from ground combat, injury, or death; and is inconsistent with our democratic ideals and values.

The Appendices add specific information on key legal decisions and legislation that affect women in the military, the articles of the Uniform Code of Military Justice that can be used to prosecute sexual harassment perpetrators, and a historical review of the few military ships that have been named for women. Also included are a chronology of historical events relating to military women and an annotated bibliography of selected books of further interest to readers and prospective scholars of military women's issues.

I would like to thank the many people who have helped bring me to this stage in my career, particularly Captain Lori Manning, USN (ret), for recommending me as a potential author for this volume, as well as Dr. Mady Wechsler Segal, my mentor and dissertation advisor, for her support as well as faith in my ability. I would like to thank my friends, particularly Katarzyna Skuratowicz, who kept me encouraged and motivated; Kimberly Bonner, who reviewed the chapter on sexual harassment; Rick Geissal, for reviewing and commenting on the entire volume; Alliance for National Defense (AND) Executive Vice President Sherry deVries, Lt. Col. USMCR (ret), and board member Col. Barbara Lee, USA (ret), who reviewed chapter 1, and the other members of the Board of Directors for AND—President Pat Gormley, Capt., JAG, USN (ret), President Emerita Pat Foote, BG, USA (ret), Capt. Georgia Sadler, USN (ret), Col. Mitzi Manning, USMC (ret), Lt. Stephanie Miller, USN, Lt. Col. Ruth Walsh, USMC (ret), and webmaster Jared Cameron. They helped me focus on the issues that still need to be resolved for military women. I would like to thank retired Master Chief Petty Officer of the Coast Guard Vince Patton— an avid supporter of women in the military, a prior member of AND's board, and currently a member of its National Advisory Council—for his friendship and his support in writing the Foreword. Last, but certainly most important, I would like to thank my family members, numerous as they are, for their support and their inability to verbalize the sentence, "What has Darlene done *now?*" when I tell them of some new project or honor I have received. I know they are proud to have me as their daughter, sister, niece, cousin, aunt, and friend, and I truly depend on that knowledge. Thanks!

Note

1. This has been thoroughly researched and documented in 544 pages by Maj. Gen. Jeanne Holm, USAF (ret), in her book *Women in the Military: An Unfinished Revolution*, rev. ed. (Novato, CA: Presidio Press, 1992).

Abbreviations

AAF	Army Air Forces
AE	Auxiliary Explosives, supply ship
AEF	American Expeditionary Force
AEG	Air Expeditionary Group
AFNC	Air Force Nurse Corps
AFS	Auxiliary Food Stores ship
ANC	Army Nurse Corps
AND	Alliance for National Defense
AO	Auxiliary Oiler, supply ship
AOE	Auxiliary Oiler and Ammunition/Explosives supply ship
AOR	Area of Responsibility
ASVAB	Armed Services Vocational Aptitude Battery
ATC	Air Transport Command
AVF	All-Volunteer Force
BAQ	Basic Allowance for Quarters
BG	Brigadier general
CAB	Combat Action Badge
CAPT	Captain
CDR	Commander
CIB	Combat Infantryman Badge
CMB	Combat Medical Badge
CMW	Combat, masculine-warrior
CNO	Chief of naval operations
CNP	Chief of naval personnel
CO	Commanding officer
COL	Colonel
DACOWITS	Defense Department Advisory Committee on Women in the Services
DCPC	Direct Combat Probability Coding
DD	Destroyer
DDG	Guided Missile Destroyer

DoD	Department of Defense
DON	Department of the Navy
DOPMA	Defense Officer Personnel Management Act
DFC	Distinguished Flying Cross
DSC	Distinguished Service Cross
EIB	Expert Infantryman Badge
EOD	Explosive ordnance disposal
ERA	Equal Rights Amendment
FMLA	Family and Medical Leave Act
FY	Fiscal year
GAO	General Accounting Office
GFO	General/flag officer
HR	House of Representatives bill
IAVA	Iraq and Afghanistan Veterans of America
IG	Inspector general
JAG	Judge advocate general
JCS	Joint chiefs of staff
LCC	Amphibious Command ship
LCDR	Lieutenant commander
Lt	Lieutenant
Lt Col	Lieutenant colonel
MCM	Mine counter measures ship
MCPON	Master Chief Petty Office of the Navy
MEU	Marine Expeditionary Unit
MHC	Coastal mine hunters
MSC	Military sealift command
NAS	Naval Air Station
NASA	National Aeronautics and Space Administration
NC	Nurse Corps (Navy)
NFO	Naval flight officer
NIS	Naval Investigative Service
NOW	National Organization for Women
OCS	Officer Candidate School
OEF	Operation Enduring Freedom (Afghanistan)
OIF	Operation Iraqi Freedom
OJT	On-the-job training
OSS	Office of Strategic Services
PC	Coastal patrol craft
PFC	Private first class
PL	Public law
POW	Prisoner of war
PTSD	Posttraumatic stress disorder
RADM	Rear admiral
RDML	Rear admiral, lower half
ROTC	Reserve Officer Training Corps

SAPRO	Sexual Assault Prevention and Response Office
SECDEF	Secretary of defense
SECNAV	Secretary of the navy
SOFA	Status of Forces Agreement
SPAR	Semper Paratus, Always Ready
SSBN	Ballistic Submarine, Nuclear
SSN	Attack Submarine, Nuclear
SWO	Surface warfare officer
TD	Temporary duty
UCMJ	Uniform Code of Military Justice
USA	United States Army
USAF	United States Air Force
USAFR	United States Air Force Reserve
USAHS	United States Army Hospital Ship
USAR	United States Army Reserve
USC	United States Code
USCG	United States Coast Guard
USCGC	United States Coast Guard Cutter
USMC	United States Marine Corps
USMCR	United States Marine Corps Reserve
USN	United States Navy
USNR	United States Navy Reserve
USS	United States Ship
VA	Veteran's Administration
VADM	Vice admiral
WAAC	Women's Army Auxiliary Corps
WAC	Women's Army Corps
WAF	Women in the Air Force
WAFS	Women's Auxiliary Ferrying Squadron
WASP	Women Airforce Service Pilots
WAVES	Women Accepted for Voluntary Emergency Service (Navy)
WIMSA	Women in Military Service for America
WWI	World War I
WWII	World War II
YMCA	Young Men's Christian Association
YT	Yard Tug

CHAPTER 1

Historical Overview through 1990

The military is not commonly perceived as a career women would voluntarily pursue. However, women have voluntarily served in all of America's wars since the beginning of our history. Today, military women have opportunities that 30 years ago were not possible, such as participating in and commanding troops in a combat zone.[1] The demands of a military career—including long hours, geographic relocation, separation from loved ones, and participating in military conflicts with the real possibility of death or injury—are not seen as conducive to the social expectation of women as family caregivers. Yet some women have been able to maintain a fulfilling personal life and still thrive in a military career.

Being a woman in the military is challenging for many reasons. Historically, the male warrior model has defined the military. The "cult of masculinity" inherent in the military defines the warrior as a man of power, exploits, and heterosexual virility.[2] Those who do not fit into this ideal are considered inferior and without value. As a result, women historically could only participate as support personnel aiding in the mission of war—primarily as nurses, but also as cooks, laundresses, and other ancillary personnel. However, as civil society changed, the military was forced to change as well, allowing women to serve in the regular military forces, starting in World War II (WWII), but especially after the start of the All-Volunteer Force (AVF). As women integrated into many new roles, military leaders found they had different issues to face. Because many of these issues revolved around sex and sexuality, privacy, close physical spaces, and physical capability, these issues became labeled "problems with women."[3]

The number of women in the military has dramatically increased in the last 60 years, from less than 2 percent to about 15 percent of the total force. Women have expanded their roles and responsibility, they have risen in rank, and some have had combat experience. Due to Department of Defense (DoD) policies, there are still some constraints on women's careers, such as the current policy prohibiting their assignment to certain combat occupations, excluding them from jobs with the greatest career opportunities. Some military men still perceive women as "inherently less capable, physically and mentally, to perform a military job and lead troops,"[4] which may lead to situations where women have to prove themselves many times over, causing frustration, resentment, and higher attrition rates.

There is also the ongoing issue of gender harassment, which creates an uncomfortable working environment for women, reduces the morale of both women and men, and affects the long-term retention of qualified personnel. The flip side of this is the fear among male superiors and peers of not being able to refute unwarranted charges of sexual harassment, which affects the interactions between men and women and may lead to difficulties in forming peer and mentor relationships.[5] Any or all of these structural and interpersonal variables could lead women to conclude it is not worthwhile to invest in a military career. This may also be the reason why the ratio of women to men in the military has not changed significantly since the new millennium.

A Short Historical Perspective

The military has always been perceived as a man's world.[6] History extols the virtues of the military officer, the battle hero, the defender of the home. War has been the impetus for boys to become men, and when war is lacking, other venues for that significant rites of passage were created, such as the Boy Scouts.[7] The "Myth of the War Experience"[8] provides little information about the support system that made it all happen: the women. Women not only birthed the boys who eventually grew up and went off to war, but women also provided the symbolic ideal of home for which the soldier fought. As Linda Grant DePauw explains, "In a traditional war story the male heroes do the fighting and embody the martial virtues. Their reward for suffering hardship and risking their lives is woman's love, including, in addition to sex, all the admiration, compassion, and provision of creature comforts that are associated with the image of wife and mother. Focusing on women in any other role spoils the story."[9] Because war was considered men's work, and the men who performed that work (with the exception of the officers leading them) were considered to be mean, tough, and socially unacceptable, the thought of women voluntarily joining such a group was scandalous. Yet women have always been where armies bivouac.

Women's roles in the American military began informally. Until enlisting in the military required a complete physical around the time of World War I (WWI), many women served as soldiers by disguising themselves as men. Their gender was only known when they were killed or wounded. If discovered, they would be discharged. Women also worked as spies, scouts, or couriers, as well as camp followers. Camp followers were so named because they performed logistical duties needed to support military personnel, such as laundry, cooking, nursing the sick and wounded, burying the dead, and so forth, so the men could concentrate on fighting. Many of these camp followers were wives, mothers, widows, sweethearts, or daughters of the soldiers. Historical sources called them prostitutes because they slept with their men. But this also could be because they earned money from selling their services (as cooks, laundresses, seamstresses, etc.) to men with no female support system.[10]

During the American Revolution, as a result of men going off to fight the British, women organized for self-defense. They fought against Indians and Loyalists, defending their homes and children by using ad hoc weapons such as hatchets, shovels, or pots of boiling lye to blind their enemies. One woman, Ann Bailey, received pay from the army for work as a scout and courier, but the Indians called her "Mad Ann Bailey" due to her ferocity in fighting.[11]

During the Crimean War (1853–1856), with Great Britain, France, Turkey, and Sardinia fighting against the Russians, women and military nursing became forever linked. Nursing was considered the domain of women, a role emanating from their responsibilities as family caregivers. The camp followers learned via on-the-job training and had no status to change the filthy conditions of camp. The lack of hygiene and the presence of disease and wounds were more than an uneducated camp follower could manage. As a result, formally trained nurses were sent to the front for the first time, where their social status above the average soldier and his wife allowed them to crusade for cleanliness, good food for soldiers, and other preventative medicine techniques.[12]

In the United States, the Civil War was the impetus for the first women to be formally accepted for wartime service. In 1861, the Union army established a civilian nursing corps under the direction of Dorothea Dix. Clara Barton, the founder of the American Red Cross, was probably the most famous Civil War nurse, but she chose not to serve under the auspices of the military. She nursed independently, avoiding military bureaucracy and going where she felt she was needed the most. She never received any pay or official recognition for her work, but she insisted that there were "hundreds of women like her at the front." Clara Barton is also credited with the statement, "[If war] seemed rough and unseemly for a *woman*, it should be remembered that combat was equally rough and unseemly for *men*."[13]

The Formal Entry of Women into the Military

Thus, it is no surprise that the first women formally brought into the military in the early part of the 20th century were nurses in the Army (1901) and Navy (1908). They were not equal to other military personnel. The Army and Navy nurse corps were separate from the regular forces, with their own rank structure, personnel policies, and pay scales. Nurses were neither officers nor enlisted, leaving them in limbo in an organization that valued status and hierarchy and relied on that hierarchy to maintain order and discipline. As a result, nurses had no status to even direct the enlisted Army medics or Navy corpsmen who worked with them, many of whom were hostile and refused to follow their instructions.[14]

The lack of military rank caused many problems for the nurses. During WWI, nurses suffered many "indignities," a term we would now call harassment, mostly at the hand of officers. These included discourteous treatment and the inability to defend themselves against superiors, particularly when a nurse rebuked an officer's advances. Providing rank for nurses was thought to be a solution to the problem, and after the war, discharged nurses willingly shared their tales of hardship and harassment in order to help and protect current and future military nurses.[15]

However, the concept that nurses could be equal in rank to military men was such an anathema to acceptable roles for women that a compromise was reached. The Army Nurse Corps (ANC) was awarded "relative rank" in 1920. This at least placed them in a situational hierarchy that allowed them many of the same rights and privileges of military officers. However, this legislation did not apply to Navy nurses, who continued their non-status until 1942, when legislation was being considered for the authorization of military women other than nurses to join the Army, Navy, and Marine Corps. The Army-Navy Nurse Act of 1947 (PL 36) established a permanent nurse corps in both the Army and the Navy, authorized a Women's Medical Specialist Corps in the Army, and provided identical rank, pay, and allowances to those received by other commissioned officers. Nurses were officially and finally military officers.[16]

WWI also saw other women employed in the service of our country. The Department of the Navy was the first to employ enlisted women as Yeoman (F) and Women Marines. They filled clerical jobs in order to free the men in those billets to fight. Of course, this did not endear the women to men who had thought they would spend the war behind a desk but soon found themselves on the front lines. Many think policies of this type contribute to the resentment of military women, which continues to be displayed as harassment toward them.[17]

Other women outside of the formal military establishment also served during WWI. Civilian women worked for the Army Signal Corps, and were affectionately known as "The Hello Girls." General John Pershing himself requested 100 American French-speaking telephone switchboard operators to operate Army communication networks. Telephone operators at this time were highly skilled, and also predominately female. They also served as interpreters. Eventually 223 women were employed in this capacity.

Reconstruction Aides were used to help prepare wounded veterans for work outside of the service. Their talents included physical and occupational therapy as well as educational and vocation program evaluation. The YMCA sent women volunteers to work during the civil war and the Spanish-American War as well as WWI to provide venues for the benefit of soldiers. Thus, they established tents for social activities, reading materials and stationery, ministering to the needs of prisoners of war, as well as providing a respite from Army food by establishing canteens that served donuts, hot chocolate, and other remembrances of home.

The Red Cross sent volunteers primarily to serve as nurses alongside Army and Navy nurses. During wartime, nurses are always in short supply, and the military was thankful for all the women who served. Of course, the Red Cross also was involved in other relief requirements, including providing so-called care packages to the troops as well as delivering letters to and from POWs. The Salvation Army also sent women, who helped with all phases of humanitarian work, including the establishment of canteens, recreation and meeting rooms, libraries, and religious services.[18]

During WWII, women's roles expanded even further. They performed in every possible position except those involved in actual ground, sea, or air combat. After the war, all the services except the Marine Corps felt that women enhanced the services' mission even in peacetime. Thus, in 1948 women were given permanent status in the military via the Armed Services Integration Act of 1948.[19]

Women's Armed Service Integration Act of 1948 (PL 80-625)

WWII was a watershed event for women in the labor force. Prior to the war, it was common for white middle-class women to work until they got married, when they would give up the single life for the middle-class American dream: "The male breadwinner who supported his family and the female homemaker who cared for his domestic needs."[20] Regardless of ethnic background or class, women were segregated into occupational roles that were low paying and had few benefits and few, if any, promotion opportunities. Poor women who worked to supplement the family income were relegated to menial jobs. Women's occupations at that time were limited to clerical work, nursing, and teaching, in addition to low- or unskilled work in factories such as textile mills, in rural agriculture, or as domestics. A small number of women, primarily college graduates, chose career over marriage as a lifelong vocation, and were funneled into teaching and nursing jobs. But the most accepted roles for middle-class white women were those of wife and mother. The pervasive attitude was that if a woman worked, she did it for extra money rather than necessity. The high-paying, high-status jobs went to men, whether or not they supported a family.[21]

In her study of women, work, and WWII, Sherna Gluck states, "Urban women in the 1940s were accustomed to their work being devalued—be it in the home or in the marketplace. During the war, for the first time in their lives, many women performed jobs that were viewed by the public as necessary and valuable, and that were often physically challenging. Finally valued by others, they came to value themselves more."[22]

Poor women, especially full-time workers in low-paying jobs before the war, eagerly shifted to the more lucrative jobs left by men who joined the military. The military, however, was still considered a male-only occupation. Manpower shortages and the worldwide necessity for fighting men dictated changes in both the civilian work force and the military institution. The government's goal was to use women as temporary workers, both in factories and in the military. In order to entice women into these new roles, recruiting efforts emphasized heroic service to one's nation, self-sacrifice, and putting the welfare of soldiers ahead of one's own desires. The government made erroneous assumptions that women would take war jobs out of patriotic duty, not because they would benefit from them personally, and that these jobs would be filled by housewives, not women already in the work force. Both of these assumptions proved to be false.[23]

Women in the military during WWII were originally envisioned as temporary workers who would be assigned to take over clerical and administrative work and free those men for combat. Soon, however, women were driving trucks, digging ditches, working on machinery, teaching navigation, and flying airplanes. Women were doing any and all jobs that did not involve direct combat. Although they taught men how to fly airplanes, they were not assigned to operational aircraft or sea squadrons. And they did not just serve in the continental United States. Many also served at or near the front in Europe and in the Pacific theater of operations. The reasons given for the exclusion from combat were social expectations and the supposed need for men to protect women and keep them safe from the horrors of war.[24]

However, not being assigned to combatant positions did not protect women from death, injury, or other horrors of war. By virtue of their job requirements, military nurses had always served at or near the front to care for and help triage the wounded. After the fall of the Philippines in 1942, 66 Army nurses and 15 Navy nurses were captured and imprisoned by the Japanese and remained prisoners of war (POWs) for the remainder of the war. Additionally, 565 women in the Women's Army Corps (WAC) stationed in the Pacific theater received combat decorations. Women in all the services distinguished themselves and proved that women had the courage, strength, and stamina to perform in a combat environment.[25]

WWII was a classic example of why the participation of women increased in the military—a national emergency and shifts in demographic patterns where there were not enough men to meet military personnel requirements. The needs of the military have a tendency to override current social norms and lead to using women and minorities as a reserve force. Once the crisis is over, there is a desire to return to "the way things were."[26] During WWII, the unprecedented military mobilization of men required that women, both on the home front and in the military, take over those vacated jobs. After the war, women were forced out of the workplace or back into lower paying women's work both in the civilian sector and the military. This was accomplished through a concerted campaign, via the media, to portray women war workers as willingly leaving the labor force to return to their rightful roles as homemakers, nurses, clerical workers, or teachers. The reconversion period occurred from August 1945 to March 1946, at which time the proportion of females in male jobs declined to approximately prewar levels. For many women, particularly minorities and immigrants who enjoyed the higher wages of men's work, this forced transition was not welcome.[27]

Some leaders within the armed forces, most notably General Dwight D. Eisenhower (USA), were convinced there was a permanent place for women in the services, and eventually Congress was persuaded that keeping women in administrative roles would contribute to, not degrade, military effectiveness and would provide a framework for mobilization in the event of another national emergency. Although women had served admirably in many occupational roles during the war, the final legislation (PL 80-625, Women's Armed Forces Integration Act of 1948) allowed women as permanent members of the armed forces but severely limited their occupational roles and opportunities, similar to the restrictions legislatively imposed on nurses the previous year.[28]

There were many higher, and double, standards for women vis-à-vis men who joined the military. For example, a woman could not enlist if she was under the age of 21 without the written consent of her parents,[29] and enlisted women were limited to 2 percent of the total authorized enlisted force. Women officers were limited to 10 percent of the authorized number of enlisted women and could not have a permanent commission above the grade of commander/lieutenant colonel (O-5), nor could they supervise men. This legislation included provisions that prohibited women from serving on any naval vessel except hospital ships and naval transports, and they could not be assigned to aircraft that would likely engage in combat missions.[30] For more than 25 years, these provisions were interpreted to exclude women from serving as crew in *any* ship or aircraft.

The higher standards for recruiting women were insisted upon by the women's service directors in order to maintain the prestige of the program in the eyes of the public and ensure acceptance of the women by men. There were policy disparities as well. Women could opt out of their service contracts if they married, which served to foster increased attrition of first-term women enlistees as high as 80 percent. Additionally, by DoD regulation, women were forced out of the military if they became pregnant or even if they married someone with children, as the military paradigm was that the social role of women was as primary caregiver. If an unmarried woman became pregnant, she would receive a punitive discharge and little to no support for her prenatal care. No such discharge was given for the men who impregnated them. Still, women were authorized "all provisions of law relating to pay, leave, money allowances for subsistence and rental of quarters, mileage and other travel allowances, or other allowances, benefits, or emoluments, of male personnel,"[31] which, for the era, was unusual.

Although women remained members of the military, social expectations defined what occupational *and* family roles women performed. Since women could not be assigned to ships, aircraft, or other *military* roles, their career paths differed from their male counterparts, and their promotion opportunities were severely limited. Unlike their WWII counterparts, by the mid-1960s women in all the services were excluded from the occupations considered mainstream by the military. Women were occupationally segregated into administrative or medical fields considered women's jobs by current social standards. The continuance of the draft ensured an adequate supply of men for the military, and the higher attrition of women was just considered the cost of doing business, as women's obligations as wives and mothers superseded all other responsibilities. Thus, the women's programs limped along during the 1950s and 1960s until the start of the major combat operations of the Vietnam War. Once again, a national emergency raised the desire and need for military women, particularly nurses.[32]

The Defense Department Advisory Committee on Women in the Services (DACOWITS)

The DACOWITS was established in 1951, composed of civilian women and men appointed by the Secretary of Defense (SECDEF) to provide advice and recommendations on matters and policies relating to the recruitment and retention, treatment, employment, integration, and well-being of highly qualified professional women in the Armed Forces.[33] The original committee consisted of 50 prominent women, such as former WWII women directors, prominent academicians, and other professionals from business, law, the arts, and politics. Their first major task was to recruit women for the Korean War, a task that ultimately failed miserably. There were fewer draft-eligible men, and women were not flocking to the services as expected, so DoD became concerned about their ability to meet recruiting goals for women volunteers. Assistant Secretary of Defense for Manpower Anna Rosenberg convinced Secretary of Defense George Marshall that a committee of committed volunteers could help, individually and collectively, to accomplish the following:

1. Inform the public of recruiting needs
2. Reassure parents of their daughter's well-being and security as a military member
3. Provide information to young women of the career opportunities in the services
4. Raise the prestige of military women in the public mind[34]

DACOWITS studied and made recommendations to the SECDEF about issues pertaining to women and family as well as quality-of-life issues that affected all members of the military. For example, in their fall 1968 report, 4 of the 29 recommendations concerned quality of life issues that affected both male and female members:

10. Off-Base Living

DACOWITS recommends that personnel of the rate of E-5 and above be given the option to live off-base and receive BAQ when this would not conflict with the military mission even though quarters are adequate and available.

22. Living Space

DACOWITS recommends in the review of the matter of minimum net living area, DACOWITS found 72 sq. ft. for grades E-6 and below to be inadequate. Therefore, it is recommended that this net minimum area be substantially increased.

23. Bachelor Living Quarters

DACOWITS recommends that Bachelor living quarters configuration allocation for permanent party grades E-6 and below be based on no more than two occupants to a room.

24. Bachelor Living Quarters

DACOWITS recommends Bachelor living quarters accepted for Beneficial Occupancy on or after 1 January 1958 be re-rated to conform to revised standards. For example, two occupants to a room and net minimum area changes as DACOWITS recommended above.

In this same report, there were 5 recommendations regarding equality of treatment for married women members of the uniformed services. This was well before policies finally changed in the 1970s after military women filed class actions suits against the government for discrimination. DACOWITS in the 1950s and 1960s was not the strong advocate for women that it became in the 1970s.[35]

DACOWITS became a powerful force and voice for military women especially after conscription ended in the 1970s. During the initial years of the

AVF, DACOWITS served as the voice of reason for the integration of larger numbers of women into the military. No longer were women satisfied with just fitting in. They wanted and needed career options that were challenging and provided opportunities for advancement and promotion. The 1970s were an era of women's liberation and demands for increased equality and inclusion in public life. Opportunities were opening for women to attend schools they had previously been excluded from, like Harvard University and other ivy-league schools. They were entering the professions as lawyers and doctors, even clergy. In the 1970s, with the passage of the Equal Rights Amendment (ERA) in Congress and the military facing personnel shortages due to the unpopularity of the Vietnam War, women entered the military because of increased opportunities due to the reduced numbers of men willing to join. Because the military needed women to fill their personnel needs, it also had to confront the obstacles to women's equality that were ubiquitous during the era of conscription. DACOWITS was there to ensure the military understood those obstacles, and it also made recommendations to overcome them.[36]

During this time, DACOWITS was able to set their own agendas and make unannounced visits to military installations to observe firsthand how military women were treated. This allowed them to observe whether policies were being adhered to or if local commanders allowed procedures that discriminated against women. Their autonomy helped tremendously in improving the status and treatment of women in the military. If DACOWITS questioned a discriminatory policy or seemingly unfair treatment, the commander better have a viable explanation for it.

The status and impetus of DACOWITS changed in 2002 when the charter was revised. It reduced DACOWITS's autonomy, allowing only those issues to be studied that were approved by SECDEF. Additionally, while it regularly had addressed both women's concerns and overall quality-of-life issues for all service members, the new charter remanded DACOWITS to provide advice and recommendations only on family issues related to the recruitment and retention of a highly qualified professional military. The charter now calls for 15 members, men or women, with a chair appointed by the president.[37] It remains to be seen if the committee can regain some of its previous clout in addressing both quality-of-life issues as well as operational use of personnel. Regardless of its future, DACOWITS's recommendations have been historically instrumental in effecting changes to laws and policies pertaining to military women.

The All-Volunteer Force

The limitations on women's military service legislated in 1948 remained until the women's movement of the late 1960s and early 1970s empowered women to push for greater equality. The status of military women had deteriorated to the point they were not considered much more than a "ladies' auxiliary."[38] This period in history is interesting because women in the military were truly a forgotten entity, stuck in a 1950s model while women in civil society were clamoring for equality in citizenship rights, occupational roles, and personal status. In the 1960s, the restrictions on women's numbers and rank were lifted, offering them the opportunity to compete for the highest ranks in the military as general and flag officers.[39]

Several court cases in the mid-to-late 1970s gave women many of the same rights as men for dependent benefits, career continuation without regard for motherhood status, and the opportunity to serve at sea on noncombatant ships and as aviators (crew as well as pilots) on noncombatant aircraft. In 1975, President Gerald Ford signed into law a provision allowing women to enter the federal service academies. The law was vigorously opposed by the military, which argued that the academies should be limited to men due to the academies' mission of training career combat officers.[40] Nevertheless, over these objections, the women of the class of 1980 entered the academies in July 1976.

The change to an AVF also required the military to compete for, and recruit, qualified personnel from the same labor market as the civilian sector. With demographic reductions in the number of available 18- to-24-year-old white men, the military became increasingly dependent on male minorities and the untapped pool of women, particularly minorities, to make the AVF succeed.[41] For example, when the draft ended in 1973, women comprised only 1.6 percent of the force. At the end of fiscal year (FY) 1980, this number had risen to 8.4 percent. It currently stands at 15.1% for women officers and 14.2% for enlisted women. Minority women make up a large part of the female force—35.3% of women officers and 52.8% of enlisted women.[42] This increase in the number of women made it difficult for the military services to effectively utilize them, particularly in the Navy and Air Force due to the legal restrictions against women on ships or combat aircraft.

Women at Sea

Since men of sufficient quality and quantity were not enlisting after the end of the draft, by the end of the 1970s the Navy was having trouble manning its ships. The Navy judge advocate general (JAG) had interpreted the prohibition against assigning women to ships (other than hospital ships and transports) literally, even prohibiting assignments of short duration. If a Navy vessel was at sea, a Navy woman could not be on that vessel—not even temporarily to deliver parts or be transported by sea from one duty station to another.[43] Ironically, civilian, Army, and Air Force women could be temporarily assigned to do maintenance or other work on the ship. In 1977, in a unilateral decision without regard for the Navy's views on the subject of women at sea or in aviation, the Coast

Guard opened all of its positions to women. This was clearly a decision made after carefully reviewing the requirements and coming to the conclusion that women could do these jobs as well as men. The Coast Guard, as a much smaller naval service, could not afford to have a dual career path for women and men without sacrificing effectiveness.[44]

In the Navy, the first chink in the armor of prohibition occurred in 1972, when then Chief of Naval Operations (CNO) Admiral Elmo Zumwalt authorized a pilot program for women at sea in which women were assigned to the crew of the United States Ship (USS) *Sanctuary*, a hospital ship. Nurses assigned to hospital ships in the wards were not unusual, but this was the first time that non-nurse women were part of the ship's crew.[45] The pilot program was successful and proved women could successfully perform arduous sea duty, previously regarded as men's work. It also revealed the negative impact the legal prohibition against going to sea had on women's naval careers. In 1976, six women filed a class-action suit in federal court claiming the prohibition in Section 6015 of U.S. Code (USC) Title 10 was unconstitutional.[46]

On July 28, 1978, Judge John Sirica ruled that Section 6015 unconstitutionally denied women their right to the "equal protection guarantee embodied in due process clause of Fifth Amendment." As stated in the decision, "The core protection afforded by the equal protection component of the Fifth Amendment is that laws favoring members of one gender and disadvantaging members of the other be reasonably and, beyond that, substantially related to the achievement of some important objective."[47] Thus, the Navy had a mandate to utilize women at sea, and a precedent was set for opening new opportunities in the future.

The lawsuit, the increase in the numbers of navy women, and personnel shortages on ships became overarching reasons for the expansion of women's roles. Although Section 6015 was deemed unconstitutional, Judge Sirica's ruling did not automatically overturn that section of the law. The law would need to be changed. In the late 1970s, the Navy submitted legislation to Congress asking to amend the law that restricted women from ships so it could have the flexibility to assign women to noncombatant ships. This would allow the Navy to back-fill noncombatant ships with women, freeing more men to serve on combatant ships.

The House Armed Services Committee (HASC) began hearing testimony about expanded roles for women in July 1977 and they continued through 1978. In a written statement by then CNO Admiral James Watkins, the Navy endorsed the proposed change to the law for the following reasons:

> The need to "maximize (its) readiness through more efficient use of both manpower and womanpower"

The "decline of the male population eligible for military service in the 80's [*sic*] and beyond has increased the urgency of efforts" to improve the utilization of women

An "increased recognition by our society, including our armed services, of the obligation to provide greater opportunities for women to enjoy full and rewarding careers in the service of their country"

The requirement to provide young women at the Naval Academy the same training and opportunities (at sea) as their male counterparts

The "archaic provision" that Navy women cannot go aboard a ship to make repairs, for training or even transport, yet civilian, Army, or Air Force women can.[48]

The Navy testified that this change would allow them to use their womanpower to meet the needs of the Navy more efficiently, thus resulting in greater combat readiness. The Navy did not, however, push for the total repeal of the exclusionary parts of the law. Women would still be prohibited from serving on combatant ships. The Navy did push to allow women to be temporarily assigned on combat ships not expected to be involved in combat missions because it gave the Navy more flexibility in assigning women, especially midshipmen, to sea for training and other purposes. The types of ships to which women would be assigned were "tenders, repair ships, auxiliaries and support ships." The manning goal would be a "minimum ratio of 1:3 women to men (25%), with a maximum goal of 1:1 (50%)."[49]

On Tuesday, March 21, 1978, the Chairman of the Military Personnel Subcommittee of the HASC, the Honorable Richard C. White, convened a hearing on HR 7431, "a bill which would permit increased flexibility in the utilization of women aboard naval vessels." Although the DoD wanted a complete repeal of the section, Chairman White made it clear that since the hearing was being held pursuant to the Defense Authorization Bill, he wanted the bill to be passed quickly and therefore would not undertake any consideration on the issue of women in combat. He stated, "Manpower management issues are . . . appropriate for consideration at this time. The issue of using women in combat has broader implications, and . . . it is not a subject which can be effectively addressed during these authorization proceedings."[50] Thus, the total repeal of Section 6015 of Title 10, USC, was tabled for another 15 years.

In addressing the issue of women in combat on ships, Secretary of the Navy Graham Claytor indicated he was worried about "discipline and operation of a ship, particularly a small ship, under wartime conditions, with no liberty, no opportunity for recreation, to get ashore, crowded together in very small places. . . . I just think that sex is sex, and when they're put together for that long, under those kind of conditions, you're going to have trouble."[51] He later stated, "We would not have women on the destroyers, but we would have women on the transports. They're at hazard, but we cannot avoid hazard. What we're trying to do is avoid having them as a part of the combat team."[52]

The Administration, HASC, and naval leaders were concerned that this change would open the door to women in combat, and they consistently opposed that outcome. The safety of women in a combat zone was not the issue so much as concern about the *idea* of women in combat. At that point in time the idea was unpalatable, even though combat on a Navy vessel in hostile waters only involved engaging an enemy at great distance, which had not happened since the Vietnam War. Nevertheless, the focus, as always, was on the Navy's needs.

Bills were introduced in the House and Senate the summer of 1978 which eventually became Public Law 95-485. On October 20, 1978, in the DoD Appropriation Authorization Act of 1979, Section 808 amended Title 10, section 6015, to read:

> However, women may not be assigned to duty on vessels or in aircraft that are engaged in combat missions nor may they be assigned to other than temporary duty on vessels of the Navy except hospital ships, transports, and vessels of a similar classification not expected to be assigned combat missions.[53]

In late 1978, the Navy began assigning women as permanent members of ships' crews on tenders and repair ships, large ships that supposedly were almost always in port. Women could be temporarily assigned to combatants for training purposes only. Enlisted women were assigned to ships involuntarily based on their occupational specialty and the size of the enlisted women's berthing compartment. Officers, because of the smaller number of available billets at sea, plus their additional training requirements, had to compete for the few slots that were available. The women officers assigned to sea duty on tenders were thus the cream of the crop, as opposed to the male officers who were either staff officers, such as supply or medical, or were line officers who were at the bottom of their training classes. In their book on the history of women in the Navy, Jean Ebbert and Mary-Beth Hall stated:

> This . . . required the Navy to change three things: the ships themselves, to accommodate women; women's training; and women's career paths. In addition, Navy leaders would have to make every effort to gain men's acceptance of the new reality, and they would have to decide how to deal with pregnant sailors aboard ships. Women also faced change. The opportunity to serve in ships would allow them to expand their range of professional skills and, in the case of female officers aspiring to a seagoing career, prepare themselves for the Navy's sternest professional challenge, command of a ship. They would also have to accept radical changes in their per-

sonal lives, for now they would face what Navy men had always endured—
long periods of duty at sea that separated them from family and friends.[54]

Unfortunately, the Navy had not thought through the career aspects of only
assigning women officers to one class of vessel. By the early 1980s, a number of
officers had completed their initial sea tours and then found their careers stag-
nant. The tenders they had been assigned to as junior officers held no other job
opportunities until much later in a military career. Division officers were usually
ensigns, lieutenants (junior grade), and lieutenants, while department heads
were usually officers ranked as commanders. The women would not be eligible to continue their career progression due to the lack of available follow-
on and increasingly responsible jobs at sea.

This shortsightedness almost caused the program to fail, as women officers
became frustrated and either transferred to another naval community that offered a viable career path or left the service. A program that thought only of
the needs of the Navy soon found that the Navy's needs could not be met without a way for women to sustain a career at sea. As a result, by the mid-1980s, the
Navy had redesignated several ship classes as noncombatants, and though still
limited, this at least provided a viable career path to command for women sea-
going officers.

Women in Aviation

It appears utterly nonsensical, from our contemporary viewpoint, why the
military insisted women would not be able to cope with the hazards of flying
military aircraft when women aviators took to the skies as readily as men during the 1920s and 1930s. Military leaders conveniently forgot the daring feats
of women like Amelia Earhart, Jacqueline Cochran, Nancy Harkness Love, and
Beryl Markham, who flew, broke aviation records, and made history prior to
WWII. There were two basic rationales for excluding women—the multitude
of qualified men, and the ideology that women could not fly in combat. Also
conveniently forgotten was the fact that women did fly combatant aircraft for
the military during WWII but in a civilian capacity, and not in actual combat.

As early as 1941, Jackie Cochran had petitioned General Hap Arnold, the
Commanding General of the Army Air Forces (AAF), to bring women into the
war as ferrying pilots. General Arnold was unsure of the need, though he apparently promised Cochran the job if it came to fruition. Simultaneously, the Air
Transport Command (ATC) was in dire need of pilots, and began considering
the use of women. The name of Nancy Harkness Love, an experienced pilot with
more than 1,000 flying hours, came up. Not knowing about Arnold's and Cochran's agreement, work was soon underway to stand up a women's ferrying

unit. It was lack of communication between the AAF and the ATC that allowed Love's organization to stand up first.[55]

In September 1942, the Women's Auxiliary Ferrying Squadron (WAFS) was established by the ATC under Love's command. The WAFS pilots delivered new aircraft from factories to ports of embarkation and ferried planes to training and Army bases stateside. In the meantime, Cochran had brought 24 female pilots to work under the Royal Air Force Air Transport Auxiliary in Great Britain. The British were under siege and were grateful for all pilots, even women. However, when Cochran found out about the WAFS, she was understandably upset. Later that year, Arnold's staff found a way to appease Cochran by authorizing a newly formed unit to train new women ferry pilots. In September 1942, Cochran headed the newly formed Women's Flying Training Detachment (WFTD). In August 1943, the two organizations would be combined to become the Women Airforce Service Pilots (WASP). Cochran was named director of women pilots within the Army Air Force, and Love was transferred to the Ferrying Division Headquarters as WASP executive with jurisdiction over all women ferry pilots. Even though the Army, Navy, and Marine Corps had successfully petitioned for women to enter the services in 1942, for many reasons the WASP were never militarized.[56]

Before it was disestablished in 1944, 1,074 WASP had earned their wings; they had flown over 60 million miles in all weather and in every aircraft in the inventory of the AAF. Thirty-eight of them had died on duty. Yet since they had not been militarized, they left service with no benefits, just a note from General Arnold saying, "Thank you for your service." It would be another 30 years before the WASP would be militarized in 1977 with the passage of HR 8701.[57]

The AVF once again was the impetus for change in the military services. The Navy was the first to select eight women for flight training in 1973, six of whom would earn their wings and become naval aviators. Of course, the planes were not to be involved in combat per the 1948 Women's Armed Services Integration Act. Among this first group was Rosemary Mariner, who served for 30 years, became the first woman to command an aircraft squadron, and retired as a captain (O-6). Captain Mariner also became an avid spokesperson for equal rights *and* responsibilities for women in the military. The Army followed suit in 1974, selecting women for its rotary wing program (helicopters). In 1974, the Air Force selected Jane Holley to attend the flight-test engineer program and in November 1975 announced it would begin training women as pilots. To answer the touchy question of women in air combat, the Air Force developed a two-track career program, male combat and female noncombatant pilots, similar to what the Navy would later do with the Women at Sea program in 1978. Both the Air Force and the Navy, announced the change was due to the shortage of qualified men.[58] Once again, the needs of the military overcame social inertia to provide greater occupational opportunities for women.

The transition was not without its critics and naysayers. There was little, if any, training on integration, and many men were openly hostile to the women. In 1978, Navy wives began to write in to the *Navy Times*, a weekly newspaper that caters to Naval personnel, accusing the women who wanted to go to sea of being nothing but whores.[59] The dual career path was also a deterrent to keeping women on active duty after all of their training costs. Like the Women at Sea program, the inability of a woman pilot to land on an aircraft carrier or other combatant ship at sea was career limiting. They fell behind their male peers, logging about 25 percent fewer flying hours. As a result, many women opted out after their initial service obligation ended, a loss to the government of expensively trained and qualified women.[60]

Defense Officer Personnel Management Act (DOPMA)

One other piece of legislation that made a significant difference in women officers' career opportunities was the Defense Officer Personnel Management Act, enacted in 1980. DOPMA called for consolidation of the officer promotion systems and uniform laws for managing the different services' officer career structures. Included in DOPMA were provisions to abolish gender-separated promotion lists and integrate them into one list.[61] This legislation dissolved the Women's Army Corps and incorporated women into the regular Army, and also allowed women to command men for the first time. Since that time, women have competed with men for promotion and have been selected by the same promotion boards.

Although the structural impediments to women's advancement had been abolished, the law did not allow women officers into the most competitive jobs, since that was forbidden by Title 10 Section 6015 as amended in 1978. DOPMA was designed with the assumption that it was beneficial to create uniform requirements about officer assignments, promotions, and retirement across the services. Yet women were competing with men but did not have equal career opportunities, so this system put them at a disadvantage for promotion.[62]

The structures of opportunity and power were slowly being opened, but there were still many obstacles to women actually attaining opportunity and power. Combat exclusion laws and policies were prevalent for all of the branches. Women were still an anomaly at the service academies and Reserve Officer Training Corps (ROTC), and new career paths had certain dead ends. This was especially true of the Women at Sea program, which by 1980 had only 14 ships that could accommodate a very small number of women officers. Many women who were excited at the prospect of participating in the Navy's primary missions at sea soon became discouraged when it was apparent there was no viable career path. Also, women officers who had navigated the promotion system under the old rules did not feel they could compete, since they had been denied equal job opportunity early in their careers.[63]

Nevertheless, all of the services managed to negotiate the transition. The abolition of the women's support structure was necessary to eliminate a "separate and unequal" attitude about women in the military and to promote the military as a gender-neutral team. However, this led to a false assumption that all the issues concerning women were being dealt with effectively, that total integration had been achieved, and that there was no longer a need for oversight.

Women's Expanding Opportunities

Regardless of the initial reluctance of the military services to include women into operational roles at sea and in the air, the programs had taken root. The Defense Authorization Bill of 1978 increased women's opportunities at sea and in the air, and DOPMA created other opportunities. By the end of the 1980s, women were entering the military in greater numbers and were being sent to sea and to aircraft squadrons. Even though they had separate noncombatant career paths, women were pushing toward the goal of all military officers—an upward path to command.

The Coast Guard had its first female ship commander in 1978, but the Navy did not until the end of 1990. The first female naval air squadron commander was selected in 1990, but not until 1993 in the Air Force. In the years since DOPMA was enacted, and even though women still are not fully integrated into all military occupations or positions, they are successfully competing. Each year the number of women who achieve the rank of flag or general officer (GFO) grows, and the number of women in operational rather than support jobs also grows. Strides continue to be made toward equality of opportunity and responsibility, and military women are able to successfully navigate this maze and achieve their career goals.

By the mid-1980s, the remaining statutory restrictions for women prohibited their assignment to combatant ships and aircraft and, by default, in ground combat roles in the Army and Marine Corps. It would take about 10 more years before Congress would rescind the remaining combat exclusion laws, allowing military women to fly jets and other combatant aircraft in all of the services and the Navy to follow in the Coast Guard's footsteps and open all surface ships to women. There continue to be some restrictions to women's military opportunities, even with their history of excellent service.[64] This will be further explained in the next chapters.

Notes

1. Rebecca Santana, "She's a General, Not a Gender," *Associated Press*, August 13, 2006.

2. Nancy Loring Goldman, "The Changing Role of Women in the Armed Forces," *American Journal of Sociology* 78, no. 4 (1973): 908.

3. Darlene M. Iskra, "Attitudes toward Expanding Roles for Navy Women at Sea," *Armed Forces and Society* 33, no. 2 (January 2007): 203–223.

4. Susan D. Hosek, Peter Tiemeyer, Rebecca Kilburn, Debra A. Strong, Selika Ducksworth, and Reginald Ray, *Minority and Gender Differences in Officer Career Progression* (Santa Monica, CA: RAND, 2001), 76.

5. Ibid., 76–77.

6. Two excellent books that give a more thorough history of women in the military are Linda Grant DePauw, *Battle Cries and Lullabies: Women in War from Prehistory to the Present* (Norman, OK: University of Oklahoma Press, 1998), and Jeanne Holm, *Women in the Military: An Unfinished Revolution*, rev. ed. (Novato, CA: Presidio Press, 1992).

7. Jeffrey P. Hantover, "The Boy Scouts and the Validation of Masculinity," in *Men's Lives*, 4th ed., ed. Michael S. Kimmel and Michael A. Messner (Boston: Allyn and Bacon, 1998), 101–108.

8. George L. Mosse, *Fallen Soldiers: Reshaping the Memory of the World Wars* (Oxford: Oxford University Press, 1990).

9. DePauw, *Battle Cries and Lullabies*, 17.

10. Ibid., 20.

11. Ibid., 117.

12. Ibid., 144.

13. Ibid., 160.

14. Kimberly Jensen, "A Base Hospital Is Not a Coney Island Dance Hall," *Frontiers* 26, no. 2 (2005): 206–235.

15. Ibid.

16. Mary Sarnecky, *A History of the U.S. Army Nurse Corps* (Philadelphia: University of Pennsylvania Press, 1999), 147; Doris Sterner, *In and Out of Harm's Way: A History of the Navy Nurse Corps* (Seattle, WA: Peanut Butter Publishing, 1996), 123.

17. Jean Ebbert and Mary-Beth Hall, *Crossed Currents: Navy Women in a Century of Change*, 3rd ed. (Washington, DC: Brassey's, 1999); Iskra, "Attitudes toward Expanding Roles."

18. Lettie Gavin, *American Women in World War I: They also Served* (Niwot: University Press of Colorado, 1997).

19. Holm, *Women in the Military*; Michael L. Patrow and Renee Patrow, "The Leathernecks: A Few Good Men . . . and Women," in *Life in the Rank and File*, ed. David R. Segal and H. Wallace Sinaiko (Washington, DC: Pergamon-Brassey's, 1989), 153–183.

20. Francine D. Blau, Marianne A. Ferber, and Anne E. Winkler, *The Economics of Women, Men, and Work*, 3rd ed. (Englewood Cliffs, NJ: Prentice Hall, 1998), 22.

21. Blau, Ferber, and Winkler, *The Economics of Women*; Maureen Honey, *Creating Rosie the Riveter: Class, Gender, and Propaganda during World War II* (Amherst: University

of Massachusetts Press, 1984); Brenda Moore, *To Serve My Country, To Serve My Race* (New York: New York University Press, 1996); Joan Williams, *Unbending Gender: Why Family and Work Conflict and What to Do About It* (Oxford: Oxford University Press, 2000).

22. Sherna B. Gluck, *Rosie the Riveter Revisited: Women, the War, and Social Change* (Boston, MA: Twayne, 1987), xii.

23. Gluck, *Rosie the Riveter Revisited*, x; Honey, *Creating Rosie the Riveter*, 55.

24. Gluck, *Rosie the Riveter Revisited*; Holm, *Women in the Military*, 91; Honey, *Creating Rosie the Riveter*.

25. Holm, *Women in the Military*.

26. Ibid.

27. Gluck, *Rosie the Riveter Revisited*; Honey, *Creating Rosie the Riveter*.

28. Holm, *Women in the Military*.

29. As opposed to under 18 years of age for men.

30. Section 210 of Public Law 80-625, codified in USC Title 10, Section 6015.

31. Ibid., 268.

32. Holm, *Women in the Military*, 162–163, 175.

33. DACOWITS, About, http://dacowits.defense.gov/index.html.

34. Holm, *Women in the Military*, 151. See also pp. 148–165, for a complete history of the establishment of DACOWITS during the Korean War and the fate of the women's military programs during that time period.

35. DACOWITS, Recommendations, "Fall 1968" http://dacowits.defense.gov/index.html.

36. Holm, *Women in the Military*.

37. DACOWITS, Charter, http://dacowits.defense.gov/tablecharter_subpage.html.

38. Holm, *Women in the Military*, 180.

39. Ibid., 192.

40. This included the Military Academy at West Point, New York, the Naval Academy at Annapolis, Maryland, and the Air Force Academy in Colorado. The restriction on women at the Coast Guard Academy had been lifted in 1975, but the first women did not enter until 1976, the same year as the other academies. The services warned Congress that since women were not allowed to fight in ground, sea, or air combat, their presence was only taking away valuable resources from qualified men. The argument fell on deaf ears (Holm, *Women in the Military*, 305–312).

41. Goldman, "The Changing Role"; David R. Segal, *Recruiting for Uncle Sam: Citizenship and Military Manpower Policy* (Lawrence: University Press of Kansas, 1989).

42. Lory Manning, *Women in the Military: Where they Stand*, 6th ed. (Washington, DC: Women's Research and Education Institute, 2008). The high number of minority women in the military is unfortunately indicative of the lack of equal opportunity for well-paying jobs with benefits in the civilian sector.

43. Why this was the case has never been adequately explained, since women were clearly not prohibited from serving on hospital ships per the 1948 legislation. I can only surmise that Naval leaders of the 1950s and 1960s interpreted the law, and the intent of Congress, to mean that only nurses could serve on hospital ships and women

could be passengers on transports but never part of the ship's crew of either vessel. Again, the gender norms of the era were the primary prohibition, as well as the fact that it had never been done before.

44. Ebbert and Hall, *Crossed Currents*. Even though the Coast Guard had opened all their positions to women, the Coast Guard was not considered a combatant force. Thus, even though it was clear that women could fulfill seagoing roles on ships and aircraft, the Navy opted to delineate between combatant and noncombatant units, so there was no discord with the Navy's reasoning.

45. Ebbert and Hall, *Crossed Currents*, 237.

46. *Owens v. Brown*, 455 F. Supp. 291 (1978), 308.

47. Ibid (Owens v. Brown)

48. HASC, "HR 7431: Assignment of Women."

49. Ibid., 1179–1185.

50. Ibid., 1177.

51. Ibid., 1197–1198.

52. Ibid., 1211.

53. DoD Appropriation Act of 1979, Public Law 95-485.

54. Ebbert and Hall, *Crossed Currents*, 238.

55. Leslie Haynsworth and David Toomey, *Amelia Earhart's Daughters* (New York: Morro and Co., 1998). For the complete story of the establishment of these two organizations and the WASP, see pages 22–148 of this book.

56. Ibid.

57. Deborah G. Douglas, *American Women and Flight since 1940* (Lexington: University Press of Kentucky, 2004), 187–189.

58. Darlene M. Iskra, "Attitudes toward Expanding Roles."

59. Ibid.

60. Holm, *Women in the Military*, 313–323.

61. Bernard Rostker, Harry Thie, James Lacy, Jennifer Kawata, and Susanna Purnell, *The Defense Officer Personnel Management Act of 1980: A Retrospective Assessment* (Santa Monica, CA: RAND, 1993).

62. Holm, *Women in the Military*, 277.

63. Ibid.

64. Darlene Marie Iskra, *Women in Submarines: Have the Arguments about Expanding Women's Sea-Going Roles in the U.S. Navy Changed over Time?* Unpublished Master's thesis, University of Maryland, 2003.

CHAPTER 2

Rescinding the Combat Exclusion Laws

The years between the start of the AVF and 1990 saw many new opportunities for women in the military. In many ways, women in the military were benefiting from equal-opportunity policies even more than their civilian sisters. This was especially true in terms of equal pay and benefits. Since the military pay system is based on rank and time in service, when women were authorized a permanent place in the regular military in 1948, their pay became equal with men of the same rank and service time. Through lawsuits and subsequent legislation in the 1970s, women in the military were no longer forced out when they got pregnant, were able to claim their civilian husbands and children as military dependents, were accepted to the federal service academies, were authorized to fly noncombatant aircraft and serve in noncombatant ships, and were employed in many traditionally male occupations. However, in one major way they were still considered second-class citizens because they could not perform duties that involved *combat,* which is of course the primary focus of military service. The Persian Gulf War in 1991 started to change that.

The Persian Gulf War, 1991

About 41,000 women served in Kuwait during the buildup of forces in the Middle East (Operation Desert Shield) from August through December 1990 and during the war in Kuwait and Iraq (Operation Desert Storm) through the end of combat in early March 1991.[1] They were not allowed to work in ground combat jobs (such as infantry, tanks, artillery, and Special Operations forces), on combatant ships, or in aircraft that participated in air combat. But women did just about everything else on land, at sea, and in the air. Their jobs in medical, combat support, and combat service support units provided the tools and logistical support needed for the combatants to do their job. These support jobs did not keep them out of harm's way; 2 women were taken as POWs and 15 women were killed.[2]

Approximately 2,500 Navy women served in the Persian Gulf during Desert Shield/Desert Storm. Most were in medical units and on support ships such as oilers, tenders, ammunition, hospital, and supply ships. Smaller numbers of women served in aviation units, construction battalions, cargo-handling groups, and the communication and administrative units of merchant marine vessels under contract to the Navy.[3]

The Gulf War was the first contemporary war in which large numbers of women served alongside men in a combat zone. It also ended military women's invisibility to the general public. The Pentagon found it had overestimated the angst with which the public would react to women POWs and women killed in war, as there was no greater outburst than for men.[4] Perceptions of women's performance were generally positive, but there were varying interpretations of how to apply the combat exclusion restrictions. As a result, commanders found their personnel flexibility limited, and some qualified women were not given assignments they were trained to perform.

The Gulf War was also the first time women reservists, called to active duty, were filmed leaving their young children with their husbands or other relatives and joining their waiting comrades. This actually took more of a toll on public opinion than the fact that women had been killed and taken prisoner.[5] The idea of mothers leaving their babies was an underlying reason for the historical restrictions on women's military service. Yet military women, both mothers and nonmothers, fully understood their responsibilities. After all, they had volunteered and knew they would be called to duty if their country needed them. As a result of the successes and troubles of the Persian Gulf War deployment, it was clear the restrictions on the military roles of women would have to be reevaluated.[6]

Arguments for and against Combat Roles for Women in the Military

Several important changes occurred in the careers of military women in the two years after the Gulf War. Both the House and Senate held hearings regarding women in combat in 1992 and 1993. The combat exclusion laws were eventually rescinded, but not without heated debate on both sides. Two major themes emerged and were used by both sides: military effectiveness and citizens' rights and responsibilities. These same arguments and concerns have not significantly changed today. With the continuing conflicts in Iraq and Afghanistan, decisions made about women in combat continue to be important for our nation's defense, military effectiveness, and the ability of women to be able to do their jobs without needless restrictions. The issues and rationale of the arguments during the Congressional hearings, and the 1992 study by the

Presidential Commission on the Assignment of Women in the Armed Forces, are explained in the following.

Military Effectiveness

Military effectiveness is dependent on several variables. Although the amount and type of military hardware is an important part of the equation, individual personnel readiness and behavior is the key to success. Thus, variables like retention, attrition, unit manning, physical strength, fraternization, harassment, unit cohesion, quality of life, and the morale of both the military members and their families are important issues to resolve in maintaining mission effectiveness.

A consistent theme of opponents to expanding combat roles to women is the charge that the military is being used to further social change in our society without regard for military effectiveness.[7] The criticism of using the military for social change had been used with regard to the integration of African American men into the military during the Truman administration[8] and during the debates of women's integration during the 1940s and 1970s when broad changes were made. It is also being used in the debate surrounding homosexuals' ability to serve openly in the military. Proponents argue it is the acceptance of changing values and goals by the American public that ultimately is reflected in policies that affect the military and, by default, other social institutions. The military reflects social change—it does not initiate it.[9]

Physical strength differences between men and women are a concern because of the fear that weaker women cannot perform hard physical labor and that more women in a unit will degrade its capabilities.[10] This argument only applies to a small number of jobs, such as infantry or combat engineers, where strength and physical endurance are necessary. Many units, including staffs and squadrons, ships and aircraft, do not require enormous physical strength. Proponents argue that technology has reduced the requirement for brute physical strength. They also argue that bona fide strength requirements will screen out those who cannot manage the load but that gender should not be the sole criteria.[11]

Opponents question women's performance in a combat role, both physically and psychologically. The fears that women interfere with male bonding and would unduly jeopardize the combat performance of men who might risk themselves, or the unit, to protect women have also been used as arguments about disruptions to military effectiveness.[12] Fraternization, sexual misconduct, and the competition for sexual favors are cited as detriments to unit morale and cohesion.[13] Additionally, there is a fear that these other-than-professional relationships would unduly influence the chain of command.[14] Other detriments to unit morale and cohesion include sexual and gender harassment (hostile attitudes, sexist remarks, undermining of authority) and the fear of false sexual harassment charges.[15]

Mady Segal, a military sociologist who specializes in women and family issues, argues that these issues are somewhat alleviated by the "power of social norms to prevent undesired behavior."[16] Others cite peer pressure as an effective deterrent.[17] Research has found that committed leadership, education, and rigorous and fair enforcement of the expected standards by all in the chain of command are keys to ensuring all in a unit are treated, and act, professionally.[18]

The perception of double standards has also been used as an argument against the military effectiveness of women. Men perceive women as getting special treatment in duty hours, assignments, and sick call. They resent having to assume additional duties if a woman is pregnant or otherwise not physically able to perform her tasks. Men also perceive that women with less-than-average performance are being retained while men with equal or better records are being dropped from special training programs, such as jet training.[19] Norming, the establishment of standards that take into account differences in age and gender, is also perceived as a lowering of standards.[20] However, proponents point out that women who have scored better than men in military schools have been refused certain duty options, such as combat flying, simply because they were women. They argue that when the required standards are met, duty assignments should be made based on ability rather than gender.[21]

Finally, flexibility of assignment regardless of race or gender enhances military effectiveness rather than degrades it. The inefficiency of segregation was shown during the Korean War and was the impetus for the integration of African Americans. It was an issue after the start of the AVF, when not enough white men enlisted and the military was forced to accept women and minorities in order to fill vacant jobs. It was evident in the later 1970s as well, when the Navy needed personnel to crew its ships and had to petition Congress to revise the laws against assigning women to ships. It continues to be an issue with the continued occupational segregation of women in ground combat. The military would be better served if it had the flexibility to use the best talents of both men and women.[22]

Citizens' Rights and Responsibilities

The changing social values of the American public have greatly affected this debate. Before and during WWII, women performed their citizenship roles in both civilian and military sectors as patriotic workers. They performed their civic duty, made sacrifices for the good of American soldiers, and were the caretakers of national ideals and normalcy. The idea of self-sacrifice reinforced women's traditional family responsibilities as caretaker of the family and supporter of the husband.[23] The passage of the ERA by Congress in the 1970s; the passage of Title 9, the Equal Opportunity in Education Act; and the rise of the women's rights movement began a change in the cultural views about appropriate roles for women. Legislation and civil suits in both the civilian and military sectors helped promote women's equality in the workplace with a concurrent increase in citizenship participation. Thus, the "right to fight" for women who choose to enter the military can be seen as a demand for equal citizenship participation.[24] While not all women are willing or capable of serving in combat roles, the equality debate centers on whether gender should be used as the sole criteria for inclusion or exclusion from full military roles. Proponents argue that women's equality is not about ignoring readiness issues but is about being judged as individuals—by the same standards as men, but without artificial barriers based solely on gender. Opponents claim that equal opportunity should not risk other's lives and mission effectiveness.[25]

There are several reasons why women pursue equality of assignments in the military. First, dividing jobs between men and women creates resentment. Women's noncombatant positions cause problems because of the perception that women get equal pay for unequal work. Even though military personnel have no control over these policies, some men react with resentment toward those easiest to blame: military women. Institutional policies that prevent women from pursuing the same career goals as their male peers creates the impression, for both men and women, that women are second-class citizens and that their contributions are not as important to the common goal.[26] It is a built-in double standard. This reciprocal resentment creates, rather than alleviates, morale problems.

Second, women want their career opportunities to be equal to their male peers. They want to do the jobs they are trained and qualified to do, regardless of the location of that job. Women believe they will not be treated as equals until they are integrated into all aspects of the military for which they are qualified.[27] Third, military service is linked with citizenship rights. It has been considered both a right and a responsibility of citizenship.[28] Military service as a responsibility of citizenship for women is part of the ongoing debate of women's evolving roles.

Women in Combat Aviation

In the aftermath of Desert Shield/Desert Storm, Congress took action in the form of an amendment to the 1992 Defense Authorization Act that repealed the existing combat exclusion laws pertaining to women flying combat aircraft—Title 10, USC section 6015—in the Navy, Air Force, and Marine Corps. But what was the impetus for this amendment, and how did it come about?

Patricia Schroeder, Democratic Congresswoman from Colorado, was a pilot herself and had been a strong advocate of women moving into more aviation roles in the military.[29] The no-combat flying statute was perceived as the weakest point in the combat exclusion laws because women had been at the forefront of aviation in the 1930s, had ferried all of the various military aircraft as ferry pilots, had served as flight instructors during WWII, and had successfully participated in combat support missions during Operation Desert Storm, particularly by refueling fighter planes over combat zones in KC-135s. Noncombatant units flying over or near the battlefield were easier targets than combatant planes. They could get shot at but could not shoot back.

Schroeder, a member of the House Armed Services Committee, proposed the amendment rescinding the aviation combat exclusion for women to the committee with no advance notice, no formal debate, no input from the services, and no pressure from outside groups. It passed in committee with a unanimous vote. With support from Speaker of the House Les Aspin, and as a committee-sponsored amendment, it was virtually assured of passage, since removing such amendments were difficult and took tremendous political clout.[30]

Schroeder's original amendment was limited to the Air Force, since the Air Force's personnel chief, Lt. General Thomas J. Hickey, was receptive to the idea and had publicly acknowledged that "there were no flying jobs in the Air Force that women were not capable of performing."[31] Co-sponsor Beverly Byron (D-MD), originally against expanding women's roles, proposed expansion of the amendment to include the Navy and Marine Corps, to the surprise of the Schroeder staff. The Navy had been allowing women to fly combat jets, but not in combat squadrons, since 1975. Women in the Navy could also fly combat helicopters, but only from noncombatant ships, and were being trained to fly air-to-air gunnery and air combat maneuvering, but not against an enemy.[32] The law, if passed, would certainly require the Navy and Congress to review the laws against women in combat ships. The revised amendment slipped through with little debate or opposition. The bill passed the full house on May 22, 1991, and passed to the Senate. Dick Cheney, then Secretary of Defense (SECDEF), endorsed the proposal, stating in an official release that it gave the authority of personnel assignments to DoD where it belonged, rather than to Congress.[33]

The ease with which this amendment passed in the House belies the extent of the opposition to it in and out of the Pentagon. There was concern that its passage would make defending the existing exclusion of women on ships and in ground combat very difficult. And though the Army was not directly involved with the legislation, the amendment's passage would remove any rationale behind keeping Army women out of combat aircraft as well.[34] This, of course, was true for women in combat ships and aircraft, regardless of service branch, but there remains a stubborn resistance to women in ground combat.

Once the bill got to the Senate, the opponents of change, who had been taken by surprise by the House vote, rallied their forces and vigorously campaigned against the bill. Over three weeks of intensive lobbying, they voiced exaggerated fears about the effect of pregnancy and motherhood to military readiness, fraternization in foxholes affecting morale, and the specter of a gender-neutral draft on military effectiveness. They also accused women officers of selfish ambition at the expense of enlisted women who wanted no part of combat. The opponents were successful in changing the minds of Senators John McCain (R-AZ) and John Warner (R-VA), who had initially expressed support for the bill after the House vote. They also managed to change the focus of the bill from rescinding the combat exclusion laws for aviators to a general women-in-combat debate, which included women on ships but especially women in ground combat.[35] Their strategy was to make the idea of women in combat so onerous that the Senate would balk at supporting the issue.

In a departure from protocol, the Senate Armed Services Committee (SASC) decided to host a hearing on the issue of combat roles for military women. The witness panel was heavily weighted with opponents to the bill, mostly Army and Marine Corps ground soldiers and enlisted women who had no desire to serve in combat. There was no meaningful discussion about women in combat aviation; the focus was on women in ground combat. The Joint Chiefs, the senior military leaders of all the services, also went on record opposing any change to the law. When the bill came out of Committee, the provision for rescinding the laws against women in combat aviation was no longer there.[36]

In a strategic counter-maneuver, Senators Edward Kennedy (D-MA) and William Roth (R-DE) decided to propose a bill on the full Senate floor to repeal the law. The proponents of change went to work. Many active duty women and men headed to the hill to express their support. A phone, mail, and fax campaign was initiated that inundated Senate offices. Roth stated, "We are here today to talk, not about gender, but about excellence. We are here to talk, not about whether we want women pilots flying combat missions, but whether we want the *best* pilots flying combat missions. . . . When our nation's future is at stake . . . we want the most highly skilled and seasoned men and women on the job."[37]

Prior to the Senate vote, however, Senators Sam Nunn (D-GA), John Warner (R-VA), John McCain (R-AZ), and John Glenn (D-OH) felt that to "rush ahead without proper study and a national consensus" on this amendment would be premature. They offered a second amendment that would study the effect of repealing the combat exclusion laws on the national psyche. This amendment created a commission, the Presidential Commission on the Assignment of Women in the Armed Services, that would study the issue and provide a venue for the "American people" to indicate their views on this issue. Both amendments passed in July, and the 1992 Defense Authorization Act became law on December 5, 1991.[38]

The crux of the first amendment to the law was that it allowed the DoD to have more flexible assignment options for its officers, but it did not dictate that women be assigned to combat aviation jobs. The second amendment, which formed the Presidential Commission, was a sure way to avoid any immediate action and was in keeping with the Administration's desires. SECDEF Cheney opted to delay any decision on the assignment of women to combat aviation units until after the Commission issued its recommendations.

The Presidential Commission on the Assignment of Women in the Armed Forces

The Presidential Commission was tasked to provide equality for women in all ranks and military specialties while ensuring the nation's security needs and sustained military effectiveness were met. Even though combat restrictions for women in aviation had been rescinded, the Commission felt it needed to review the issue of women in combatant aircraft, as well as all other aspects of women's military service, including family considerations, cultural values, women in sea combat, and conscription. There were no statutory restrictions on women in ground combat, but the DoD utilized a Risk Rule that governed the assignment of women in each of the services. The Commission also reviewed that policy.[39]

The Commission consisted of 15 people—6 women and 9 men—chaired by General Robert T. Herres, United States Air Force (USAF, ret), and included several retired general officers, a few active duty military members, a military sociologist, and other distinguished individuals. However, many of the members were openly against the repeal of combat exclusion laws.[40] They reviewed 17 issues and conducted their research through the review of available literature, surveys, letters sent to the commission, hearings, and testimony from a wide range of people. They approved all 17 issues, some more controversial than others.[41]

Though Congress had repealed the laws against women flying combat aircraft the previous year, the Commission unsurprisingly recommended that the combat exclusion law be reinstated. They also recommended that the DoD Risk Rule regarding women in ground combat be codified in law. Ironically, they also recommended that the laws be modified to *allow* women to serve on combatant vessels except submarines and amphibious vessels. The report barely made the news, however, because it was finalized in November, just after President Bush was defeated in the 1992 election by Bill Clinton. As a result, the Commission's recommendations were largely ignored.

Tailhook 1991

Prior to the final passage of the 1992 Defense Authorization Bill, a scandal that had far-reaching consequences not just to the Navy but to all of the military branches occurred at the Tailhook convention of September 1991. The Tailhook Association was named for the combat pilots who land on aircraft carriers by using a "tailhook" to catch one of four arresting wires that stop the plane on landing. It is an elite group of military pilots because it takes daring and skill to land a high-performance aircraft on a moving ship. The association itself is a "private, nonprofit social/professional organization of naval aviators, contractors, and others involved in naval aviation." While it had started as a mostly social club, it had since morphed into a professional organization with a mission statement, nonprofit status, and a monthly magazine. An annual convention offered lectures, symposia, and contractor exhibits.[42]

The Navy had consistently provided significant support and cooperation for the conference and the association. For example, active and retired naval aviators serve on the Board of Directors, and a senior active duty admiral was usually appointed as president. Prior to the 1991 scandal, the Navy provided free office space for the association at then-Naval Air Station (NAS) Miramar, near San Diego, CA, home of the Navy's Fighter Weapons School, colloquially known as "Top Gun." In addition, the Navy issued orders, and authorized and supplied transportation to the conference by military aircraft and busses, some of which were driven by enlisted personnel.[43]

The Tailhook convention originated as reunion in 1957, first held at Rosarito Beach in Mexico, with the usual drinking and partying as its goal. It had been hosted at the Las Vegas Hilton since 1968. Over the years, the social aspect of the conference became the overriding reason many people attended and the partying had grown increasingly out of control. In fact, it was reported by the investigators that the 1991 conference was one of the tamer events. However, the inappropriate behavior of attending aviators, both male and female, got the attention of the press and Congress because of one person—Lt. Paula Coughlin.[44]

Lt. Coughlin was a helicopter pilot then serving as the admiral's aide to Rear Admiral John W. Snyder, Jr., commander of the Patuxent River Naval Air Test Center. While at the convention, Coughlin was caught in a gauntlet of men in a corridor outside an elevator; the men were grabbing women's breasts and buttocks as they walked down the hallway. Coughlin was grabbed and confronted her attacker, but she continued to be grabbed by others even though the men knew she was serving as an admiral's aide. As an aviator, Coughlin was devastated that her fellow naval aviators would attack one of their own. She also knew this behavior was not just about her but was a professional issue. When Coughlin reported the assault to her boss, he did not seem surprised and did not seem to consider it inappropriate, remarking, "That's what you get when you go on the third deck full of drunk aviators."[45] After repeated attempts to get her boss to do something, Coughlin filed a formal complaint through Navy channels. When the Naval Investigative Service (NIS) investigation revealed no suspects, she decided to go public with her story in June 1992.

Two mitigating circumstances that may have affected the behavior at that year's convention were the success of the Persian Gulf War and the passage of the combat exclusion amendment in Congress. Those aviators who had participated in the Gulf War were proud of their service in the first successful war since WWII. The women aviators were feeling extremely proud and excited about the possibility that the Navy would announce they were opening combat aviation to women. Some of the male aviators found the potential change unbearable. Women aviators attending the convention found themselves in the middle of a group of angry young men who felt it was "intolerable that all the things they think are worth dying for were suddenly going to be done by women."[46] Their response was to reduce the women to a common denominator—sex objects.

Coughlin was not the only woman to be assaulted at the convention. By the end of the investigation, 90 victims of indecent assault were identified. There were also other inappropriate behaviors, such as indecent exposure, streaking, mooning, public sex, pornography, and other sexually motivated misconduct. It was not until Coughlin filed her official complaint, along with the complaints of 4 other women, that any action took place. Facing disclosure of the complaint by the *San Diego Union*, then Secretary of the Navy (SECNAV) H. Lawrence Garrett III took the first official action by ending all the Navy's support for the Tailhook association. A report issued by the Navy Inspector General (IG) and the NIS in April 1992 failed to identify any of the assaulters, though it did indicate there were many senior officers present at the convention who were aware of the assaults and inappropriate behavior but failed to stop them. The report also appeared to whitewash the fact that SECNAV Garrett was in a room where inappropriate rituals were taking place. The fallout from that eventual disclosure was that prior to his resignation as SECNAV, Garrett turned the investigation over to DoD's IG.[47]

The IG's report cited "a failure of leadership"[48] for the increasingly blatant sexual misconduct over the years of the convention. In the end, many senior officers in the Navy resigned, including the SECNAV, the CNO Admiral Frank Kelso, and the Assistant Chief of Naval Operations (Air Warfare) Vice Admiral (VADM) Richard Dunleavy. Coughlin's boss, Snyder, was relieved of duty. Three admirals were censured for failing to prevent or stop the misbehavior of the junior officers at the convention. Thirty other admirals received letters of caution to be placed in their permanent records. Nearly 40 lower ranking senior officers (captains and commanders in the Navy and colonels in the Marine

Corps) were fined or otherwise disciplined with letters of censure or reprimand. Although 117 junior officers were implicated in one or more incidents of indecent assault, indecent exposure, conduct unbecoming an officer, or failure to act in a proper leadership capacity, none were court-martialed or otherwise brought to public account. Fifty-one officers were found to have made false statements trying to stonewall the investigation. Twenty-three officers were referred for further investigation, but only 10 were issued letters of admonition and docked $1,000 from their pay.[49]

The Aftermath of Tailhook

The Tailhook scandal did not start out as an immediate public affairs nightmare. The media attention occurred after Coughlin came forward and put a face to the terrifying experiences the women had endured. After Tailhook, the Navy struggled to overcome the impression it hosted a bunch of "drunken sailors" who felt free to behave in an inappropriate manner without consequences. Except for a few senior and junior officers, there was no real judicial closure for the 90 victims.

In June 1992, the new acting SECNAV, Dan Howard, held a closed meeting with senior naval officers and indicated that Tailhook was a symptom of an underlying and outmoded code of conduct. He wanted to change attitudes and, thus, behavior. It began with a daylong, service-wide "stand-down," an educational seminar on sexual harassment. The Standing Committee on Women in the Navy and Marine Corps was formed, the Tailhook association was asked to disband (it did not), and Howard called for making sexual harassment a separate offense under the Uniform Code of Military Justice (UCMJ).[50] He also called for the pilots and aviators at the convention to come forward and tell the truth. Unfortunately, he was replaced after only three weeks by Sean O'Keefe, who, like SECDEF Cheney, called Tailhook an aberration and not indicative of the behaviors and attitudes of naval personnel as a whole.[51]

Howard's approach might have stemmed the tide of incidents that occurred, and were duly reported by the press in the summer of 1992 and beyond, had he remained at the Navy's helm. If the issues of sexual harassment and assault had been seen as symptoms of an underlying tumor, actions could have been taken to remove the tumor and start the healing. Instead, it was allowed to fester, and rather than a Navy-wide approach, individual leaders, perhaps covering their own inadequacies, relieved subordinates "for cause" without exactly disclosing the problem in the interest of privacy.[52]

Additionally, attitudes toward women in the Navy changed. Naval aviators were the worst offenders. They continued to undermine and isolate their female peers at every opportunity. They leaked stories to the conservative press about perceived lowered standards for passing women pilots. They hounded Coughlin out of the Navy through hate mail, a slander campaign, and ostracism. Though she was avenging a wrong that male aviators created, the backlash that resulted was that women were seen as the enemy, not just in naval aviation, but throughout the fleet. Working conditions worsened as men refused to talk to co-workers for fear they would be accused of inappropriate behavior. It was a low point for the Navy.[53]

In November, the Clinton administration ousted the one-term Bush presidency. The new SECDEF, Les Aspin, was the former speaker of the House. In April 1993, the administration issued the new policy that permitted the services to allow women to compete for assignments in aircraft, including aircraft engaged in combat missions. Aspin also directed the Navy to develop a legislative proposal to repeal the existing laws forbidding women from serving on combat ships.[54]

Military Women and the Abaya

One woman who took advantage of the expanded opportunities for women in aviation was an Air Force officer named Martha McSally. By 1995, she was the first female fighter pilot in the Air Force, and she is now the highest-ranking female fighter pilot in the Air Force, with the rank of colonel. Her status gave her a platform to challenge what she felt was a misguided local policy that was fully supported by the DoD.

The policy McSally wanted to change began in the wake of the 1991 Gulf War. The instruction for off-base travel in Saudi Arabia, 320th Air Expeditionary Group (AEG) Instruction 31-1, was written as force protection guidance for "reducing [off-installation terrorist] exposure by setting standards that will allow personnel to maintain a low profile." In it, the commander of the 320th AEG required the following clothing and behavioral restrictions for off-base travel:

> 6. Clothing Requirements. Neither males or females will wear any Desert Camouflage Uniform (DCU) item during Recreational Travel. These items may be worn when necessary for Mission Essential Travel and specifically authorized by unit commanders.
>
> 6.1 Male Clothing. Males will wear a collared shirt, long pants, and conservative shoes. Males will not wear any hats or jewelry, other than a wedding band and watch. Wear of the thobe and ghutra (traditional Saudi robe and headdress) is not authorized. Exception: For trips outside the city of Riyadh . . . the wear of headgear is authorized.
>
> 6.2. Female Clothing. Females will wear the abaya[55] buttoned/zipped from the hemline to neckline. The abaya will extend to the ankles and cover the arms to the wrists. Covering of the head and wearing of the veil is not necessary; however the veil must be carried and worn if asked.

Females will wear conservative shoes, long pants, and a short sleeved shirt under the abaya.

7. General Behavior. All personnel traveling off-base will behave in a courteous and professional manner. Horseplay or loud and boisterous behavior will not be tolerated.

7.1. Male/Female Interaction. Males will not approach, touch, or stare at females encountered off-base, including other westerners, nor will they speak to women they don't know. Any male/female interaction must be discrete.

7.2. Female Restrictions. While off installation, females will not smoke in public. Females will be accompanied by at least one male at all times. Females are not permitted to operate a vehicle and must sit behind any other males in the vehicle.[56]

Additionally, according to McSally, the abaya was to be worn whenever off base, whether in off-duty status or not. And when off base, women had to walk behind men.[57] The policy was supposed to ensure American servicemen and women did not offend Saudi culture by wearing inappropriate clothing, such as shorts, cut-offs, and tank tops, while off base in the Area of Responsibility (AOR). It also attempted to reduce exposure to terrorist and criminal activity while in a travel status within Saudi Arabia by instructing personnel on security, proper behavior and clothing, and other requirements. The impetus for this may have been the Saudi royal decree, in 1992, announcing Islamic law as the overriding law of the land. There was also the issue of a lack of Status of Forces Agreement (SOFA) for military personnel stationed in Saudi Arabia. A SOFA protects American service members if they get in trouble with local laws or law enforcement personnel.

Of course, it is important for Americans to respect the laws of the country in which they are assigned. However, it was never a requirement by the Saudi government that non-Muslim women wear the abaya. Yet, as a precaution against possible international issues and incidents that could result from the inappropriate dress or behavior of the men and women stationed there, the 320th/Eskan Village commander made a unilateral decision to have military women under its command wear the abaya. Although the U.S. military was stationed in other Islamic countries (Kuwait and Afghanistan) with similarly stringent cultural and religious values, similar restrictions were not in place for other military personnel.

However, the policy, whether wittingly or not, created a double standard that segregated men from women and normalized the ideology that women were subordinate to men. The instructions ordered women to wear the abaya and conform to the host nation culture by engaging in subordinate (by Western standards) actions toward men. The policy also did not take into account the ideology behind the wearing of the abaya in the first place—it is a religious garment designed to reinforce women's chastity and beliefs in the tenets of

Islam. Additionally, the instructions did not differentiate between women officers and enlisted women, so a situation was created in which women officers appeared subordinate to the men they were supposed to be leading. In an institution that favors men over women, this policy added a potential and unnecessary strain on women officers who needed to maintain credibility in their leadership roles. Wearing the abaya would symbolically, if not actually, mock that leadership credibility. Wearing the abaya effectively reduced all women, whether officer or enlisted, to the status of femme fatale who needed to be hidden.

Host nation sensibilities aside, the issue of terrorists targeting military personnel was a legitimate concern, but the resultant policy was misguided. It was apparent who was and was not Arab for several reasons. First, Arab men do not shave. U.S. military grooming regulations forbid facial hair, except mustaches, unless authorized by secret military operations. Second, the 320th AEG regulations required women to wear the abaya yet prohibited men to wear Arab robes. Because the regulation also required all military women to be accompanied by a man when off base, it was obvious the women were not Arab, as no Arab woman would be seen with a Western man who was not her husband or a relative. Finally, this directive was targeted only at the military personnel stationed in Saudi Arabia under the 320th AEG. Other service women, State Department workers, and government employees stationed in and around Saudi Arabia, including other Arab countries, were not required to abide by this policy. Women working for the State Department were forbidden from wearing the abaya while on duty, although they could voluntarily wear it when not, and many women did.[58] There was a disconnect not only between State Department regulations concerning official business in Saudi Arabia but also between the different military branches stationed there. Thus, the instructions, while seemingly aimed at protecting the force, actually made the men and women stationed with the 320th AEG in Saudi Arabia more of a target.

McSally was on the fast track for promotion, having been selected for lieutenant colonel several years ahead of her peers. As the most senior female combat pilot in the Air Force, she used her status and visibility to challenge a policy that she felt was inherently wrong and discriminatory even under the rubric of military personnel safety in a host country. As early as 1995—when she was deployed to Al Jabber, Kuwait—she saw a picture of enlisted women wearing the abaya in the local military newspaper with instructions on how to properly wear it. Even though she was not required to wear the abaya at that point, she could not believe what she saw and was determined to challenge the policy. She understood that by speaking out she might place her career in jeopardy. She thought her status as a "first" might give her the credibility to get the policy rescinded; that if anyone could do it, she could. She also strongly believed the policy was discriminatory, against her Christian ideals, and demeaning to women. For the next six years, she continued to try to get the policy rescinded via the military chain of command. It appeared to have some sympathetic ears for a policy review, but she soon became thought of as a troublemaker for addressing this controversial issue.[59]

In 2000 as an Air Force major, the issue became personal between McSally and the command in Saudi Arabia when she was proposed for assignment to the Joint Task Force Southwest Asia (JTF-SWA) at Eskan Village, under the auspices of the 320th AEG. "I was tapped to direct search-and-rescue missions over Iraq. It was a plum job—a real testament to my leadership and skills. The only drawback: I'd be stationed in Saudi Arabia."[60] She was willing to wear appropriate civilian clothing, as required by State Department regulation, but was rankled by the 320th AEG's continued insistence on the mandatory wearing of the abaya. Her primary argument was that it was an article of religious clothing, and as a Christian she could not wear a symbol of the Muslim faith. She suggested a variety of ways to work around the policy, including that the abaya be made optional. But the command seemed to dig in its heels. She indicated that if assigned to JTF-SWA, she would continue to fight the policy and would not go off base because of her beliefs. It was almost as if the Air Force was daring her to violate the order.

In an interview with Cynthia Hanson of the *Ladies' Home Journal* in 2002, McSally said that after receiving her orders to Saudi Arabia she was under the impression she would be able to do her job without having to wear the abaya. However, she was told that when she arrived in country she would be required to wear the garment when she traveled from the airport to the base. She protested but was warned that she would obey the order or "suffer the consequences."

She explains in her own words:

> I then received an email from the JAG with legal language about the result of disobeying lawful orders, a plea not to endanger the lives of the transportation enlisted personnel because of my "crusade," and a statement that it was very important to blend in due to the threat level. She then told me I should make my decision as to whether I will follow this order before I get on the plane, since "Having the government pay for your travel to an assignment you don't intend to complete will add to the case against you."
>
> The next day, I visited my commander in Washington, D.C. "Sir, I'm about to torch myself over my conviction," I said. "If you're committed to changing the policy, put aside your personal conviction one time," he advised. "If you disobey the order, you'll never get it changed."
>
> After a night of prayer, I decided to take his advice. Arriving at Prince Sultan Air Base in the middle of the night, I was ushered into a small tent, given a quick briefing and handed an abaya. Then I was escorted to a car with dark-tinted windows and, as the only woman in the group, directed to sit in the backseat for the ride to our base. I felt humiliated

and angry. It struck me as ludicrous that the Air Force will let me go up alone in a single engine fighter jet over enemy territory, but won't let me sit in the front seat of a car on a Saudi street.[61]

McSally suffered through her tour, though she continued to protest the policy to her chain of command. They were not swayed. As a result, upon her return to the United States she went public with the issue to *USA Today* in 2001[62] and simultaneously sued the DoD and the Secretary of Defense, contending that the policy was unconstitutional as it discriminated against women and violated their religious freedom. She ultimately persuaded her local congressional representative, Jim Langevin (D-RI), to take on the issue with federal legislation. It unanimously passed in the House. In order to get the full support of Congress, she also needed supporters on the Senate side, which she did with Senate co-sponsors Senators Bob Smith (R-NH) and Maria Cantwell (D-WA).

In 2002, I was working as a congressional fellow for Senator Cantwell. I knew about the issue from the *USA Today* article a year earlier, and I was excited at the prospect of being able to help rescind this misguided policy. While then-Major McSally and Senator Smith focused on the religious aspects of the case, in a memo to Cantwell's office I argued, "This policy is especially onerous towards women officers . . . because it usurps the authority of the women officers who are stationed over there, it degrades their ability to maintain good order and discipline, and it makes it impossible for them to lead their troops. The uniform is a symbol of their authority. Wearing the abaya is symbolic of the second class status of women. Wearing the abaya not only reduces an officer's authority, but condones an atmosphere conducive to negating a woman's authority even when she is in uniform."[63]

Additionally, I noted, "DoD has argued that for force protection, women need to blend in to avoid being targeted for terrorist attack. They also argue that if women do not comply, they would be subject to attack by the Saudi religious police or other zealots. Regardless of whether or not women are wearing the abaya, all Americans are readily visible in the host country. Additionally, the military should be loudly protesting any attack on our military personnel, regardless of the cause. Our military personnel, men and women, are representing the United States, and any attack on our personnel should be considered an attack on the U.S."[64] Senator Cantwell agreed and fully supported the legislation to forbid the Pentagon from requiring women to wear the abaya. Bipartisan agreement was reached due to the gender inequality aspects of the issue for Democrats and the religious freedom issue for Republicans. In the Defense Authorization Act of 2003, the amendment forbidding the DoD from forcing women to wear the abaya was unanimously approved by both the House and the Senate and was signed by the president in December 2002.

Opponents of the law called it "congressional meddling." The DoD argued that the legislation would unreasonably limit commanders' ability and authority to act in their best judgment to protect their personnel. This partially explains the reluctance of the 320th AEG to change the policy at the local level, where it could have been accomplished without Congressional interference. However, the bottom line was that the American military was there at the behest of the Saudi government, and military women were an integral part of that contingent. They should not have been singled out for discriminatory treatment. They were military personnel representing the American government and, like their State Department colleagues, should have been treated as such.

Repeal of the Combat Exclusion Law for Women at Sea

By early 1994 more than ten thousand women were serving at sea,[65] but women still were not full members of the Navy team. Women could not be assigned to combat ships, a key occupational role for advancement to flag ranks in operationally significant billets. There was still residual concern about the safety of women in a war zone. But this changed soon after the start of the 1991 Gulf War, when several noncombatant U.S. Navy ships sailed into the war zone.[66] Besides the goals of a new administration, it was clear that during Desert Storm, assignment to noncombatant duty did not prevent women from being in harm's way or in a combat zone, subject to all the hazards of combatants but clearly unable to defend themselves against attack.[67] Additionally, British coalition forces had integrated women onto combatant ships in 1990,[68] and several of these ships served alongside U.S. combatants in the Gulf War. A hearing on women in combat was held in May 1993 by the HASC Military Forces and Personnel subcommittee on women in combat. At the hearing, the Navy requested a repeal of the legislation that excluded women from serving on combatant ships.

The Navy's position focused on mission effectiveness. Vice Admiral Ron Zlatoper, then chief of naval personnel (CNP), argued that women have succeeded in tough assignments in both aviation and on ships and that force reductions, austere budgets, and changing missions required the Navy to draw from the most talented personnel available, regardless of gender, to maintain a high level of readiness and effectiveness. There would be no quotas and no double standards. He testified that cohesion "is a function of shared purposes—common risks and rewards—and good leadership, not a function of some mystical male bonding."[69] Supporters concurred by relating instances of teamwork, heroism, and the abilities of women who had faced the ultimate life-threatening situation on board a ship: fire. The emphasis, it was argued, should be on allowing the Navy maximum flexibility in personnel assignments. This would maintain readiness by allowing them to utilize their best-qualified personnel.[70]

Those opposing opening combatant ships to women focused on the nature of war, family and cultural values, and military effectiveness. They questioned whether the assignment of women would *enhance* the combat capability of a unit and felt that equal opportunity, women's rights, and career development should not be pursued at the expense of putting people's lives at risk. They pointed out that the Civil Rights Act of 1964 does not apply to the military and that the needs of the service subordinate any individual needs or desires. There was concern that the repeal of combat exclusion laws might result in the involuntary assignment of women to combatant ships as well as possible conscription, and that the documented differences in physical strength capabilities between women and men would negatively impact women's ability to do the required physical work without assistance from men. They also pointed out that there was no compelling evidence that the military *needed* women to fight—demographically, the military was not facing a manpower shortage that required the type of changes being discussed.[71]

Marine Brigadier General Thomas V. Draude testified that the argument regarding "added value" was specious. He stated that the broader utilization of talented women in the Navy and Marine Corps would increase military effectiveness. He also testified that the prohibition of women in combatant vessels tied the hands of Marine Expeditionary Unit (MEU) commanders, as they are denied the "skills, talent, dedication and courage of our women. These units deploy with the best men, but not necessarily the best Marines."[72]

Opponents retorted that there is a cultural norm that men in our country protect and defend their families. They argued that family morale, essential for retention, would be adversely affected; that lack of privacy on board ships could lead to increases in inappropriate sexual relationships; and that the resultant pregnancies and fraternization would adversely affect morale. They also argued that the assignment of women only to surface ships, not submarines, would create an unstable situation unlikely to withstand political pressure or legal challenges.[73]

The issue of pregnancy has probably caused the most angst due to attrition and unplanned losses on the ship. During the 1940s, pregnancy was not an issue because women who were mothers, by any means,[74] were discharged. Unplanned losses occur for a number of reasons, but the primary reason for women on ships is pregnancy. Navy policy states that pregnancy and parenthood are compatible with a naval career. However, it does concede that pregnancy could affect a command's operational readiness by temporarily limiting a servicewoman's ability and availability to perform her assigned tasks. At the 20th week of pregnancy, the woman is a loss to the ship; she is also removed if the ship is deployed or underway and cannot guarantee medical evacuation within a six-hour period.[75]

When faced with the loss of a crewmember, commanding officers (COs) must file an Unplanned Loss Report, which begins the process of finding a replacement person. The earlier the report is filed, the sooner a replacement is identified. However, the more specialized the qualifications, the harder it is to find a qualified sailor. A woman's increased visibility during pregnancy creates performance pressures,[76] and her exemption from physical training requirements translates into a perception of a double standard of special treatment.[77] Additionally, the cultural expectation is that a pregnant woman's role and priorities are shifting and that her military responsibilities will suffer.[78]

Even though the Navy's pregnancy rate at sea is considerably less than the rate for women in the civilian sector,[79] it doesn't alter the opinion of most critics that *any* pregnancy aboard ship is problematic. This is not alleviated by the fact that men can be unplanned losses as well, for a variety of reasons, but primarily due to disciplinary infractions. Testimony during the Congressional hearings on women in combat indicated that no mixed-gender ship has ever failed to sail or missed a commitment because of a lack of personnel readiness.[80]

The women's successful performance during Operations Desert Shield/Desert Storm, and the public acceptance of women in dangerous situations, including combat, was the impetus for the Congressional review, and the eventual overturning, of combat exclusion laws and policy. The prohibition against women serving in combatant ships was repealed in November 1993 via the FY94 Defense Authorization Bill (PL 103-160) but included the provision that the services give Congress 30 days' advance notice of proposed changes to policies in the assignment of women to combatant ships. Soon after, the Navy successfully authorized the assignment of women to all ships except submarines and patrol craft (PCs).[81]

The move was met with approval from people "on the deck plates." In their book on the history of women in the Navy, Jean Ebbert and Mary-Beth Hall found that men who had worked with women praised them highly, and those who had not tended to be the naysayers.[82] Women are now on nearly every ship in the Navy. Women have also served in every echelon in the chain of command on almost every ship in the Navy, including as the commanding officer. The first female surface warfare (SWO) flag officer was selected in FY 2002.[83]

The social construction of what it means to be a sailor and the traditional image of what it means to be a woman appear to be mutually exclusive. Men are raised by women, grow up with women, and marry women. They envision women as nurturing and loving, not as warriors.[84] Many men have anecdotal evidence that supports what they already perceive to be true. But the evidence shows that women who join the military do not necessarily fit those gender stereotypes. Military women do not expect to lead a sheltered and protected life; they understand the potential dangers.[85] Through self-selection, military women are generally strong, independent, and anxious for adventure. They join for a variety of reasons, not unlike men. They are looking for opportunities to excel. And they have shown that they want to, and can, do nontraditional jobs as well as men when given the opportunity. Women proved this during WWII, when they filled every possible job except those involving direct combat, and they continued to do so as full members of ships' crews on noncombatants between 1978 and 1994 and on all ships (except submarines) since.[86]

The repeal of the combat exclusion law enables women to aspire to the highest echelons of the Navy: chief of naval operations, fleet commanders, and unified commanders. The motivation for change was due to the personnel needs of the Navy. Although couched in egalitarian terms, there was not necessarily a change in attitude about appropriate roles for women. While individual officers may feel that women can perform the tasks required of any sailor, there is still an institutional bias that can be seen in the debates about women in submarines and in ground combat. There are strong opinions on both sides of the issues.

Women in Submarines

One of the last bastions of male heterogeneity is submarine service. There was discussion regarding the integration of submarines during the 1994 hearings about women in combat. However, the Navy decided its policy would be evolutionary rather than revolutionary[87] and decided to wait to integrate submarines until after the integration of surface ships. Five years later, at their fall 1999 conference, DACOWITS asked the Navy about the status of assigning women to submarines. The committee wondered why the integration had not yet started. However, in the five years since the beginning of combat ship integration, the Navy's top brass had changed dramatically. Admiral Ron Zlatoper, CNP, had retired, and Admiral Jeremy Boorda, CNO, had committed suicide and was replaced by a naval aviator, Admiral Jay Johnson. While Zlatoper and Boorda were highly favorable to the full integration of Navy women, Admiral Johnson was not.

The debate that occurred during the DACOWITS conferences of fall 1999 and spring 2000 was reminiscent of earlier arguments against women going to sea. In contrast to the 1994 hearings, the Navy was adamantly against integrating submarines. The issues of military effectiveness—particularly morale issues—and citizenship responsibilities continued to be cornerstones of the debate. Ironically, DACOWITS made the same argument for the integration of submarines that the Navy had used earlier when lobbying for integrating surface ships: "Full utilization of all personnel resources plays a vital role in Navy readiness, [and] integration of women into the submarine community would more fully utilize all of the Navy's personnel assets."[88] During their fall 1999 conference, DACOWITS recommended that future plans for submarine platforms incorporate appropriate berthing and privacy arrangements to accommodate mixed gender crews.[89]

DACOWITS members wanted to know why women could not serve aboard large ballistic missile submarines (Trident class SSBNs) and why the attack (Virginia class SSNs) submarines, then under construction, were not being built to gender-neutral standards. They wanted the Navy to explain the rationale and assumptions that drove the reported costs, and they wanted *specific* information on why it was impractical to reconfigure current submarines for mixed-gender crews.[90]

The Navy's response to DACOWITS acknowledged the success of women in aviation and surface communities and recognized that opening submarines to women would expand the available pool of personnel who might be interested in and eligible for submarines. The Navy's primary argument against the integration of submarines was that it was not feasible due to the high cost and impracticality of undertaking the necessary habitability upgrades. The Navy argued that to ensure adequate privacy for both genders in submarines would cost millions of dollars, would not be cost effective, and that to accommodate mixed-gender crews would reduce operational readiness due to the necessity to remove operational equipment as a space/weight trade-off, and that even with habitability modifications, privacy would still be inadequate.[91]

Related to this argument was a concern that lack of privacy would cause family morale problems, false sexual harassment charges, or inequality of berthing and head facilities, all of which would be a detriment to unit morale and cohesion.[92] An argument that surfaced during the 1978 Congressional hearings on women at sea rose again during the submarine debate. The issue was that sailors' wives were against women going to sea. Although the Navy dismissed the arguments then, they appeared to have more clout in 1999 and 2000. Submarine wives were highly resistant to assigning women to submarines, citing lack of privacy, the morale of the men, and safety. The Navy was concerned that prolonged loneliness and the lack of two-way communication would cause stress, hurt morale, and diminish support from home, thus affecting the ability of the sailor to do his job. The wives also feared that the female sailors would cause more work for their husbands because they could not handle certain tasks. That military women would be spending more time with the men than their wives was another negative morale factor for the families.[93]

Low family morale can negatively affect the morale of the crew and decrease their long-term productivity. However, the needs of the Navy come first, and the Navy relies on leadership to make it all work. Commander Gerard Roncolato and Lt. Commander Stephen Davis, the Commanding Officer and Executive Officer of *The Sullivans* (DDG-68), found during the commissioning process of the then-new ship, that good leaders could alleviate gender integration concerns through frank discussions at support group meetings, command events, and other family venues, and by taking necessary disciplinary action when infractions are discovered. Those leaders who do not are remiss in their duties. They advocate a commonsense approach: train the women the same way as the men to ensure they can do the job; treat everyone professionally and with respect; and provide counseling to all parties—men, women, and spouses—so everyone knows what to expect, what the standards are, and how to deal with problems. Emphasize adult, professional behavior. They found that the anticipation and antagonism of people who have never served with women usually give way to respect and relief once the women arrive and perform to the set standards.[94]

The Navy was also concerned that submarine mission effectiveness would be degraded by personnel losses due to pregnancy. The justifications included inadequate medical evacuation capabilities, fetal damage due to possible exposure to ionizing radiation from the nuclear reactor in the engineering spaces, and of most concern, unplanned personnel losses due to the Navy's reassignment policies for pregnancy when on sea duty. The need to keep the submarine fully manned and operationally ready is cited as the most important reason women should not be assigned to submarines.[95]

However, the fault of the Navy's logic was in basing these arguments on the presumption of uncontrolled pregnancies on surface ships, where the majority of pregnancies occur in non-rated personnel as opposed to more senior enlisted personnel or officers.[96] Most submariners are assigned a rating[97] and once rate training is complete these sailors generally are promoted to E-4 as an incentive. As a woman becomes more senior—with more responsibility, education, and experience—she is less likely to get pregnant while on sea duty.[98] The most glaring difference between surface ships and submarines is that submarine duty is voluntary, screened, and requires higher Armed Services Vocational Aptitude Battery (ASVAB)[99] scores. The training pipeline for submarine personnel can be 11–18 months,[100] so most of the unmotivated or problem sailors will either screen out or drop out. Additionally, there is a hefty reenlistment bonus associated with continuing as a nuclear trained crewmember.[101]

What this all means is that just because a woman *can* get pregnant does not mean she *will* get pregnant. Only a small percentage of women get pregnant while on sea duty; most Navy women either do not have children at all, or wait until they are on shore duty to take that step. The 1997 Navy Pregnancy Study found that women on deployable units had *significantly lower* pregnancy rates than women on shore duty.[102] It also makes an assumption of a lack of professionalism of women sailors. Contrary to the Navy's arguments, one should not assume there will be a pregnancy problem for female submarine sailors.

At the spring 2000 conference, DACOWITS again addressed the issue of women in submarines, and acknowledged the Navy's helpfulness in allowing the members to embark on submarines while underway in order to see first hand the unique aspects of submarine life. They did, however, recommend that in the short term the Navy assign women officers to the larger TRIDENT class ballistic submarines (SSBNs); and in the long term they redesign the smaller attack Virginia-class submarines (SSNs) to accommodate mixed gender crews.[103]

In response, the Navy explained that submarine officer career paths required assignment to both SSN and SSBN vessels. Allowing women officers to serve only on Trident-class SSBNs would create a two-tiered officer community. This would limit the female officers' opportunities for command, which would be unfair. In addition, the quality of life on a Trident is relatively high, and allowing women to serve only on that class could be perceived as an inequity. In both cases, morale would be affected.[104]

Although supportive of assigning women to combatant ships, the Navy's official stance in 2000 with regard to the assignment of women to submarines was that it was not feasible, not only due to cost, quality of life, and mission effectiveness, but also because of the arduousness of the duty and family morale concerns. There was also the argument that the submarine force could not support a two-track career system, to the smaller SSNs for men, and the larger SSBNs for gender integration.

A report by Science Application International Corporation in their 1995 study regarding women in submarines concludes:

> Submarines are unique; they operate alone for months at a time, limited only by food supplies and the endurance of the crew. The recreational facilities on other vessels used to relieve stress are absent on submarines. There are no sociological or psychological data that can be used to determine the effects of gender mixing. Thus, the unknown effects of the extreme conditions are a major factor that should drive submarine assignment policy.
>
> The introduction of women in submarines is less a question of whether they can do the job than it is a question of whether the added complications of a mixed gender ship will undermine the combat effectiveness. Issues such as pregnancy, fraternization or harassment, shipboard supplies, bunk management, changes in group dynamics may detract from the focus on operations and nuclear safety.
>
> Therefore, the focus should not be on women, per se, but on the ramifications of having mixed gender crews in the unique submarine environment.[105]

Thus the reasons why submarines are viewed as different from all other ships and remain closed to women encompasses more than the cost and military effectiveness stance the Navy has taken. It includes concerns about the effect women will have on the already tight quarters and lack of privacy that the crew must endure. Nevertheless, at its fall 2000 conference, DACOWITS reiterated its recommendations to assign women officers to the larger ballistic submarines, and to plan for the implementation of women on to all submarines as a long term goal.[106] After that the issue was dropped.

The debate was effectively halted because, in October 2000, HASC member Congressman Roscoe Bartlett (R-MD) added to the House version of the National Defense Authorization Act for FY 2001 during a closed session of the HASC, a provision that would prohibit the assignment of women to submarines, in an attempt to codify the exclusion much as was done in 1948. It was adopted 31–21. The provision was later modified during the joint House/Senate conference committee to require a congressional review period of 30 days of continuous session of Congress prior to any change in the assignment of women to submarines. It also prohibited any funds to be expended on planning for reconfiguration or new design of submarines for women without this 30-day notice. This was signed into law on October 30, 2000.[107]

That there were no hearings on this subject, nor was there documented debate in committee or on the floor of Congress during the legislative process is surprising given the apparent contentious debate in the public sector. Very emotional views were coming from members of the submarine community and their wives, as opposed to the equal opportunity stance taken by DACOWITS and its supporters. However, if the Navy wanted to oppose this legislation, hearings on the subject probably would have been requested.[108]

Nine years later, in the fall of 2009, the Chairman of JCS Admiral Mike Mullin, as well as the SECNAV Ray Mabus, the CNO Admiral Gary Roughead, and the Master Chief Petty Officer of the Navy (MCPON) Rick West, a submariner himself, publically announced that they support the idea of assigning women to submarines. In contrast to the Navy's earlier stance, Roughead told *Navy Times*, "accommodations are a factor, but not insurmountable."[109] The *Washington Post* reported that one reason the Navy seeks to integrate women on submarines is that they make up a growing percentage of college graduates, including engineers, noting that there is a vast pool of talent being neglected in Navy recruiting efforts.[110]

Some of the same arguments against the plan have been voiced in Facebook chat rooms and in *Navy Times* editorials, particularly with regard to sexual harassment charges and wives' concerns. *API* reports some sailors and wives are concerned that putting men and women together in extremely close quarters for weeks at a time will result in sexual harassment cases and wrecked marriages. However, the Navy is moving ahead with plans, preparing the required notification to Congress, and reporting that women could serve on submarines as soon as 2011.[111]

The actual plan of how this will be accomplished has yet to be published, however, contacts at the Bureau of Naval Personnel report that the Navy will move forward in a measured way, taking DACOWITS's earlier recommendations to place women officers on the larger ballistic submarines, which can be done as soon as women can be trained, and taking the long view for renovating the smaller submarines. There is also the possibility that currently warfare qualified staff officers, such as supply and medical officers, would be assigned along with junior officers to provide role models and mentors for both men and women. One suggestion for a proven method of integration is to study the experiences of the gender-integrated submarines of other Western countries such as Australia, Norway, and Sweden, who have had women on their submarines for years.

In the past, many barriers have been broken as a result of the needs of the military, and this appears to be the case in the desire to move forward with integrating submarines. Although Admiral Mullin is a huge proponent of diversity in the military, apparently there is also a concern that there are not enough men volunteering for submarine service, and this is a way of ensuring the future of the submarine force. In the end, just as with the integration of African Americans and women at sea in previous iterations, the move is made with military readiness in mind. Equal opportunity is a supplemental benefit that the military can tout as well. As in the past, if there are personnel issues with submarines, the Navy will probably find a solution. Regardless of the reason, if leadership supports it, service members may complain, but ultimately they will salute with a cheery "aye, aye" and make it happen.

Notes

1. Lory Manning, *Women in the Military* (Washington, DC: Women's Research and Education Institute, 2008), 2.

2. Manning, *Women in the Military*, 3; Jeanne Holm, *Women in the Military: An Unfinished Revolution*, rev. ed. (Novato, CA: Presidio Press, 1992).

3. Jean Ebbert and Mary-Beth Hall, *Crossed Currents: Navy Women in a Century of Change*, 3rd ed. (Washington, DC: Brassey's, 1999), 262.

4. Linda Bird Francke, *Ground Zero: The Gender Wars in the Military* (New York: Simon and Schuster, 1997), 220–221.

5. Ibid., 266.

6. Presidential Commission on the Assignment of Women in the Armed Forces, *Report to the President* (Washington, DC: Government Printing Office, November 15, 1992).

7. Darlene M. Iskra, "Attitudes toward Expanding Roles for Navy Women at Sea," *Armed Forces and Society* 33, no. 2 (January 2007): 203–223.

8. Mady Wechsler Segal and Amanda Faith Hansen, "Value Rationales in Policy Debates on Women in the Military: A Content Analysis of Congressional Testimony, 1941–1985," *Social Science Quarterly* 73, no. 2 (June 1992): 296–309.

9. Iskra, "Attitudes towards Expanding Roles."

10. Brian Mitchell, *Women in the Military: Flirting with Disaster* (Washington, DC: Regnery Publishing, 1998).

11. Iskra, "Attitudes towards Expanding Roles"; Mady Wechsler Segal, "Gender and the Military," in *Handbook of the Sociology of Gender*, ed. Janet Saltzman Chafetz (New York: Kluwer Academic/Plenum Publishers, 1999), 563–581.

12. Iskra, "Attitudes towards Expanding Roles"; Mitchell, *Women in the Military*; Segal, "Gender and the Military"; Clyde Wilcox, "Race, Gender, and Support for Women in the Military," *Social Science Quarterly* 73, no. 2 (June 1992): 310–323.

13. Gerard D. Roncolato and Stephen F. Davis, Jr., "A View from the Gender Fault Line," *U.S. Naval Institute Proceedings* 124, no. 3 (March 1998): 102–104.

14. John L. Olliges, "Nobody Asked Me, But . . . No Double Standards," *U.S. Naval Institute Proceedings* 120, no. 1 (January 1993): 94–95.

15. Iskra, "Attitudes towards Expanding Roles"; Segal, "Gender and the Military"; House Committee on Armed Services, Military Forces and Personnel Subcommittee (HASC), *Women in Combat: Hearing, May 12, 1993* (Washington DC: U.S. Government Printing Office, 1994).

16. Mady Wechsler Segal, "Women in the Military: Research and Policy Issues," *Youth and Society* 10, no. 2 (1978): 121.

17. Roncolato and Davis, "A View from the Gender Fault Line."

18. Holm, *Women in the Military*; Iskra, "Attitudes towards Expanding Roles"; Roncolato and Davis, "A View from the Gender Fault Line"; Ebbert and Hall, *Crossed Currents*; HASC, *Women in Combat*, 102.

19. Margaret Harrell and Laura Miller, *New Opportunities for Military Women: Effects Upon Readiness, Cohesion and Morale*. National Defense Research Institute, prepared for the Office of the Secretary of Defense (Santa Monica, CA: RAND, 1997); Iskra, "Attitudes towards Expanding Roles"; Olliges, "No Double Standards."

20. Presidential Commission, *Report to the President*.

21. Holm, *Women in the Military*; Iskra, "Attitudes towards Expanding Roles."

22. Holm, *Women in the Military*; Iskra, "Attitudes towards Expanding Roles."

23. Maureen Honey, *Creating Rosie the Riveter: Class, Gender, and Propaganda during World War II* (Amherst: The University of Massachusetts Press, 1984).

24. Holm, *Women in the Military*; Iskra, "Attitudes towards Expanding Roles"; Segal and Segal, "Social Change and the Participation of Women"; Wilcox, "Race, Gender, and Support."

25. HASC, *Women in Combat*, 68; Holm, *Women in the Military*; Iskra, "Attitudes towards Expanding Roles"; Segal, "Women in the Military."

26. Holm, *Women in the Military*; Iskra, "Attitudes towards Expanding Roles."

27. Ibid.

28. Segal and Segal, "Social Change and the Participation of Women"; David R. Segal, *Recruiting for Uncle Sam: Citizenship and Military Manpower Policy* (Lawrence, KA: University Press of Kansas, 1989); Wilcox, "Race, Gender, and Support."

29. Patricia Schroeder, *24 Years of House Work . . . and the Place Is Still a Mess* (Kansas City, MO: Andrew McMeel Publishing, 1998).

30. Francke, *Ground Zero*, 220–221.

31. Holm, *Women in the Military*, 475.

32. Francke, *Ground Zero*, 221.

33. Holm, *Women in the Military*, 476.

34. Ibid., 476–477.

35. Francke, *Ground Zero*, 230–233.

36. Ibid.

37. Holm, *Women in the Military*, 491.

38. Presidential Commission, *Report to the President*, iii. For an electrifying account of the Senate hearing and all the lobbying both for and against the exclusion, see Francke, *Ground Zero*, 220–240.

39. Presidential Commission, *Report to the President*, iii.

40. Francke, *Ground Zero*, 240.

41. See the full Presidential Commission *Report to the President* for all the issues.

42. Department of Defense, Office of the Inspector General, *The Tailhook Report [The Official Inquiry into the Events of Tailhook '91]* (New York: St. Martin's Press, 1993), vii.

43. Ibid., 18.

44. Ibid, viii; Jean Zimmerman, *Tailspin: Women at War in the Wake of Tailhook* (New York: Doubleday, 1995), 6–7.

45. Gale Cengage Learning, "The Tailhook Scandal: 1994," *Women's History*, report of the lawsuit between Paula Coughlin and Hilton Hotels Las Vegas, http://www.gale.cengage.com/free_resources/whm/trials/tailhook.htm; Zimmerman, *Tailspin*, 27.

46. Francke, *Ground Zero*, 240; Zimmerman, *Tailspin*.

47. Department of Defense, Office of the Inspector General, *The Tailhook Report*.

48. Ibid., 2.

49. Learning, "The Tailhook Scandal: 1994."

50. There currently is no one article in the UCMJ that prohibits sexual harassment. The infractions are dealt with under other articles in the UCMJ. This actually serves a better purpose, showing the seriousness of the conduct. See Appendix I.

51. Zimmerman, *Tailspin*, 96–97.

52. Ibid.

53. Unfortunately, I lived through this time in the Navy. Articles and letters to the editor depicting the backlash against women were published in *Navy Times* throughout 1993 and 1994. It took several years before gender relations became somewhat normalized.

54. Zimmerman, *Tailspin*, 218.

55. The abaya is a traditional, heavy black religious garment for Saudi Muslim women that covers the body from head to toe.

56. "Off-Base Travel Program," *320th Air Expeditionary Group Instruction 31-1*, October 31, 2000. Military instructions normally come up for review every five years, but this policy was updated even as McSally was trying to have it abolished.

57. Martha McSally, e-mail from Lt. Col. McSally to her boss, J3 of Joint Task Force–South West Asia, July 2, 2001.

58. U.S. Department of State, "Saudi Arabia: Country Specific Information," http://travel.state.gov/travel/cis_pa_tw/cis/cis_1012.html.

59. Martha McSally and Cynthia Hanson, "The Fight of My Life," *Ladies Home Journal* (2002), http://www.lhj.com/relationships/work/worklife-balance/the-fight-of-my-life/.

60. Ibid.

61. Ibid.

62. Edward T. Pound, "Saudi Rules Anger Top Air Force Pilot," *USA Today*, April 18, 2001, 1A.

63. Darlene M. Iskra, "Prohibition to Wearing Abaya in Saudi Arabia by Women in the Military," memo to Senator Cantwell's legislative and office directors, May 13, 2002.

64. Ibid.

65. Ebbert and Hall, *Crossed Currents*, 324.

66. Ebbert and Hall, *Crossed Currents*; Holm, *Women in the Military*.

67. Ebbert and Hall, *Crossed Currents*.

68. Presidential Commission, *Report to the President*.

69. HASC, *Women in Combat*, 13.

70. Ibid.

71. Ibid.

72. Ibid., 104.

73. Ibid. The issue of dual career paths in the navy has been well established, so this argument is specious. Additionally, similar arguments were made when women were first assigned to ships in 1978. Women are still not serving on submarines.

74. Women who became mothers through adoption or marriage to a man who had custody of children by a prior marriage were discharged, as well as women who became pregnant.

75. Secretary of the Navy, "Department of the Navy (DON) Policy on Pregnancy," *SECNAV Instruction 1000.10*, February 6, 1995.

76. Rosabeth Moss Kanter, "Some Effects of Proportions on Group Life: Skewed Sex Ratios and Responses to Token Women," *American Journal of Sociology* 82, no. 5 (1977): 965–990.

77. Harrell and Miller, *New Opportunities for Military Women*.

78. Segal, "Gender and the Military."

79. Jacqueline A. Mottern, *Parenthood and Pregnancy: Results of the 1999 Survey* (Millington, TN: Navy Personnel Research, Studies, and Technology, 2000).

80. HASC, *Women in Combat*, 102.

81. Ebbert and Hall, *Crossed Currents*; HASC, *Women in Combat*.

82. Ebbert and Hall, *Crossed Currents*.

83. Women have served as commanding officers on all ships except, of course, submarines. There also has not yet been a woman in command of an aircraft carrier, typically reserved for aviators on their way to flag rank. The first woman SWO was Rear Admiral (Lower Half) (RDML) Deborah Loewer. A few have since followed in her

footsteps, including RADM Carol Pottenger, and RDML Michelle Howard, who is also the first female Naval Academy graduate to be promoted to flag rank.

84. Anna Simon, "Women Can Never 'Belong' in Combat," *Orbis*, Summer 2000, 451–461.

85. Holm, *Women in the Military*, 405; Darlene M. Iskra, *Breaking Through the Brass Ceiling: Strategies of Success for Elite Military Women* (Saarbrüken, Germany: VDM Verlag Dr. Müller, 2008).

86. Ebbert and Hall, *Crossed Currents*; Holm, *Women in the Military*; Iskra, "Attitudes towards Expanding Roles"; Roncolato and Davis, "A View from the Gender Fault Line."

87. HASC, *Women in Combat*.

88. DACOWITS, *2000 Spring Conference Issue Book*, http://dacowits.defense. gov/issue_books/Spr2000_IssueBk_toc.html.

89. DACOWITS, History of Recommendations, *Fall 1999*, http://dacowits.de fense.gov/history_of_recommedations/hist-rec-fall-99.html.

90. DACOWITS, *1999 Fall Conference Issue Book*, http://dacowits.defense.gov/ issue_books/Fall99_IssBk_ForceDU.html.

91. Darlene Marie Iskra, *Women in Submarines: Have the Arguments about Expanding Women's Sea-Going Roles in the U.S. Navy Changed over Time?* Unpublished Master's thesis, University of Maryland, 2003.

92. HASC, *Women in Combat*.

93. Science Application International Corporation (SAIC), *Submarine Assignment Policy Assessment* (Washington, DC: Science Application International Corporation, 1995).

94. Holm, *Women in the Military*; Roncolato and Davis, "A View from the Gender Fault Line."

95. HASC, *Women in Combat*; SAIC, *Submarine Assignment*.

96. Mottern, *Parenthood and Pregnancy*.

97. A rating in the Navy is an occupational specialty area, such as sonar technician, mechanic, cook, or radioman.

98. Mottern, *Parenthood and Pregnancy*; Patricia J. Thomas and Zannette A. Uriell, *Pregnancy and Single Parenthood in the Navy: Results of a 1997 Survey* (San Diego, CA: Navy Personnel Research and Development Center, 1998).

99. The ASVAB is a test required of all prospective recruits to determine their eligibility for a variety of occupational specialties.

100. Robert Benson, "Light Years Ahead," *All Hands* 995 (April 2000): 34–39.

101. Ibid.

102. Thomas and Uriell, *Pregnancy and Single Parenthood*.

103. DACOWITS, *2000 Spring Conference Issue Book*.

104. Iskra, *Women in Submarines*.

105. SAIC, *Submarine Assignment*, 4.

106. DACOWITS, *2000 Fall Conference Issue Book*. http://dacowits.defense.gov/ issue_books/Spr2001_IssueBk_toc.html.

107. Iskra, *Women in Submarines*, 30–31.

108. Ibid.

109. William H. McMichael and Andrew Scutro, "SecNav, CNO: Women Should Serve on Subs," *Navy Times*, September 27, 2009, http://www.navytimes.com/news/2009/09/navy_roughead_subs_092409w/.

110. Ann Scott Tyson, "Navy Seeks to Allow Women to Serve on Submarines," *Washington Post*, September 26, 2009, http://www.washingtonpost.com/wp-dyn/content/article/2009/09/25/AR2009092503385.html.

111. Russ Bynum and Pauline Jelinek, "Navy Moves to Put Women on Submarines," *Associated Press*, October 13, 2009, http://news.yahoo.com/s/ap/20091013/ap_on_re_us/us_women_on_submarines.

CHAPTER 3

Citizenship Rights, Responsibilities, and Women in Ground Combat

Women want to go into the combat forces just like they want to be SEALs or submariners—they were the first child and their dad wanted a boy and treated them as such. Then along came the brothers, and dad had already treated them as a boy and still does. Then comes the Army, and they can't understand why anyone would think they would be anything other than equal to the boys. I know when I was young I was as strong as any of my brothers and worked twice as hard. I loved to be outside, didn't mind the mud, was the women's rifle champion in Minnesota, and was not in the least bit modest in front of the boys. When I was young my dad treated me as an equal, and when I first came in the Navy I could not figure out why I could not go to sea. But I joined the Navy because all the women did in the Army was desk work, and the Navy had more options, i.e., pilots, etc. Also women who are in the tough jobs and succeed are promoted and looked up to.

—Mary, retired Navy captain

Women such as my friend Mary joined the military in increasing numbers in the 1970s. They have continued to be attracted to the lifestyle, benefits, and opportunities the military provides that are not necessarily available on such a broad scale in the civilian workforce. Although not all women have the same attitude as Mary, many did join with this "I am equal" attitude and were surprised and dismayed when their opportunities were limited because of gender.

Military service is necessarily discriminatory. Rules that apply in the civilian workplace do not necessarily apply to work in the military. There are both policies and legislation that make discrimination legal. For example, there are mental, physical, educational, and age standards that must be met before one is eligible to enlist. The military also discriminates on the basis of dependency status, sexuality, and gender.[1] African Americans were segregated in the military until the Korean War made it militarily ineffective to continue to do so. Women in the military were segregated until DOPMA in 1980 equalized, at least theoretically, promotion opportunity. Of course, there are reasons behind these rules and policies; many make sense, but some do not.

The concept of citizenship rights is taken for granted by all who are born in the United States. While the Bill of Rights addressed 10 of the most important rights as part of our Constitution, many others are assumed without being codified. Citizenship responsibilities are much less touted but are no less important. However, note that the rhetoric regarding rights can also be viewed as responsibilities. One of the historical responsibilities of citizenship is the obligation of military service and to give one's life for one's country when called upon.

Military service has been associated with the concept of citizenship since before the American Revolution. Women have participated in the military in significant percentages since the end of the draft, yet equal rights in all aspects of American society remain elusive. Egalitarian feminists believe it is a "woman's right and even responsibility to perform martial service, because the military is the *sine qua non* of full citizenship, and thus, equality."[2] In contrast, antifeminists rue the loss of their "right to be excused from the draft"[3] and desire to exercise their citizenship responsibilities as wives, mothers, and/or peacemakers.[4] Thus, the goals of women's equality and citizenship status are driven by very different perspectives.

While many rights and responsibilities of citizenship such as voting, serving on a jury, or working and paying taxes are burdens of all citizens, the right to fight remains unresolved. The words rang out at rallies for equality in the military for African Americans during WWII and are still being debated as we begin to think about including openly homosexual men and women into military ranks. For women, the right-to-fight debate is ongoing.

The gendered construction of roles and social values has been a hindrance to women's full participation as citizens since this country was established. Although the American Revolution was fought over the issues of state sovereignty and citizen obligations, it was inherently understood that these issues only applied to white male property owners. At the Constitutional Convention of 1787, the relationship between the state and citizen was radically changed: as individuals, men could choose the extent to which the state exercised control over them through the electoral process. They could choose and redefine obligation. Yet, either through neglect or the implicit social constructs that were both legally and socially dominant at the time, a woman's civic obligations were *covered* by either her husband or her father. This practice was based on the old English system of domestic relations—the principle of *coverture*. Women had no rights and no obligations; they were *protected*.[5] The progress made over the last two centuries in the legal, political, and social rights of women is a story unto itself.[6]

The stance that most proponents of increased roles for women in the military take is that status as first-class citizens can only be reached if women who *choose* to participate in the military are given equal access to all jobs, including combat. Mady Wechsler Segal and Amanda Faith Hansen theorize that as gender equality becomes more of a reality in the "broader society," pressure to increase nontraditional roles and equality for women in the military will follow. This, in turn, will lead to greater roles for women in the military, though not at the expense of military effectiveness.[7] Yet these citizenship rights and responsibilities arguments are somewhat problematic. This is evidenced by the chasm that exists between various feminist groups—they cannot agree on an acceptable standard of equality for women. There are differences in attitudes that start with the *right* not to be drafted versus the *right* of equal selective service registration, the *right* to participate fully in the military versus the *right* to be stay-at-home wives and mothers, and continue with the question of whether women have *equal responsibility* to participate in ground combat or not.[8] It is no wonder that feminist ideals are not taken seriously by nonfeminists: there is no consolidated platform.

There are several feminist schools of thought, all of which seem to have contradictory views when it comes to women in the military and citizenship rights. Three approaches to women's military service developed from the women's movement of the 1960s and 1970s. The first, defined as either *feminist antimilitarist* or *critical feminists*, believe it is dangerous for women to be involved in the military at all, as it promotes masculine values and results in the reinforcement of the gendered hierarchy. It allows women to be manipulated rather than empowered. They believe the military culture is diametrically opposed to women's culture and feminist goals. They oppose the military as violent and an impediment to justice and peace. They believe women can achieve equality through a redefinition or reprioritization of what is important for society—namely, that the military plays too important a role in society and that the importance of the military must be changed. Similarly, the *antifeminists*, also called right-wing women, the far right, or the New Right, support traditional family values and do not believe there is any place in the military for women. Their viewpoint is that women are natural nurturers and that their participation in the military not only destroys the family and civil society but also impairs military efficiency.[9]

On the other hand, *egalitarian feminists* (also known as liberal or equal rights feminists), believe in women's capacity and capability to compete equally with men within our current social system and social norms. They assert that women may *earn* equality by assuming the social roles that have traditionally been assigned to men. They use equality to demand a full and unimpeded role for women in the military, and they also define the *benefits* afforded by military service as rights of citizenship.[10] I will primarily address the issues of equality and citizenship as defined by the egalitarian feminists, but I will also attempt to provide the opposite views of the antifeminist New Right, since these two groups are the most frequently heard in public discourse. This is not to discount the views of the critical feminists, but the idea of a world without the military (critical feminists) is beyond the scope of this discussion.

What Is Full Citizenship?

In his seminal essay "Citizenship and Social Class," T. H. Marshall and Tom Bottomore describe citizenship as the right to enjoy the *qualitative* factors associated with equality and the right to be admitted to share in the social heritage, which can be interpreted to mean the right to be accepted as full members of the society—that is, as citizens. Interestingly, they assume that economic inequality is compatible with full rights of citizenship.[11] I, however, find this problematic; in this country, economic viability is the key to equality in a number of social institutions, especially education and justice.

Marshall and Bottomore analyze citizenship as a social structure by dividing it into three parts: civil, political, and social. The civil element defines the rights necessary for individual freedom—liberty of the person, freedom of speech, thought and faith, the right to own property and to conclude valid contracts, and the right to justice. The political element involves the right to vote, and otherwise participate in the political process, either as a member of a political body, such as city council or the House of Representative, or as an elector of the members of such a body. Finally, the social element is the whole range of life elements, from the right to a minimum degree of economic welfare and security to the right to share in the county's heritage and to *live the life of a civilized being according to the standards prevailing in the society*. The institutions most closely connected with the social element are the educational, health, and labor system.[12] It stands to reason, then, that second-class citizenship occurs when individuals or groups are not able to take advantage of any or all aspects of the full definition of citizenship described by Marshall and Bottomore.

The civil, political, and social elements, which I define as *rights*, comprise the basic foundation for our democratic society. Civil rights seem to be the most invoked in contemporary times; the right to due process is often used as certain systemic inequalities are eliminated through court challenges.[13] Civil rights for both minorities and women were granted in the latter half of the 20th century as demanded by the civil rights and women's movements. According to the 14th Amendment's due-process clause,[14] employers could no longer discriminate on the basis of race or ethnicity for the "right to follow the occupation of one's choice in the place of one's choice, subject only to legitimate demands for preliminary technical training."[15] The defeat of the Equal Rights Amendment precluded the same civil rights for women, but subsequent

Supreme Court decisions provided equality for women in virtually every area *except* the military.[16] This remains the case today.

Early in our nation's history, political rights were nonexistent for women, African Americans, immigrants, and nonproperty-owning white men. They were not full citizens; they did not have voting rights, economic freedom, or even the right to education. Over the years this changed as suffrage was granted to African Americans by the 15th Amendment to the Constitution in 1870, to women by the 19th Amendment in 1920, and to 18-year-olds by the 26th Amendment in 1971. Additional access to voting rights was given to the poor when poll taxes were alleviated by the 24th Amendment in 1964.[17] These were clearly steps in the direction toward full citizenship.

Social equality, however, remains elusive. By this I mean the ability live life according to our American standards and to enjoy the Constitutional rights we so often take for granted. This is evidenced by the dual lifestyle standards between rich and poor, minority and white, and men and women that continue today in education, housing, legal justice, occupational status, wages, and equality of opportunity,[18] although equality of opportunity does not always mean equal outcomes in a capitalistic society.

The historical connection between citizenship and military participation in America was manifested by the opportunity for non- and second-class citizens to gain full citizenship rights through military service. Citizenship was granted to immigrants and free blacks who fought with the colonial forces during the American Revolution, and for those who fought for the Union during the Civil War. During subsequent wars, including the world wars and the Korean and Vietnam wars, naturalization requirements were waived for immigrants who served in the military. These special benefits are still conferred to those who serve honorably.[19]

Rights versus Responsibilities

One would think the idea of civic rights would correspond with appropriate civic responsibilities. Unfortunately, this is not the case. Morris Janowitz, in his 1980 essay on the sociology of citizenship, states: "Equality, rather than citizenship is a core concern of contemporary sociology."[20] He goes on to say that citizenship is the basis for citizen rights and political, economic, and social equality. Yet social science literature concerning civil rights primarily invoke citizenship in terms of citizen rights and the barriers faced in equality of those rights. Janowitz concludes that the result has been a distortion in the sociology of citizenship; that citizenship involves a balance between rights and responsibilities, which is *"missing from the discourse."*[21]

The concept of citizen obligations rises from the political authority given to governments to ensure the security and protection of citizen rights and property. In order to carry out that function, the government must impose certain obligations.[22] As defined by Marshall and Bottomore, these obligations include 1) the duty to pay taxes, 2) the duty to be educated, 3) the duty of military service, and 4) the duty to promote the welfare of the community.[23] Morris Janowitz adds the duty to participate in the electoral process and in fact seems to suggest that this is the most important facet of contemporary citizenship obligation.[24]

Linda K. Kerber defines obligations as those duties that invite state punishment if they are not performed; the obligations she lists differ from Marshall's, with the exception of military service and paying taxes. She adds obligations to: avoid vagrancy (that is, to appear to be a respectable working person); serve on juries; and to refrain from treason. These obligations, which appear to be equitable requirements for all citizens, have actually been experienced differently by men and women. While subject to the laws and obligation to pay taxes, women were not able to vote, work, own property, or participate on juries until well into the 19th and 20th centuries.[25]

Kerber argues that the "equal protection of the laws" guaranteed by the 14th Amendment has resulted in a gendered definition of *rights* and argues that the history of gendered *obligation* is less understood. Rights should be paired with obligations: "The right to enjoy a trial by jury is mirrored by an obligation to serve on juries if called upon. The right to enjoy the protections of the state against disorder is linked to an obligation to bear arms in its defense. The right to enjoy the benefits of government is linked to an obligation to be loyal to it and to pay taxes to support it."[26] Similarly, the performance of military service (as an *obligation*) has been linked to the *rights* of full citizenship—an area in which women have been deprived.

The second class position of women began in the 19th century with protectionist legislation sheltering women and children from exploitation because, as noncitizens, they had no legal recourse. In the social context of the day, it was believed that in order for women to enjoy full and responsible citizenship, they would have to forego the right to protection. Marshall and Bottomore note that this argument had become obsolete with women's suffrage in 1920,[27] but, as we will see, this *right to protection* is one of the counter arguments by the antifeminists to the *right to fight* arguments of egalitarian feminists.

The Obligation of Military Service

The relationship between the military and citizenship in American history has been discussed. Although the United States did not maintain a large standing army prior to WWII, the military was widely seen as a coming-of-age experience for males, especially in the era of the draft.[28] The shift to an AVF, however, has slowly eroded that relationship. Eight out of 10 age-eligible men served in the military during WWII. About half of eligible men served from the Korean War through the early 1960s. During Vietnam only 4 of 10 served, and currently only about 9 percent are serving or have served in the military. Additionally, in the first three decades after WWII, military service was almost a requirement for elective office. By 1982, the proportion of veterans in Congress fell below half for the first time since before that war.[29] In the 111th Congress, about 23 percent have prior military service—a number that has been steadily declining since the draft ended.[30]

The severance of rights and responsibilities identified by Janowitz has been documented, and David R. Segal cites two studies that reiterate this severance. In the first—a survey of over fifteen hundred college students conducted by Janowitz in 1979—the rights of free speech, religion, franchise, and trial by jury were deemed more important than any obligation, including the associated obligations that support those rights. In a 1982 study conducted by the Roper Organization regarding the difference between benefits that had to be earned as opposed to rights, it was found that 60 percent felt that retirement provisions, and 52 percent felt that standard of living, were rights versus privileges to be earned. These finding were even more prevalent among the poor (70 percent and 65 percent) and among blacks (83 percent and 74 percent). Segal concludes that there is a constituency for entitlement programs that primarily consists of the most disadvantaged in society.[31]

Military service did, and still does, provide a venue for upward economic and social mobility for those disadvantaged in the civilian workforce (i.e., women and racial minorities, especially black men and women).[32] However, the primary *obligation* of military service is really during mass mobilization, when conscription is required to provide adequate personnel for the military. There will always be those individuals who believe war is wrong, regardless of the circumstances, and their option is to pursue conscientious objector status. But it is clear, by the definitions provided by both Kerber and Marshall and Bottomore, that full citizenship does *require* participation in combat when called for by the state. This is the balm of the egalitarian feminists and the bane of the antifeminists.

Feminism, Citizenship, and the Equality Debate

As previously discussed, the debate regarding women's roles in the military comes from two opposite camps: the egalitarian feminists and the antifeminists. These groups have different definitions of equality, which, I argue, serves to maintain the gendered status quo rather than change it. Ilene Rose Feinman discusses this dilemma, noting that women's groups that work toward opposite ends will never have the political power to elicit change. As a critical feminist, she realizes her paradigm of women as peace loving and nurturing does not coincide with the reality of women who *want* to participate in the military. She recognizes and concludes that "in order to be taken seriously as opponents to war, feminist antimilitarists will have to . . . acknowledge women's accomplishments there while continuing to work toward the separation of militarism and citizenship."[33]

Using the arguments of the egalitarian feminists to support her view, Feinman recognizes that equality in our culture will only come (1) when women compete on men's terms and that (2) once equality is established, women can use that power to *change* the social constructs of our gendered society. In contrast, egalitarian feminists believe in the inherent equality of women and men, and that women should be able to aspire to all of the same civil, political, and social elements that are taken for granted by men. They see the military as a way for women to get ahead, allowing working-class and minority women to receive better wages, benefits, and educational opportunities than they would otherwise receive in the civilian sector. They believe the participation of women in the military will lead to their status as full citizens. Their analysis is based on the paradigm that full military service and participation is the epitome of full citizenship. This is in contrast to antifeminists, who believe in the right of women to be *Ladies*, and who define women as different from men and in need of protection rather than equality.[34]

Antifeminists believe in the traditional family—the middle-class standard of a male breadwinner who supports his family and the female homemaker who supports her husband's and family's needs. The issue of women as equal citizens is seen as irrelevant because antifeminists define women in relation to men and the family, much as in 19th-century America under coverture. This view of the traditional family is being challenged by today's family structures, many of which do not resemble the middle-class norm. This norm is also in contrast to the family structures of poor families where women have always had to work to supplement the family income.[35] Viewing their position from a privileged standpoint, antifeminists argue that it is because of feminists' selfish desires for self-fulfillment in the workplace that family and social structure have deteriorated. They have constructed women's primary social and family roles as the proper caregivers for children and the stabilizer of family values. They feel it is right that women are protected by men and fought to sustain that right by successfully blocking the ratification of the ERA in the early 1980s. Their position is that the military is a male domain and women should stay out—that women ruin the armed forces.[36]

The right-to-fight argument for military women is a demand for equal citizenship participation. While not all women are willing and capable of serving in combat roles, the equality debate centers on whether gender should be used as the sole criterion for inclusion or exclusion from full military roles. The proponents of equality cite several reasons why assigning military personnel on the basis of personal capabilities—by the same standards as men, rather than by the artificial barrier of gender—contributes to military effectiveness.[37]

As discussed in the previous chapter, the primary arguments opposing women in combat roles are not about women's capabilities to serve, fight, or kill the enemy but on their traditional gendered roles, usually couched in terms of military effectiveness. The military usually opens up new roles to previously excluded personnel when it is in their best interest to do so, primarily during war time or when there are not enough men to fill the ranks, again couching those changes in terms of military need and effectiveness. The executive, legislative, and judicial branches of our government have all been hesitant to impose civilian legal standards on the military due to national security concerns. Thus the military has been allowed to legally discriminate under the auspices of military effectiveness.[38] Military personnel are bound by a different set of legal rules and regulations under the UCMJ and do not have all the Constitutional rights of citizenship, yet they serve to protect those rights.[39] No one in the military has all the same rights as the citizens they have volunteered to defend, and not all Americans have the right to join the military. Thus, when egalitarian feminists use the rhetoric of equality and equal rights in their arguments about women's roles in the military, they may not understand that these arguments are not completely valid. At the same time, many military women have the capability, both mentally and physically, to do more than they are currently allowed or trained to do. Manpower policies change only when additional sources of personnel are needed, and then the gender (or race, or sexuality) arguments are ignored. Thus, the reasons for excluding women are specious. The military should recruit, train, and assign personnel based on their capabilities, not on their gender.

The Equal Rights Amendment

The Equal Rights Amendment (ERA) was first proposed in 1923 and was defeated every year until 1972, when it finally passed in Congress. It has been ratified by 35 of the necessary 38 states to make it a Constitutional Amendment. The 15 states that have not yet ratified the amendment are Alabama, Arizona, Arkansas, Florida, Georgia, Illinois, Louisiana, Mississippi, Missouri, Nevada, North Carolina, Oklahoma, South Carolina, Utah, and Virginia. The ERA simply states, "Equality of rights under the law shall not be denied or abridged by the United States or by any State on account of sex."[40]

This language seems simple enough, and it says nothing about women being drafted or being required to join the military and serve in combat. But in the early 1980s, when ERA proponents were trying to get the last three states to ratify the amendment before the 1982 deadline, the antifeminists, led by Phyllis Schafly, began their own campaign to defeat it. Using scare tactics and misinformation, her Stop ERA Now campaign has been successful in the still-ongoing fight to get this amendment passed. Egalitarian feminists rallied around the ERA as an indication that the responsibilities of citizenship, as well as citizenship rights, were concerns of to women. The debate that imploded the historic legislation, however, was the issue of selective service registration and conscription for women. This simple concept—that equality in citizenship also meant equality in civic responsibilities—divided the nation and ultimately resulted in the rejection of the ERA.[41]

The idea of drafting women came into the national consciousness in 1977 during the National Women's Conference. At this time, 35 states had ratified the ERA, and the conference attendees opted to generate a political platform for women's rights. It was a far-reaching platform and included a statement about women's access to the military:

> *ERA will NOT* require that there be as many women as men in combat roles in the military service, but it will give women equal access to the skills, training, education, and other benefits that military services provide. There is no draft now, but if a national emergency requires one in the future or if it is reinstated for any reason, women would be subject to the draft just as men would be, under a system that would undoubtedly provide for exemptions for specific categories, e.g., parents of dependent children, persons with physical, mental, or emotional illness, conscientious objectors, and others.
>
> The military services would have the same right to assign women as they have to assign men, but this does not mean that women would be automatically assigned to combat, unless they volunteered for such duties. As a matter of fact, in modern warfare a very small percentage of men in the armed services actually serve in combat, and the decision as to who is best equipped for combat is up to the commanders. Meanwhile, to deny women the opportunity to freely enter the military services today is to deny them equal expression of patriotism as well as career, educational, and job opportunities.[42]

The major concern of the antifeminists was whether equality for women necessarily meant equal military service and equal military risk. The antifeminists felt that the maintenance of gender difference was a matter of civil rights. "Our young women have the right to be feminine, to get married, to build families and to have homes. Our daughters should not be deprived of rights which every American woman has enjoyed since our country was born."[43] Their campaign blurred the line and caused confusion that the language of the ERA would *mandate* the drafting of women.

In 1980, when it appeared the draft was going to be reinstated, egalitarian feminists in the National Organization for Women (NOW) issued a statement in which they formally opposed the draft; however, they insisted that if there were to be a draft, or registration for the draft, both men and women must share it equally.[44] This statement just gave further fodder to the antifeminists to continue their campaign against ERA.

As a result of the antifeminist campaign, the ERA was not ratified by the states. However, from 1972, when it passed Congress, until its defeat in 1982, many court decisions, in anticipation of its ratification, essentially gave women most of the rights inherent in the ERA. The exception, of course, is women in ground combat. This was debated during the case of *Rostker v. Goldberg* (1981), which upheld the male only draft as constitutional since the draft is to provide combat troops, and women are excluded from serving as combat troops.[45]

Recent calls for a return to the draft at the outset of the wars in the Middle East were not supported by Congress. Charles Rangel (D-NY) had submitted bills in 2003 and 2006 stating the military did not have enough people to fight the two-front war. The bill was to mandate military service for men *and women* between age 18 and 42. It was soundly defeated by a vote of 402–2.[46] The public has no stomach for return to the draft, but if the draft were ever reinstated it very well might call for the selective service registration of both men and women.

In the meantime, the ERA is not a dead issue. It was reintroduced in the House of Representatives on July 21, 2009, as House Joint Resolution 61, proposing an amendment to the Constitution of the United States relative to equal rights for men and women. The bill has 62 co-sponsors. Lead sponsors are Congresswoman Carolyn Maloney (D-NY) and Congresswoman Judy Biggert (R-IL).[47]

Women in Ground Combat and the Collocation Issue: Policy versus Reality

The idea of women in combat was, and still is, a main issue for antifeminists. Their platform is that women are socially unfit for the demands of war, incapable of killing, and physiologically unable to use the equipment; they believe women have the *right* to be protected by men, and to be homemakers. Egalitarian feminists, on the other hand, publicly support opening all positions to military women *if they want it and are fully capable*, arguing that equal rights also entail equal responsibility.[48]

This appears to be one of the flaws of the egalitarian platform: if women demand equality, they should be treated, by policy, exactly as men. Men must register for and serve in combat jobs when they are drafted, even if they do not want to. If a war required the conscription of soldiers, the height, weight, and physical fitness standards alone would disqualify most women. Additionally, if there were enough able-bodied draftees, single parents, and perhaps even parents of small children under 6 years old, might be exempted from service. The requirements for conscientious objector status might also need to be reviewed and adjusted to include other mitigating factors. Thus, it seems hypocritical to argue for full equality yet not argue that there is a responsibility for all qualified women to risk their lives for their country as men have traditionally been required to do—that is, *without choice*.

That being said, in this day and age of the volunteer military, all personnel go where they are told to go, combat area or not. There is an assumption of choice since they voluntarily joined the service. Women are assigned to ships primarily without choice, other than their choice to volunteer for the Navy. Likewise, women in the Army and Marine Corps who enlisted for combat support and combat service support occupations and positions do not have a choice as to whether or not to be sent to Iraq or Afghanistan. If their unit goes, they go, barring illness or pregnancy. And, given the nonlinear, unconventional aspect of the war in those two areas, women are in combat regardless of DoD policy.

Studies of the late 20th century supposed that most women would not want to go into combat, that there was no need for women in combat, and that there was no empirical evidence to support the idea that military effectiveness would not be affected.[49] This is no longer the case. Women are needed in Iraq and Afghanistan. The military could not do its job without the support services they offer. Additionally, it could not do its job of searching for terrorists, conducting household raids, and protecting noncombatant citizens without women warriors. Women have shown just as much courage and initiative in combat as their male peers. The military has not been adversely affected by women in combat zones participating in combat and peacemaking operations, doing the jobs they were trained to do. It is time to recognize the fact that women are in combat and give them credit for it.

The current DoD policy regarding women in ground combat is called the *collocation rule*, which replaced the Risk Rule in 1994. The policy directs that women be assigned to all positions where they are qualified but excludes them from assignments to "units below the brigade level whose primary mission is to engage in direct combat on the ground." The Army has a separate policy, created in 1992, that excludes women from jobs that are "assigned a routine mission to engage in direct combat, or which collocate routinely with units assigned to a direct combat mission."[50] Note that the issue of protection is not mentioned in either of these policies.

Ground combat is defined as well: "Direct ground combat is engaging the enemy on the ground with individual or crew served weapons, while being exposed to hostile fire and to a high probability of direct physical contact with the hostile force's personnel. Direct ground combat takes place well forward on the battlefield while locating and closing with the enemy to defeat them by fire, maneuver, or shock effect."[51]

The Army's definition is more rigid. It reads, "Engaging the enemy with individual or crew served weapons, while being exposed to direct enemy fire, a high probability of direct physical contact with the enemy's personnel and a substantial risk of capture. Direct combat takes place while closing with the enemy to defeat them by fire, maneuver, or shock effect in order to destroy or capture the enemy, or while repelling the enemy's assault by fire, close combat, or counterattack."[52]

RAND's National Security Research Division was tasked to study the Army's assignment policy for women. The report, released in 2007, found that assignment policies are not clearly understood or consistently enforced. While the Army may comply with DoD policy, it does not appear to comply with its own more rigid policy. The study noted that the current definition of ground combat is not suited to the type of operations in Iraq and Afghanistan. There is a question of whether or not the definition includes self-defense missions. While military women are not assigned to ground combat offensive units on a permanent basis, they have been assigned on a temporary basis to help with the war effort, and they have engaged with the enemy in self-defense missions. In other words, while Army policy is being adhered to, the spirit of the policy is not. The problem is, there are few places in Iraq and Afghanistan that are not war zones, although actual combat operations ebb and flow. RAND noted that a very strict interpretation of the Army's policy would probably preclude some women from deploying to Iraq.[53] The Army is not about to go down that path.

In 2005, at the urging of conservatives, Duncan Hunter (R-CA) proposed an amendment to the 2006 Defense Authorization Bill that would force the Army to comply with its own regulations regarding women in ground combat. The legislation would have prohibited female soldiers from serving in smaller forward support companies that collocate, or operate with land combat battalions such as the infantry. The Army denounced the amendment and managed to halt the legislation before it arrived on the House floor.[54] As modern battlefields are asymmetrical, the Army needs to adjust its policies to reflect reality. The Army has recognized that most barriers are artificial and has adjusted women's roles when necessary to facilitate mission accomplishment whether following current policy or not.[55] The Marine Corps are following suit.

The Not-So-Secret Lioness Program

In 2008, filmmakers Meg McLagan and Daria Sommers released a film, *Lioness*,[56] that presented a new paradigm to the military and to the American public that women warriors were needed in this century's war against Muslim terror-ists. The film documented a program called Team Lioness and followed and interviewed five of the first women assigned to the team in Iraq. It discussed the onset of the program, the decision to use women for certain missions, and the aftereffects of the decision not only on the military but also on the women themselves. Although the Army knew they needed women for the mission, the Lionesses were not trained in combat operations.

The Lioness program had started several years earlier due to the realization that men seeking insurgents and terrorists in the urban environment of Bagh-dad could not search the local women due to cultural and religious constraints. That many Muslim women covered themselves completely in a garment called a burka also allowed them to hide contraband. It was also an effective cos-tume, when used by men, to avoid being searched or to hide in a crowd of women.

The Lioness program began as a tool of necessity, but it has since become a public relations tool as well. Team Lioness has several missions. The first is to accompany combat teams when they are searching the homes of suspected insurgents or terrorists. Team Lioness members guard the women and children in a separate area, search them, and calm them down. They calm the rest of the household as well and prevent the unnecessary escalation of force from male members of the household who might resist due to a perceived threat to their family. Another purpose is to deter the use of women for terrorist attacks. More recently, they have been used to conduct surveys and gather other information about the local economy in both Iraq and Afghanistan. Marine Corps women are also now used for this work.[57]

Although these women serve in combat roles, accompanying the infantry when they conduct combat operations, officially they are not in combat. They are assigned on a temporary basis (temporary duty, or TD) to a combat unit. And although the TD may or may not be documented in the women's service record, administrative personnel certainly do not want to permanently indicate that the women were involved in ground combat operations during the TD be-cause it is against Army policy. This has many unintended consequences.

For example, women cannot receive the Combat Infantryman Badge (CIB) since they are not assigned to the infantry due to its direct combat mission. The CIB is the U.S. Army combat service recognition decoration awarded to soldiers, enlisted men, and officers (commissioned and warrant) holding colo-nel rank or below who *personally* fought in active ground combat while as-signed members of either an infantry or special forces unit, of brigade size or smaller, any time after December 6, 1941. The CIB and its noncombatant ana-logue, the skill-recognition Expert Infantryman Badge (EIB), were simultane-ously created during WWII as primary recognition for the combat service and sacrifices of the infantrymen who likely would be wounded or killed in numbers disproportionate to those of the Army's other service branches. However, an alternative is the Combat Action Badge (CAB). The CAB was added to acknowledge that soldiers (both men and women) other than infantrymen engage in ground combat. The CAB can be awarded to any soldier who meets the criteria. The award was approved May 2005 and is retroactive to September 18, 2001, but does not apply to previous conflicts. Assignment to a combat arms unit or a unit organized to conduct close or offensive combat operations or performing offensive combat operations is not required to qualify for the CAB. However, it is not intended to be awarded to all soldiers who serve in a combat zone or imminent danger area.[58]

Specific Eligibility Requirements for the CAB

a. May be awarded to any soldier.
b. Soldier must be performing assigned duties in an area where hostile fire pay or imminent danger pay is authorized.
c. Soldier must be personally present and actively engaging or being engaged by the enemy and performing satisfactorily in accordance with the prescribed rules of engagement.
d. Soldier must not be assigned/attached to a unit that would qualify the soldier for the CIB/Combat Medical Badge (CMB).[59]

At a March 31, 2009, hearing regarding the Lioness program that included a short clip of the film and a panel discussion for the Congressional Woman's Caucus, four of the five original Lioness members were present. One told a story of how the Veteran's Administration (VA) refused to treat her for combat related posttraumatic stress disorder (PTSD) because "women were not in combat." Later that summer, Kayla Williams, a U.S. Army veteran and author of the book *Love My Rifle More Than You*, told the Committee on Veterans Affairs on July 14, 2009,

> As a Soldier with the 101st Airborne Division (Air Assault), I took part in the initial invasion of Iraq in 2003, and was there for approximately one year. As an Arabic linguist, I went on combat foot patrols with the Infantry in Baghdad. During the initial invasion, my team came under small arms fire. Later, in Mosul, we were mortared regularly. I served right alongside my male peers: with our flak vests on during missions, we were all truly Soldiers first.
>
> However, it became clear upon our return that most people did not understand what women in today's military experience [while in Iraq]. I was asked whether as a woman I was allowed to carry a gun, and was also asked if I was in the Infantry. This confusion about what role women play in war today extends beyond the general public; even Veterans Affairs (VA) [sic] employees are still sometimes unclear on the nature of modern warfare, which presents challenges for women seeking care. For example,

being in combat is linked to post-traumatic stress disorder (PTSD), but since women are supposedly barred from combat, they may face challenges proving that their PTSD is service-connected. One of my closest friends was told by a VA doctor that she could not possibly have PTSD for just this reason: he did not believe that she as a woman could have been in combat.[60]

The film *Lioness* has finally brought the issue of women in combat into the open and documented its reality. As a result, Congress has taken steps to help alleviate discrepancies in the availability of adequate health care and adequate documentation of service for women through two separate bills. The first, HR 1211, the Women's Health Care Improvement Act, was passed in the House on July 24, 2009. The bill seeks to improve and expand health care benefits through the VA for women veterans, especially of Iraq and Afghanistan. It has not yet been voted upon by the Senate.[61]

The second bill, an amendment to the FY 2010 Defense Authorization Bill (HR 2647), which passed in the House on June 25, 2009, includes a provision for training and documentation for the Lioness program. It reads:

> The committee is aware that there are members of the armed forces deployed in support of contingency operations who, as a result of operational requirements on the battlefield, volunteer to provide mission support outside of the requirements of their military occupation. These individuals are often temporarily removed from their regular assignment to serve in these capacities before returning to their regular duties during their deployment. One such group of volunteers are women who are serving at the point of the spear and are referred to as "Lionesses." They participate in offensive operations by providing culturally-sensitive search and engagement activities for certain combat units deployed in the Republic of Iraq and the Islamic Republic of Afghanistan.
>
> The committee is aware that service women, particularly those who volunteered during the early stages of the Lioness program, have encountered difficulties in gaining proper recognition for their service, both within the services and when they leave active duty and seek assistance from the Department of Veterans Affairs. For example, service women who volunteered to accompany units during the Battle of Fallujah in 2004 have had to rely on the support of an outside organization in order to provide the witnesses and documentation needed to seek recognition of their actions under fire and to establish their combat experience while deployed, in order to receive health care and disability benefits from the Department of Veterans Affairs.
>
> The committee is concerned that there is no mechanism in place within the services to properly document service member participation in operational missions outside of the requirements of their military

occupation. Therefore, the committee directs the Secretary of Defense, in consultation with the services, to review the way the services manages and documents the additional services some service members perform. The review should also consider a way to properly document participation in such actions, particularly since they are being pulled from their regular units for these missions. The review should consider whether a service or skill identifier to identify these individuals, who have previously served and may be called upon again to serve in future deployments, is appropriate. The review should also consider whether the current chain of command construct allows these individuals sufficient oversight to be able to seek proper recognition for their service. The review should also take into consideration the differences that may need to be addressed between those within the active component and those within the Reserve Component who are activated and subsequently demobilized.

In addition, the committee believes that there should be a systematic training program for these individuals prior to their deployment that takes into account the unique mission for which they have volunteered. The committee directs the Secretary of Defense to submit the results of the review, and any recommendations, to the Senate Committee on Armed Services and the House Committee on Armed Services by March 31, 2010.[62]

The Senate bill, S1390, does not have this provision included in its version. After the joint congressional committee worked out the differences, it was signed into law on October 28, 2009 (P.L. 111-84) without the House provision. If it had passed into law, women with PTSD due to combat stress would have gotten the proper treatment. It also would have acknowledged that women are being put in harm's way and are taking offensive action. Pending the outcome of the secretary of defense's report to Congress in March 2010, the debate about women in combat may become moot.

The VA has also begun to understand that women are serving in combat. It is preparing to publish a rule, after the appropriate public comment period, that will help provide care for women who have seen combat. *Stressor Determinations for Posttraumatic Stress Disorder* (AN 32) published in the Federal Register states:

> The Department of Veterans Affairs (VA) is proposing to amend its adjudication regulations governing service connection for PTSD by modifying the evidentiary standards related to establishing the required inservice stressor. This amendment would eliminate the requirement for corroborating that a veteran actually experienced hostile military activity. The in-service stressor would be established by the opinion of a VA psychiatrist or psychologist that a stressor that is reported by a veteran is related to fear of hostile military or terrorist activity, and is adequate to support a diagnosis of posttraumatic stress disorder.[63]

Women have made significant inroads toward equality, both in the civilian sector and in the military. But the equal status conferred by the responsibility for selective service registration, conscription, and unrestricted service in ground combat remains elusive. In an all-volunteer force, the issue of having a duty to perform a distasteful chore, such as serve in the military, has given way to volunteers who are proud to make the military a career. There is no requirement to serve, so citizenship status and military service have become separated. This is not to suggest, however, that qualified women should not be able to fully participate in the military on an equal basis with men. It is time to separate the policy from the reality and use all personnel in any capacity for which they are qualified.

Notes

1. *Age:* generally cannot enlist if under 17. The maximum age of enlistment changes according to the needs of the military. *Physical capability:* physical disabilities are disqualifying, weight standards must be met, and a physical fitness test must be passed. *Mental disabilities or deficiencies:* must have a high school education and pass an entrance exam with a minimum score; cannot be in the lower quartile of intelligence. *Dependency status:* single parents may not enlist if they have custody of children under the age of 18; they can enlist if they legally transfer responsibility to a permanent caregiver. *Gender:* women are not allowed in direct ground combat occupations, special operations, or in submarines. *Sexuality:* Openly gay or lesbian service members are not authorized to enlist, and are discharged if discovered during their service.

2. Ilene Rose Feinman, *Citizenship Rites: Feminist Soldiers and Feminist Antimilitarists* (New York: New York University Press, 2000), 1.

3. Linda K. Kerber, *No Constitutional Right to Be Ladies: Women and the Obligations of Citizenship* (New York: Hill and Wang, 1998), 286.

4. Feinman, *Citizenship Rites*; Kerber, *No Constitutional Right.*

5. Kerber, *No Constitutional Right*, xxiii; Wendy Williams, "The Equality Crisis: Some Reflections on Culture, Courts, and Feminism," *Women's Rights Law Reporter* 14, nos. 2 and 3 (1992): 151–174.

6. See Kerber, *No Constitutional Right.*

7. Mady Wechsler Segal and Amanda Faith Hansen, "Value Rationales in Policy Debates on Women in the Military: A Content Analysis of Congressional Testimony, 1941–1985," *Social Science Quarterly* 73, no. 2 (June 1992): 295–309.

8. Francine D'Amico, "Feminist Perspectives on Women Warriors," in *The Women and War Reader,* ed. Lois Ann Lorentzen and Jennifer Turpin (New York: New York University Press, 1998), 119–125.

9. D'Amico, "Feminist Perspectives," 120; Feinman, *Citizenship Rites,* 1.

10. D'Amico, Feinman, and Kerber, *No Constitutional Right.*

11. T.H. Marshall and Tom Bottomore, *Citizenship and Social Class* (London: Pluto Press, 1950/1992), 6–7.

12. Ibid., 8.

13. Jeanne Holm, *Women in the Military: An Unfinished Revolution*, rev. ed. (Novato, CA: Presidio Press, 1992); Kerber, *No Constitutional Right*; Williams, "The Equality Crisis."

14. Kerber, *No Constitutional Right*.

15. Marshall and Bottomore, *Citizenship and Social Class*, 10.

16. Feinman, *Citizenship Rites*; Holm, *Women in the Military*; Kerber, *No Constitutional Right*.

17. *Webster's Encyclopedic Unabridged Dictionary of the English Language* (New York: Gramercy Books, 1996), xiii–xiv.

18. Holly Sklar, "Imagine a Country," in *Race, Class, and Gender in the United States*, 4th ed., ed. Paula S. Rothenburg (New York: St. Martin's Press, 1998), 192–201.

19. James Burk, "Citizenship Status and Military Service: The Quest for Inclusion by Minorities and Conscientious Objectors," *Armed Forces and Society* 21, no. 4 (Summer 1995), 503–529; David R. Segal, *Recruiting for Uncle Sam: Citizenship and Military Manpower Policy* (Lawrence: University Press of Kansas, 1989).

20. Morris Janowitz, "Observations on the Sociology of Citizenship: Obligations and Rights," *Social Forces* 59, no. 1 (1980), 1–24.

21. Ibid., 1, italics added.

22. Kerber, *No Constitutional Right*.

23. Marshall and Bottomore's definitions as described by Janowitz, "Observations on the Sociology," 8–9.

24. For a full explanation of the arguments, see Janowitz, "Observations on the Sociology."

25. Kerber, *No Constitutional Right*, xx.

26. Ibid., xxi.

27. Kerber, *No Constitutional Right*; Segal and Hansen, "Value Rationales"; Williams, "The Equality Crisis"; Marshall and Bottomore, *Citizenship and Social Class*, 15.

28. Charles C. Moskos, "From Citizens' Army to Social Laboratory," *Wilson Quarterly* 17 (Winter 1993), 83–94; Segal, "*Recruiting for Uncle Sam*."

29. Moskos; Segal; David R. Segal and Mady Wechsler Segal, "America's Military Population," *Population Bulletin* (Population Reference Bureau, December 2004).

30. Mildred Amer and Jennifer E. Manning, *Membership of the 111th Congress: A Profile* (Washington, DC: Congressional Research Service, 2008), http://assets.open crs.com/rpts/R40086_20081231.pdf.

31. Segal, *Recruiting for Uncle Sam*, 97.

32. Burk, "Citizenship Status and Military Service"; Moskos, "From Citizens' Army"; Segal, *Recruiting for Uncle Sam*.

33. Feinman, *Citizenship Rites*, 211.

34. D'Amico, "Feminist Perspectives"; Feinman, *Citizenship Rites*; Judith Hicks Stiehm, *Arms and the Enlisted Woman* (Philadelphia, PA: Temple University Press, 1989).

35. Francine D. Blau, Marianne A. Ferber, and Anne E. Windler, *The Economics of Women, Men, and Work*, 3rd ed. (Englewood Cliffs, NJ: Prentice Hall, 1998).

36. Feinman, *Citizenship Rites*.

37. M. C. Devilbiss, "Women in Combat: A Quick Summary of the Arguments on Both Sides," *Minerva: Quarterly Report on Women and the Military* 8, no. 1 (1990):

29–31; Holm, *Women in the Military*; Mady Wechsler Segal, "Women in the Military: Research and Policy Issues," *Youth and Society* 10, no. 2 (December 1978): 101–126; Mady Wechsler Segal and David R. Segal, "Social Change and the Participation of Women in the American Military," *Research in Social Movements, Conflicts, and Change* 5 (1983), 235–258; Clyde Wilcox, "Race, Gender, and Support for Women in the Military," *Social Science Quarterly* 73, no. 2 (June 1992): 310–323.

38. See Darlene M. Iskra, "Attitudes toward Expanding Roles for Navy Women at Sea," *Armed Forces and Society* 33, no. 2 (Jan 2007): 203–223, for a complete discussion on the arguments for expanded combat roles for women.

39. Article 1: limited in rights of free speech, free assembly, and the right to petition the government for redress of grievances. Article 4: exempt from the right not to be searched without probable cause. Article 5: freedom from being tried twice on the same charge or being a witness against himself. Article 7: right of trial by jury; Article 8: no cruel or unusual punishment. *Webster's Encyclopedic Unabridged Dictionary*.

40. The Alice Paul Institute, "The Equal Rights Amendment," http://www.equalrightsamendment.org/.

41. Feinman, *Citizenship Rites*.

42. National Commission on the Observance of International Women's Year, "Document 38: Plank 11: Equal Rights Amendment," from *The Spirit of Houston: The First National Women's Conference* (Washington, DC: U.S. Government Printing Office, 1978), 49–52, http://womhist.alexanderstreet.com/dp59/doc38.htm.

43. Kathleen Teague, as cited in Kerber, *No Constitutional Right*, 287.

44. Feinman, *Citizenship Rites*, 133.

45. Ibid., 129; Williams, "The Equality Crisis," 156–157.

46. John Heilprin, "Rep. Rangel Will Seek to Reinstate the Draft," *The Associated Press*, November 19, 2006, http://www.washingtonpost.com/wp-dyn/content/article/2006/11/19/AR2006111900376_pf.html.

47. Alice Paul Institute, "The Equal Rights Amendment."

48. Feinman, *Citizenship Rites*; Stiehm, *Arms and the Enlisted Woman*.

49. April Carter, "Women, Military Service, and Citizenship," in *Gender, Politics, and Citizenship in the 1990s*, ed. Barbara Sullivan and Gillian Whitehouse (Sydney, Australia: University of New South Wales Press, 1996), 100–119; Laura L. Miller, "Feminism and the Exclusion of Army Women from Combat," *Gender Issues* 16, no. 3 (1998): 33–65; David R. Segal, Nora Scott Kinzer, and John C. Woelfel, "The Concept of Citizenship and Attitudes toward Women in Combat," *Sex Roles* 3, no. 5 (1977), 469–477.

50. Margaret C. Harrell, Laura Werber Castaneda, Peter Schirmer, Bryan W. Hallmark, Jennifer Kavanagh, Daniel Gershwin, and Paul Steinberg, *Assessing the Assignment Policy for Army Women* (Santa Monica, CA: RAND, 2007), xi–xii.

51. Ibid.

52. Ibid.

53. Ibid.

54. Center for Military Readiness, "Hunter Admonishes Army on Women in Land Combat," June 1, 2005, http://cmrlink.org/WomenInCombat.asp?docID=249.

55. Alliance for National Defense, "Position Paper on Women in Combat," http://www.4militarywomen.org/Women_in_Combat.htm.

56. *Lioness*, directed by Meg McLagan and Daria Sommers (Room 11 Productions, 2008).

57. Melissa A. Latty, "Lionesses Work to Improve Community in Local Iraq City," http://www.marines.mil, June 12, 2009; Felicia R. Lee, "Battleground: Female Soldiers in Line of Fire," *New York Times*, late edition, November 5, 2008, C1; Erin Solano, *Women in the Line of Fire* (Emeryville, CA: Seal Press, 2006).

58. My thanks to my friends for explaining the differences between the CIB and the CAB, and the context of their award, via e-mail correspondence with Army retirees Robert McFetridge, Col, JAG and Patricia Jernigan, Col, WAC, of August 17, 2009.

59. CAB Issue Regulations, http://www.amervets.com/replacement/cab.htm#isr. CMB History, http://www.americal.org/awards/cmb.htm. The Combat Medical Badge (CMB) was created by the War Department on March 1, 1945. It could be awarded to officers, warrant officers, and enlisted men of the Medical Department assigned or attached to the medical detachment of infantry regiments, infantry battalions, and elements thereof designated as infantry in tables of organization or tables of organization and equipment. Its evolution stemmed from a requirement to recognize medical personnel who shared the same hazards and hardships of ground combat on a daily basis with the infantry soldier. Though established almost a year and a half after the CIB, it could be awarded retroactively to December 7, 1941, to fully qualified personnel. See http://www.americal.org/awards/cmb.htm.

60. Kayla Williams, "Written Remarks for Senate Committee on Veterans' Affairs Hearing on VA Health Services for Women Veterans," July 14, 2009, http://veterans.senate.gov/hearings.cfm?action=release.display&release_id=efef9edf-ff53-474b-befb-62edc87ed9d9; Kayla Williams, *Love My Rifle More Than You: Young and Female in the U.S. Army* (New York: W.W. Norton, 2005).

61. Washington Watch, "H.R. 1211, The Women Veterans Health Care Improvement Act," As of November, 2009. http://www.washingtonwatch.com/bills/show/111_HR_1211.html.

62. "Report of the Committee on Armed Services House of Representatives on HR 2647," *National Defense Authorization Act for Fiscal Year 2010*, http://www.rules.house.gov/111/CommJurRpt/111_hr2647_rpt.pdf, 315–316.

63. Federal Register, Department of Veterans Affairs, *Stressor Determinations for Posttraumatic Stress Disorder* (AN 32), 38 CFR Part 3 RIN 2900-AN32, August 24, 2009, http://cryptome.org/0001/va082409.htm.

CHAPTER 4

Women Are Heroes, Too

Let the generations know that women in uniform also guaranteed their freedom. That our resolve was just as great as the brave men who stood among us. And with victory our hearts were just as full and beat just as fast—that the tears fell just as hard for those we left behind.

—WWII Army nurse, etched in glass at the
Women in Military Service for America
Memorial, Arlington Cemetery

According to *Webster's Unabridged Dictionary*, a hero is "a man of distinguished courage or ability, admired for his brave deeds and noble qualities." A heroine, of course, is the feminine version of the word, which is also defined as "a woman of distinguished courage or ability, admired for her brave deeds and noble qualities."[1] In the military, both heroes and heroines are often defined by their bravery on the battlefield, the most famous woman being Joan of Arc. However, there have been few contemporary women who have been accorded this honor.

Military heroes are often defined by the awards they receive for bravery and courage in battle. The Medal of Honor is the highest military decoration awarded by the United States government. This award is given, in the name of Congress, by the president of the United States to military personnel who distinguish themselves by conspicuous gallantry and bravery. It is required for the awardees to have risked their lives above and beyond the call of duty while engaged in military action against an enemy of the United States or her allies.[2] Because of the nature of the deed, many awards are given posthumously. Additionally, because two or more persons must have observed the deed, many people who probably deserved such an award have gone unrecognized or were given a lesser award. Thus, the award is rarely given. There have been millions of men and women who have served in our nation's armed forces since the Civil War. However, since the award's inception in 1861, there have been less than 3,500 Medals of Honor awarded to our nation's bravest men . . . and one woman. That woman is Dr. Mary Edwards Walker, a Civil War nurse and surgeon. Dr. Walker participated in the battles of Bull Run (July 21, 1861) and Atlanta (September 1864). She also served in the Patent Office Hospital, Washington, D.C. (October 1861) and in Chattanooga, TN, following the Battle of Chickamauga (September 1863). Additionally she was a prisoner of war from April 10, 1864, to August 12, 1864, in Richmond, VA. Her citation reads:

> Whereas it appears from official reports that Dr. Mary E. Walker, a graduate of medicine, "has rendered valuable service to the Government, and her efforts have been earnest and untiring in a variety of ways," and that she was assigned to duty and served as an assistant surgeon in charge of female prisoners at Louisville, Ky., upon the recommendation of Major-Generals Sherman and Thomas, and faithfully served as contract surgeon in the service of the United States, and has devoted herself with much patriotic zeal to the sick and wounded soldiers, both in the field and hospitals, to the detriment of her own health, and has also endured hardships as a prisoner of war four months in a Southern prison while acting as contract surgeon; and Whereas by reason of her not being a commissioned officer in the military service, a brevet or honorary rank cannot, under existing laws, be conferred upon her; and
>
> Whereas in the opinion of the President an honorable recognition of her services and sufferings should be made:
>
> It is ordered, That a testimonial thereof shall be hereby made and given to the said Dr. Mary E. Walker, and that the usual medal of honor for meritorious services be given her.
>
> Given under my hand in the city of Washington, D.C., this 11th day of November, A.D. 1865.[3]

Dr. Walker was very proud of her award, and wore it every day until she died in 1919. After the war, she became a writer and lecturer, touring the United States and abroad on women's rights, dress reform, and health and temperance issues. She was considered somewhat of an eccentric because she felt that women's clothing was immodest and inconvenient, and was arrested numerous times for wearing full male dress, including wing collar, bow tie, and top hat. She was also something of an inventor, coming up with the idea of using a return postcard for registered mail. She wrote extensively, including a combination biography and commentary called *Hit* and a second book, *Unmasked, or the Science of Immortality.* In 1917 her Medal, along with the medals of 910 others was taken away when Congress revised the Medal of Honor standards to include only "actual combat with an enemy." She refused to give hers back. An Army board reinstated Walker's medal posthumously in 1977, citing her "distinguished gallantry, self-sacrifice, patriotism, dedication and unflinching loyalty to her country, despite the apparent discrimination because of her sex."[4]

Many ordinary military personnel have exhibited extraordinary bravery under conditions other than direct combat, but they may not have necessarily been recognized with awards by the military establishment. This is very common for women, since most women, until recently,[5] have not had a hand in the offensive operations of war. Women have been relegated to support jobs, such as medical personnel, personnel and administrative specialists, legal specialists, logisticians, communicators, and the like. The military could not perform its mission of offensive combat without the support of these people behind the lines. And because there is a tooth-to-tail ratio of 20:80—which means that only about 20 percent of soldiers in the Army are combat warriors, and the other 80 percent are combat support or combat service support—the teeth of the military are held in higher esteem than their comrades. As we have seen in previous chapters, it has only been since 1993–1994 that women have been able to fly combat aircraft and serve in combatant ships.

The short biographies presented in this chapter include both military and civilian women who have made a difference in our nation's military. This chapter includes women who have won high military awards, selected women who served our country in wars prior to their acceptance as equal members through the Women's Armed Forces Integration Act, women who were POWs, and women who helped legislate changes to bring our military to where it is today. Also included are some selected women firsts that may have not been reported elsewhere. Much of the research for this chapter was conducted online, as can be seen by the numerous Web site citations in the endnotes. There is a plethora of sites that discuss the achievements of women in the military, but care must be taken to ensure that the sites are credible and adequately researched.

Military Awards

Military awards have an order of precedence that regulates the hierarchy of decorations and the order in which they are to be worn on the uniform. Of course, the Medal of Honor is the highest military award, and Dr. Mary Edwards Walker remains the only woman ever to receive it. However, she is not the only female military hero. Other women have been awarded medals for bravery and courage, not only in the face of battle but also for their extraordinary efforts in supporting the brave men who fought our nation's battles for so many years. The awards listed here are some of the highest awards given to military personnel.

Distinguished Service, Navy, and Air Force Crosses

The Service Crosses are the second highest military award (appropriate to each service), and are awarded according to the following criteria:

> Awarded to U.S. and Foreign military personnel and civilians who have displayed extraordinary heroism in one of the following situations:
>
> 1. While engaged in action against an enemy of the United States,
> 2. While engaged in military operations involving conflict with a foreign force, or
> 3. While serving with a friendly nation engaged in armed conflict against a force in which the United States is not a belligerent party.[6]

Note that this award is given for heroism during combat operations. Five nurses and a YMCA worker were awarded the Distinguished Service Cross (DSC) for their performance under fire during WWI: Jane Jeffery, Red Cross; Beatrice M. MacDonald, Army Nurse Corps; Helen Grace McClelland, Army Nurse Corps; Isabelle Stambaugh, Army Nurse Corps; Eva Jean Parmelee, Army Nurse Corps; and Emma S. Sloan, YMCA worker.[7]

Jane Jeffery was an English nurse serving with the American Red Cross. She was cited for her extraordinary heroism in action at Jouy-sur-Morin (Seine-et-Marne), France, July 15, 1918 at Red Cross Hospital No. 107. Although severely wounded by an exploding bomb during an air raid, she refused to leave her post and continued to help others.

Beatrice M. MacDonald, ANC, the head nurse at Base Hospital No. 2, was awarded the DSC while on duty with a surgical team at the British Casualty Clearing Station in Belgium on August 17, 1917. During a German night air raid, she continued caring for the sick and wounded at her post of duty until seriously injured by a bomb, as a result of which she lost one eye. Working at the same frontline casualty control station in Belgium, reserve Army nurse Helen Grace McClelland received the DSC as a result of her efforts to help MacDonald. She saved MacDonald's life by stopping the hemorrhaging from her wounds while under fire from German bombs.

Eva Jean Parmelee, ANC, at Base Hospital No. 5, was wounded in an air raid on the hospital at Dannes-Carnier, France, on September 4, 1917. She remained calm and continued to serve while wounded. On March 21, 1918, reserve Army nurse Isabelle Stambaugh, Base Hospital No. 10, was awarded the DSC for her heroism while with a British surgical team in Amiens, France. She continued her work helping the wounded and dying even while seriously wounded by shell fire from German airplanes. YMCA worker Emma S. Sloan of New Haven, Connecticut, was also awarded the DSC.[8]

The Navy Cross award was enacted at the same time as the DSC but was third in precedence because it allowed the recognition for meritorious noncombat service. After an Act of Congress dated August 7, 1942, it became an award equivalent to the DSC due to the new combat-only recognition for heroic service.[9]

Four Navy nurses received the award as a result of their meritorious service during WWI. Lenah Sutcliff Higbee received the Navy Cross for her distinguished service in the line of duty as the superintendent of the Navy Nurse Corps during the war. Three other Navy nurses received their awards posthumously as a result of their Herculean efforts during the 1918 Spanish flu epidemic. Navy nurses Edna E. Place and Marie Louise Hidell worked at the Naval Hospital, Philadelphia, and Navy nurse Lillian M. Murphy worked at the Naval Hospital, Hampton Roads, Virginia. These women worked day and night caring for patients until they, too, were struck down by the disease. Only four other (male) members of the Navy received this award as a result of their efforts during the flu epidemic of 1918.[10]

The only woman to be awarded the DSC during WWII was Virginia Hall, a civilian with the Office of Strategic Services (OSS).[11] She was cited for extraordinary heroism as she directed the French Resistance forces "with extraordinary success in acts of sabotage and guerrilla warfare against enemy [German] troops, installations and communications. Miss Hall displayed rare courage, perseverance and ingenuity; her efforts contributed materially to the successful operations of the Resistance forces in support of the Allied Expeditionary Forces in the liberation of France."[12] Hall's success and courage cannot be overstated. She was at great risk for capture, and if she had been captured, she risked torture and death at the hands of the enemy.

Distinguished Service Medal

The Distinguished Service Medals of the Defense Department and the branches of military service are awarded for exceptionally meritorious and distinguished service in a position of great responsibility to the Government of the United States, and can be awarded for such service as part of a valorous act in combat, continuous acts of valor over a period of time, for distinguished service in noncombat positions of great responsibility, and even for a career of exceptionally meritorious and distinguished service in a position of great responsibility. As such, the Distinguished Service Medals are the highest awards for noncombat actions of the DoD and the individual branches of service. They rank in precedence above the Silver Star and below the Service Crosses.[13]

During WWI many women received this award, including 27 Army nurses, among them heroine Beatrice M. MacDonald as well as director of nursing services of the American Expeditionary Forces (AEF), Julie C. Stimson; Army Signal Corps telephone operator, chief operator Grace D. Banker;

Mrs. James S. Cushman, chair of the War Work Council, YWCA of the United States; Red Cross workers Mary Vail Andress, Maude Cleveland, and Jane A. Delano, director, ARC Department of Nursing; Salvation Army commander Evangeline Cory Booth; Hannah J. Patterson of the Women's Committee, Council of National Defense; and Dr. Anna Howard Shaw, chair of the Women's Committee, Council of National Defense.[14]

Since WWII, other women have received this award for meritorious service, including VADM Pat Tracey, the first woman in the military to achieve three-star rank; and RADM Mildred McAffee, the first line officer in the navy to be promoted to flag rank. There is no complete list of awardees.

Silver Star

The Silver Star is the third highest military decoration and it is designated solely for heroism in combat, in action insufficient to warrant the Medal of Honor or Distinguished Service, Navy or Air Force Crosses. Notable recipients of this award include General George Patton, General Douglas MacArthur, and Senator John McCain.

Three Army nurses serving in WWI were posthumously awarded the Silver Star in 2007—Linnie Leckrone, Jane Rignel, and Irene Robar. Nurses were not supposed to serve in combat, but as forward surgery became more critical, some nurses were moved to the front lines to work in field hospitals. All were presented with the Citation Star, which predated the Silver Star, for serving on the front lines in July 1918 in France and caring for the wounded despite enemy artillery bombardment. In 1932, Secretary of War Patrick J. Hurley authorized recipients of the Citation Star to exchange their medals for the new Silver Star. Since then, about ten thousand service members have had their Citation Stars exchanged for Silver Stars. However, these three nurses did not receive the updated award. This oversight and its historically significant implication were recognized by a historian working with the Army surgeon general; after he brought it to the attention of authorities, the awards were exchanged and Silver Stars issued to their surviving kin.[15]

During WWII, the Silver Star was awarded to four Army nurses for their bravery under fire at Anzio, Italy, in 1944—First Lt. Mary Roberts, Second Lt. Elaine Roe, Second Lt. Rita Virginia Rourke, and Second Lt. Ellen Ainsworth. During the German shelling of Anzio Beach, Roberts is credited with continuing to supervise her staff of 50 nurses, allowing the hospital to continue functioning. When the hospital was bombed, Roberts, Roe, Rourke, and Ainsworth were cited for their bravery in successfully evacuating 42 patients by flashlight. Ainsworth, who was killed in the attack, was awarded the Silver Star posthumously.[16]

In 2005, Sergeant Leigh Ann Hester, vehicle commander, 617th Military Police Company, Kentucky National Guard, was awarded the Silver Star for her actions in Iraq, becoming the first woman to receive the award for close-quarters combat. While serving as team leader, Hester's squad of two women and eight men in three Humvees was shadowing a 30-truck supply convoy when they were ambushed by insurgents. Hester led her team through the kill zone into a flanking position, where she assaulted a trench line with grenades. She and her squad leader, Staff Sergeant Timothy F. Nein, then assaulted and cleared two trenches. She also killed at least three enemy combatants with her rifle. When the battle was over, 27 insurgents were dead, 6 were wounded, and 1 was captured. In part, her citation reads that her actions "saved the lives of numerous convoy members." Sergeants Hester and Nein were both awarded the Silver Star, as well as the unit's medic, Specialist Jason Mike. Nein's award was later upgraded to the DSC,[17] a highly unusual action, since many awards are instead downgraded by higher authority. For Hester, being the first woman serving in Iraq to receive the award was a secondary issue. "[This award] doesn't have anything to do with being female. It's about the duties I performed that day as a soldier." Three soldiers in the squad were wounded in the attack, and three other members of their squad, including Specialist Ashley Pullen, received the Bronze Star with combat V.[18]

In March 2008, Silver Star recipient Army Specialist Monica Lin Brown became the first female U.S. soldier to receive the Silver Star for combat in Afghanistan. Brown's heroism was evident when she provided aid under heavy gunfire to soldiers whose Humvee had been hit by an improvised explosive device during a convoy. A medic, and only 18 years old at the time, Brown had been assigned to the 782nd Brigade Support Battalion, 4th Brigade Combat Team, 82nd Airborne Division. Brown was temporarily assigned to C troop of the 4th Squadron, 73rd Calvary Regiment (a combat unit) because their medic was on leave; the five-truck convoy was returning to base from a security patrol in Afghanistan's isolated Jani Khail district when the last vehicle hit the improvised explosive device and the convoy was attacked by insurgents.

While under fire, Brown left the safety of her Humvee to give aid to injured soldiers Specialists Stanson Smith and Larry Spray, who both had suffered life-threatening injuries. With the help of her platoon sergeant, Staff Sergeant Jose Santos, and three other less wounded soldiers, Brown eventually was able to move Smith and Spray into a low streambed away from the burning vehicle. When rounds of ammunition from the truck began exploding, Brown sheltered the injured soldiers with her body. She and Santos were finally able to escape the gunfire and mortar rounds and get the injured men into another vehicle and to a more stable area, where she continued rendering aid until medical evacuation. Both Smith and Spray survived their injuries.[19]

Distinguished Flying Cross

The Distinguished Flying Cross (DFC) is awarded for heroism in aerial flight or for an outstanding achievement while flying and may be awarded to military members serving in any capacity with the Armed Forces. The heroic act must involve voluntary action in the face of danger and be well above the actions performed by others engaged in similar flight operations. Several women have been awarded the Distinguished Flying Cross for their outstanding achievements in aviation.

Although not in the military, Amelia Earhart was the first woman to be awarded the DFC for being the first woman to fly solo across the Atlantic Ocean in 1932, landing in Ireland, and breaking speed and elapsed time records between the two continents. Although the award was limited to military personnel only by executive order 4601 of March 1, 1927, Amelia's award was authorized by a joint resolution of Congress.[20]

Three women received the DFC during WWII. First Lt. Aleda E. Lutz, an Army flight nurse, was the first military woman to receive the award. She was posthumously awarded the Distinguished Flying Cross on December 28, 1944. Lt. Lutz had flown over 800 hours when the C-47 hospital plane evacuating wounded soldiers from the battlefront near Lyons, Italy, crashed, killing all aboard. During the war, she had flown 196 missions evacuating over thirty-five hundred men.[21] First Lt. Roberta Schilbach Ross, a flight nurse, was awarded the Distinguished Flying Cross for completing 200 flights over the Himalayan Mountains in the China Burma India theatre. Lt. Ross also received the Air Medal on two separate occasions.[22]

Colonel Jacqueline Cochran was the first woman in the newly formed Air Force to receive the Distinguished Flying Cross on three separate occasions. Her citations read:

> #1 Colonel Jacqueline Cochran distinguished herself by extraordinary achievement while participating in aerial flight from 1947 to 1951. During this period, Colonel Cochran piloted an F-51 aircraft in which she established six world speed records. At Coachella Valley, CA, flying a closed-circuit 100-kilometer course, Colonel Cochran established a new speed record of 469.549 miles per hour. In other flights from Thermal, Indio, and Palm Springs, CA, Colonel Cochran established world speed records for the 3-, 15-, 500-, 1000-, and 2000-kilometer courses. The professional competence, aerial skill, and devotion to duty displayed by Colonel Cochran reflect great credit upon herself and the United States Air Force.
>
> #2 Colonel Jacqueline Cochran distinguished herself by extraordinary achievement while participating in aerial flight during April 1962. During that period, Colonel Cochran established a number of world records

on a flight from New Orleans, LA to Bonn, Germany. Flying a Lockheed Jet Star C-140 Colonel Cochran established 69 intercity, intercapital, and straight-line distance records and routes, in addition to becoming the first woman to fly a jet aircraft across the Atlantic Ocean. The records were for both speed and distance. The professional competence, aerial skill, and devotion to duty displayed by Colonel Cochran reflect great credit upon herself and the United States Air Force.

#3 Colonel Jacqueline Cochran distinguished herself by extraordinary achievement while participating in aerial flight during May and June 1964. During this period, Colonel Cochran established three world speed records in an F-104C Starfighter. Flying a precise circular course, Colonel Cochran set a 25-kilometer record of 1429.297 miles per hour, more than twice the speed of sound. She established a record for the 100-kilometer course by flying at 1302 miles per hour. Colonel Cochran established a third world's speed record by achieving 1135 miles per hour over a 500-kilometer course. The professional competence, aerial skill, and devotion to duty displayed by Colonel Cochran reflect great credit upon herself and the United States Air Force.[23]

Colonel Eileen M. Collins was the first female space shuttle pilot and the first female space shuttle mission commander. She received the Distinguished Flying Cross for her achievement as commander of the Space Shuttle Columbia from July 23, 1999, to July 27, 1999.[24]

During the first phase of Operation Iraqi Freedom, in April 2003, Captain Kim Campbell received the DFC with valor as a result of her achievement during her return from providing air support to ground troops in her A-10 Thunderbolt II aircraft. The aircraft sustained significant damage from enemy fire near Baghdad and became uncontrollable, as it had lost all hydraulics. Even though damage to the aircraft included the horizontal stabilizer, tail section, and engine cowling, and the loss of hydraulics made braking and steering almost impossible, she put the plane in manual reversion, and it responded. Campbell decided to land the craft rather than scuttle the aircraft and eject over safe territory. She safely landed the aircraft in manual mode, a feat few other pilots have managed.[25]

Chief Warrant Officer Three Lori Hill was the first military woman to be awarded the Distinguished Flying Cross for heroism. In March 2006, two helicopters, one piloted by Hill, were flying convoy security for two Bradley vehicles on patrol in a small village. The pilots learned of an attack at a nearby command center involving both U.S. and Iraqi forces, so they responded to provide air support. On the way, they ran into a concentrated attack with rocket-propelled grenades and machine-gun fire. They laid down suppressing fire and continued on. When they arrived at the command center, they were greeted with machine-gun fire, so they broke away and headed back in, shooting at the tracer fire. Drawing the fire away from the lead helo, Hill established communications with the ground troops and provided suppressive fire for troops engaged with the enemy on the ground until the troops reached safety. On the third pass, a rocket-propelled grenade hit her, damaging the helo's instrumentation. As she was banking away, the helo took machine-gun fire that hit Hill in the foot. The aircraft was losing transmission power, as well as hydraulics, which prevented the copter from hovering—a crucial maneuver for landing. With a damaged aircraft and an injury, Hill made an emergency landing at a nearby forward operating base, saving her crew and aircraft.[26]

Bronze Star

The Bronze Star Medal was established in 1941 and can be awarded for valor, acts of merit, or meritorious service. When awarded for valor it is accompanied by a V device; it is the fourth-highest combat award of the U.S. Armed Forces and the ninth-highest military award (including both combat and noncombatant awards) in the order of precedence of U.S. military decorations. Most bronze stars are awarded for meritorious service and, thus, do not have the V.

One of the first women to receive the Bronze Star was First Lt. Cordelia E. Cook, Army Nurse Corps, during WWII in Italy. Lt. Cook was also awarded the Purple Heart, making her the first woman to receive these two awards. First Lt. Annie G. Fox, ANC, first received a Purple Heart but it was later replaced by a Bronze Star in 1945. Her citation reads in part:

> For heroic and meritorious service in military operations against the enemy during the attack on Hickam Field by Japanese forces (aircraft) on 7 December 1941. During the attack Lieutenant Fox, in an exemplary manner, performed her duties as Head Nurse of the Station Hospital, Hickam Field, P.H. In addition she administered anaesthesia [*sic*] to patients during the heaviest part of the bombardment, assisted in dressing the wounded, taught civilian volunteer nurses to make and wrap dressings and worked ceaselessly with coolness and efficiency, and her fine example of calmness, courage and leadership was of great benefit to the morale of all with whom she came in contact. The loyalty and devotion to duty displayed by Lieutenant Fox on this occasion reflected great credit upon herself and the military service.[27]

Colonel Ruby Bradley is considered one of America's most decorated military women. She served in WWII and was a POW for 37 months in a Japanese prison camp. Later, she was a frontline U.S. Army nurse in Korea. Col. Bradley earned 34 medals and citations for bravery, including two Bronze stars. She died on July 3, 2002, and was buried at Arlington National Cemetery. Her obituary reads as follows:

> A survivor of two wars, a prison camp and near starvation, Colonel Ruby Bradley, one of the most decorated women in U.S. military history, was laid to rest in Arlington National Cemetery yesterday, nearly 40 years after she retired from the Army. Colonel Bradley, a native of Spencer, West Virginia, died May 28 in Hazard, Kentucky, at age 94 after a heart attack.
>
> Her military record included 34 medals and citations of bravery, including two Legion of Merit medals, two Bronze stars, two Presidential Emblems, the World War II Victory Medal and the U.N. Service Medal. She was also the recipient of the Florence Nightingale Medal, the Red Cross' highest international honor.[28]
>
> Colonel Bradley entered the Army Nurse Corps as a surgical nurse in 1934. When the Japanese attacked Pearl Harbor in 1941, Colonel Bradley was 34 and serving at Camp John Hay in the Philippines. Three weeks later, she was captured; in 1943, she was moved to the Santo Tomas Internment Camp in Manila, the Filipino capital. It was there that she and several other imprisoned nurses earned the title "Angels in Fatigues" from fellow captives.
>
> For the next several months, she provided medical help to the prisoners and sought to feed starving children by shoving food into her pockets whenever she could, often going hungry herself. The weight she shed made room in her uniform for smuggling surgical equipment into the prisoner-of-war camp that she used to assist in 230 operations and deliver 13 children. On February 3, 1945, U.S. troops stormed the gates of the Japanese camp and liberated Colonel Bradley and her fellow prisoners, ending her three years of captivity. At 80 pounds, Colonel Bradley returned home to West Virginia and waited five years before returning to the battlefield during the Korean War.
>
> Colonel Bradley served as a frontline Army nurse in evacuation hospitals in Korea. It was there that she refused to leave until she had loaded the sick and wounded onto a plane while surrounded by 100,000 Chinese soldiers. She escaped just in time, as her ambulance exploded behind her. "You got to get out in a hurry when you have somebody behind you with a gun," Colonel Bradley said once in a TV interview. After three decades of military service, Colonel Bradley retired from the Army in 1963.[29]

Numerous men and women have been awarded the Bronze Star. Unfortunately, there is no central location where the names of all those who have earned this award reside. Several women have been recognized with this award in the ongoing wars in the Middle East, not just for meritorious service but also for valor in combat. In 2005 Specialist Ashley J. Pullen, a female driver with the 617th Military Police Company, Kentucky National Guard, was awarded the Bronze Star with combat *V* for her bravery during the same firefight in which Sergeant Leigh Ann Hester received the Silver Star. Pullen laid down fire to suppress insurgents and then ran through a heavy line of enemy fire in order to provide medical assistance to her critically injured comrades saving several lives, and using her body as a shield to save a wounded soldier.[30]

The Purple Heart

The Purple Heart was established by General George Washington at Newburgh, New York, on August 7, 1782, during the American Revolution. It was reestablished by President Roosevelt per War Department General Order 3 in 1932 and at that time could also be given as a military commendation for bravery. It was made retroactive so Army personnel who were killed or injured during WWI could receive the award. In 1942, the president established the Legion of Merit medal, restricting the Purple Heart to those killed or wounded in combat making it retroactive to December 7, 1941, and authorizing Navy and Marine Corps personnel as eligible for the award. President Truman later made the award retroactive to WWI for Navy and Marine Corps personnel. Now the award is given to any military member or civilian national of the United States who, while serving under competent authority with one of the U.S. Armed Services after April 5, 1917, has been wounded or killed. Thus, the Purple Heart today signifies one thing—the personal and physical sacrifice of the recipient due to death or wounds received as a result of combat.[31]

The first woman to receive the Purple Heart as a result of combat was First Lt. Annie G. Fox, ANC. Lt. Fox was the Chief Nurse at Hickam Field during the Japanese attack on Pearl Harbor on December 7, 1941. However, it was later changed to a Bronze Star because her award was not related to wounds received during the attack but for extraordinary military courage. No central repository of names is maintained for those who have given their lives or been injured during war, but women as well as men have received this award during their service.[32]

Other Wartime Heroines

American Revolution

Margaret Cochran Corbin was the wife of John Corbin, an artilleryman, who was killed while firing a small cannon against the British near Fort Washington, New York, leaving his cannon unmanned. With no time to grieve, Margaret continued loading and firing the cannon by herself until she was wounded by grapeshot, which tore her shoulder, mangled her chest, and lacerated her jaw. Other soldiers moved her to the rear where she received first aid. The fort was captured by the British, but the wounded American soldiers were paroled. They were ferried across the river to Fort Lee. Margaret was then transported further in a jolting wagon all the way to Philadelphia. She never recovered fully from her wounds and was left without the use of her left arm. Her plight came to the attention of the state's Executive Council, which granted her temporary relief in June 1779. The next month, the Continental Congress granted a lifetime soldier's half-pay pension to her. She was thereafter included on military rolls and in April 1783 was formally mustered out of the Continental Army. She lived in Westchester County, New York, until her death. With this act, Congress made Margaret the first woman in the United States to receive a pension from Congress. In 1916, her remains were moved from Highland Falls, New York, to West Point, where a monument was erected in her honor.

Mary Hays, also known as Molly Pitcher, became a heroine of the American Revolution at the Battle of Monmouth, New Jersey, in 1778, when she repeatedly aided soldiers overcome by heat and exhaustion by giving them water from a nearby stream. When her husband, John Hays, was overcome with exhaustion and could not be revived, Molly took over his position as gunner until dark, when the battle ended. Afterward, General George Washington made her a sergeant in the army. In 1822, she received a military pension of $40 a year. Other women disguised as men also served. Probably the most famous is Deborah Samson, alias Robert Shurtliff, who fought in the 4th Massachusetts regiment under Colonel William Shephard and later Colonel Henry Jackson.[33]

The first woman to be killed in action was Jemima Warner. On December 11, 1775, she was killed by an enemy bullet during the siege of Quebec. Mrs. Warner had originally accompanied her husband, PVT James Warner of Thompson's Pennsylvania Rifle Battalion, to Canada because she feared that he would become sick on the campaign trail and she wanted to nurse him. When PVT Warner eventually died in the wilderness en route to Quebec, Mrs. Warner buried him and stayed with the battalion as a cook.[34]

Civil War

During the Civil War, approximately thirty-two hundred women served as Army contract nurses, the most famous of whom was Clara Barton, founder of the American Red Cross. The nurses, untrained and working along with volunteer nursing agencies and nuns of various denominations, are credited with easing pain and saving lives. However, once the conflict was over, the nursing services were disbanded. Also remember Dr. Mary Walker, who served as a nurse, and was later recognized with the Medal of Honor.

Women also served as spies and soldiers, though only when disguised as men. It may be more common than originally thought, as there are a number of interesting books on the subject. One such woman was Sarah Emma Edmonds, who joined the Army in 1861 disguised as a man named Frank Thompson. She eventually also worked as a nurse and spy, cleverly disguising herself in both gender and race. She also eventually was given a pension and in 1988 was inducted into the Military Intelligence Corps Hall of Fame at Fort Huachuca, Arizona.[35]

Spanish-American War

Approximately fifteen hundred nurses were recruited to serve in the Spanish-American War, and their extraordinary service paved the way for a permanent military nurse corps—the Army Nurse Corps, established in 1901. The nurses who served in the Spanish-American War found themselves in Hawaii, Cuba, the Philippines, and Puerto Rico, as well as on the hospital ship *Relief*. During service in the Spanish-American War, upward of 20 nurses lost their lives to typhoid and yellow fever.

One of the women who served as a contract nurse was Clara Louise Maass. She served with the Seventh U.S. Army Corps from October 1, 1898, to February 5, 1899, in Jacksonville, Florida; Savannah, Georgia; and Santiago, Cuba. She was discharged in 1899 but then volunteered again with the Eighth U.S. Army Corps in the Philippines from November 1899 to mid-1900.

Shortly after finishing her second assignment with the army, Maass returned to Cuba in October 1900 after being summoned by Major William Gorgas, chief sanitation officer, who was working with the U.S. Army's Yellow Fever Commission. The commission, headed by Major Walter Reed, was established during the postwar occupation of Cuba in order to investigate yellow fever, which was endemic in Cuba. It was proposed by Cuban doctor Carlos Juan Finlay that mosquitoes transmitted the disease. Human subjects were necessary to support this hypothesis.

Maass volunteered, the only American woman to do so, with six other men. She contracted a mild case of the disease from which she quickly recovered. On August 14, 1901, Maass allowed herself to be bitten by infected mosquitoes for the second time. She became ill with yellow fever on August 18 and died on August 24. Her death helped prove that mosquitoes transmitted yellow fever, which made Major Walter Reed famous.

Maass was buried in Colon Cemetery in Havana with military honors. Her body was later moved to New Jersey. In 1976, the one-hundredth anniversary of her birth, Maass was honored with a $0.13 United States commemorative stamp. Also in 1976, the American Nurses Association inducted her into its Nursing Hall of Fame.[36]

World War I

Few women other than nurses served in the military during WWI except for the Navy Yeoman (F) and Women Marines, who primarily were stationed stateside. More than ten thousand Army and Navy nurses served in Europe, and a few of the Navy Yeomen (F) worked in hospitals in France. However, about twenty-five thousand Americans went to Europe beginning in August 1914 on their own, crossing the Atlantic in ships to help assuage the suffering. Women served as nurses, doctors, dentists, dietitians, administrators, chauffeurs, entertainers, interpreters, translators, accountants, canteen workers, reporters, and relief workers, to name a few. They went to relieve the sufferings of the civilian victims of the war, to support and nurture troops, and to report on the war.

During WWI, several nurses and other workers were wounded as a result of enemy action. About 172 women died while overseas largely due to influenza, pneumonia, and even mustard gas exposure—only four were killed due to enemy action. The first female member of the military killed in the line of duty was WWI Army nurse Edith Ayres. Nurse Ayres was killed on May 20, 1917, while with Base Hospital #12 aboard the USS *Mongolia* en route to France. The ship's crew fired the deck guns during a practice drill, and one of the guns exploded, spewing shell fragments across the deck and killing Nurse Ayres and her friend Nurse Helen Wood.

In addition to other U.S. decorations, many women received recognition for their service by awards from the British and the French. Beatrice Mac-Donald, along with 21 other Army nurses, 15 YMCA workers, physician Dr. Alice Weld Tallant, and a Salvation Army worker, Minnie Saunders Burdick, received the French Croix de Guerre, equivalent to the Bronze Star. MacDonald also received the British Military Medal, along with Eva Jean Parmelee. Army nurses also received the British Royal Red Cross, First Class, or Second Class. Four women received the Florence Nightingale Medal. Many Army nurses were named in British Army dispatches for their meritorious service. Awards were also given by the governments of Belgium, Greece, Romania, and Russia.[37]

World War II

Some four hundred thousand women served stateside, in Europe, and in the Pacific during WWII. They served in every capacity except actual combat operations against the enemy in the air, on land, or at sea. Women's patriotism knew no bounds at home or in the military. Rosie the Riveter was created as a mascot for the many women who served in our nation's military industrial complex once the men went off to war. More than fifty-nine thousand nurses in the Army Nurse Corps volunteered to serve. Over 217 lost their lives—16 to enemy action—and more than 1,600 were decorated for meritorious service and bravery under fire. Military women came from all walks of life, and, like their male peers, minority women felt it was just as important to prove their worth to the military. One such group was the women who made up the 6888th Central Postal Directory Battalion. They were the only African American women to be stationed in Europe during the war. Asian women joined as well. There are numerous books, both personal stories and researched material, on women in WWII.[38]

Korean War

After WWII, the military began an enormous task: the return and discharge of all service personnel back to the United States. In the years between 1945 and 1950, the military was returning to its prewar ranks—a small, professional army. Except for a small cadre of women remaining as a result of the Armed Services Integration Act, women's forces, including the nurse corps, were practically decimated. Men were again conscripted, but the Army was depending on women to volunteer as they had during WWII. This did not happen as planned. When the war broke out, there were only twenty-two thousand women on active duty, and about a third of them were in health care. Women comprised less than 1 percent of the total force. Women nurses who had served in WWII were recalled to active duty. Within days of combat troops landing in Korea, nurses were caring for battle casualties. About 120,000 women served during the Korean conflict, not many of whom were in country. Nevertheless, the service branches never did get the numbers of women they needed for the war. But the nurses were the stars of the show.

One such star was Army nurse Captain Viola McConnell. At the start of the war, she was stationed in Seoul as part of the Army's military assistance group. The day after the communists invaded and almost overran South Korea, she swiftly supervised the evacuation and escort of 643 American military dependents—including 277 children under the age of one plus 4 near-term pregnant women—out of the country to Japan on a Norwegian freighter. The freighter was not built for passengers, and the able bodied had to sleep in the storage holds. Assisting her was a UN nurse, an Army wife who was a nurse, six missionary nurses, and one female missionary physician. The hasty departure did not leave much time for planning, and infant formula was a rare commodity. Luckily, the arduous journey lasted only two days. The war left an Army nursing shortage worldwide. McConnell went back to Korea, where she received the Bronze Star. She later received the Oak Leaf Cluster, noting additional award of the medal for her contributions in evacuating the infirm, women, and children from the war zone.[39]

Vietnam War

Few women, except Army nurses, were sent to Vietnam. About seven thousand women served in country, eight of whom died in the line of duty including one, Sharon Lane, from hostile fire. Sharon grew up in Ohio, graduated from Canton South High School in June 1961, and entered the Aultman Hospital School of Nursing the following September. After graduating in 1965, she worked at the hospital until May 1967, when she decided to attend the Canton Business College. After three semesters she quit in 1968 to join the U.S. Army Nurse Corps Reserve. She began training as a 2nd Lieutenant on May 5 at Fort Sam Houston in Texas. In June she reported to Fitzsimons General Hospital in Denver, Colorado, and while there she was promoted to 1st Lieutenant. In 1969 she reported to Travis Air Force Base in California with orders for Vietnam, arriving at the 312th Evac Hospital at Chu Lai on April 29. She was assigned to the Intensive Care ward for a few days before being assigned to the Vietnamese Ward. She worked five days a week (12 hours per day) in this ward and on the sixth day worked in Intensive Care. At 6:05 A.M., June 8, 1969, the 74th Medical Battalion reported a rocket hit between Wards 4a and 4b of the 312th Evacuation Hospital. The explosion killed two and wounded 27 U.S. and Vietnamese personnel. First Lt Lane was killed by fragmentation wounds. The Binz-Engleman Road entrance to Fort Sam Houston is designated Lane Gate in her honor. Her awards include the Bronze Star with V and the Purple Heart.[40]

As Saigon was falling in 1975, President Ford ordered an airlift of all in-country orphans, many of whom had American fathers. Called Operation Babylift, over two thousand children eventually were evacuated to the United States and other countries for asylum and adoption. Two young flight nurses—Captain Mary Klinker, United States Air Force (USAF), and Lieutenant Regina Aune—assigned to Clark Air Base in the Philippines volunteered for the humanitarian effort. Tasked to bring children from Vietnam to the Philippines, a C-5A Galaxy plane departed with more than three hundred children and accompanying adults on April 3, with Captain Dennis Traynor at the controls, an aircrew of 16, and 7 attendants. A few minutes out of Saigon, an explosion blew off the plane's pressure door, center cargo door, and a large section of the loading ramp rear of the cargo compartment. Aune and Klinker were in the cargo hold caring for patients. The plane decompressed instantaneously and the temperature dropped, communications between the flight deck and the troop deck were severed, the flight controls were crippled, and the plane filled with fog and debris.

The pilots were able to turn the plane back toward Saigon. The damaged plane crash landed two miles from Tan Son Nhut Airport, skidded and bounced its way to a final resting place in rice paddies, and broke apart. Lt. Aune was standing in the aisle in the troop compartment when the plane went down. The impact hurled her the length of the compartment, breaking her right foot. Bleeding heavily from cuts in her left arm and leg, she made her way to an emergency exit and began helping the crew and surviving medics remove children from the shattered aircraft. Five minutes later, rescue helicopters arrived, but they were unable to land. Aune and other team members waded again and again through the mud to the hovering helicopters, carrying terrified children. Finally, unable to go on, she staggered toward an approaching officer, asked to be relieved, and passed out. Later it was discovered that, in addition to her broken foot, she had a fractured leg and a broken bone in her back. Klinker, her medical technicians, and 141 of 149 orphans and attendants in the cargo hold were killed. Three children of 152 in the troop compartment were killed. In all, 175 of the 328 aboard survived, although most were injured. Traynor and his copilot were awarded the Air Force Cross. Klinker was the last U.S. servicewoman to die in the Vietnam conflict and was posthumously awarded the Airman's Medal and a Meritorious Service Medal. Lt. Aune became the first woman to receive the Cheney Award, and eventually a Colonel in the Air Force.[41]

Persian Gulf War (Desert Storm, 1991)

The Persian Gulf War of 1991 was a second watershed event for women in the military. A record 41,000 women served in Saudi Arabia and later Kuwait, and it would be the first time since WWII that women were taken prisoner of war. Several events made the Gulf War notable in women's history. First, it became clear that the rules protecting women from war were not being followed by the enemy. Second, it became clear that women would, and could, work in a hazardous environment and succeed. The two POWs, Specialist 4 Melissa Rathbun-Nealy and Major Rhonda Cornum, an Army flight surgeon, will be discussed in the next section.

The 1990s were a time of the expansion of women's roles, and women firsts, including Commander Rosemary Mariner, the first woman to command an aviation squadron; the first woman to command a surface ship in the Navy, Lt. Commander Darlene Iskra; and the destroyer tender USS *Acadia*, the first ship with women assigned in a war zone when it entered the Persian Gulf in 1990. The performance of women during Desert Shield/Desert Storm also paved the way for the removal of the combat exclusion laws for women at sea and in aviation.

Two weeks before the start of hostilities, Army Major Marie Rossi put a face to what women in the military were feeling about the prospect of going to war. She stated in an interview with CNN, "Personally, as an aviator and a soldier, this is the moment that everybody trains for—that I've trained for—so

I feel ready to meet the challenge." Major Rossi was one of the first U.S. soldier to participate in an air assault into enemy territory, when she led a squadron of Chinook helicopters 50 miles inside Iraq during operation Desert Storm on February 24, 1991, ferrying fuel and ammunition during the very first hours of the ground assault. She was also one of the few women killed when the Chinook helicopter that she was piloting crashed into an unlit microwave tower on March 1, 1991. Her death became a symbol of sacrifice for military women, who understood that with the rights to join the military also came some of the tragedies that occur in war. Marie was buried in Arlington cemetery.[42] In all, 15 women were killed during the conflict.

Women Prisoners of War

Civil War

Because women were not officially in the military during the Civil War, few know that women were prisoners of war during that conflict. Early in the war, imprisonment was not a concern for women because most prisoners were paroled and exchanged after promising not to take up arms again. After that practice ended, and since women were not supposed to be soldiers, army regulations did not address the issue. In nearly every case, the prisoner was released once her gender was discovered. Dr. Mary Walker, most famously known as the first and only woman to be awarded the Medal of Honor, was also a prisoner of war. Confederate spy Belle Boyd was imprisoned by the Union Army, as was Washington, D.C., social matron, and Confederate spy, Rose O'Neal Greenhow. The widowed Frances Jamieson, alias Frank Abel, worked as a spy for Union General Banks. She was captured by Confederate cavalry in October 1862, imprisoned in Richmond, and was exchanged two months later for southern spy Belle Boyd.

Women soldiers who disguised themselves as men were often discovered during their time as POWs, if they contracted a disease, were wounded, or if they died while imprisoned. This was the case with Union soldier Frances Hook, alias Frank Miller, who was captured by civilians when she went into a home foraging for food. She was turned over to the Confederates, and during her journey to prison camp was shot in the thigh while trying to escape. Her sex was discovered by the surgeon who tended to her wounds. Housed separately from the other Union prisoners, she was eventually exchanged with 27 other POWs on February 17, 1864.[43]

The fact that women have been prisoners of war should not be a surprise, but it does appear to be forgotten from one war to the next. Protectionist policies for women that excluded them from serving as combatants did little to protect women from harm, nor did they protect them from becoming prisoners.

World War II

Two groups of Navy nurses were held prisoner by the Japanese in WWII. Five Navy nurses stationed at the Naval hospital on Guam were taken prisoner by the Japanese shortly after Pearl Harbor, when Guam surrendered on December 10, 1941; they were eventually transported to Japan. They were repatriated in August 1942 from the ship SS *Gripsholm*, although a *New York Times* article did not identify them as Navy nurses.[44]

**United States Navy Nurses at U.S. Naval Hospital,
Guam, Marianas Islands**

Lorraine Christiansen, LtJG   Virginia Fogarty, LtJG
Leona Jackson, LtJG   Marion Olds, chief nurse
Doris M. Yetter, LtJG

Twelve navy nurses were stationed in the Philippines when the Japanese invaded. At the start of hostilities on December 10, the naval hospital was evacuated and personnel and nonambulatory patients were sent to the larger Army hospital in Manila—Sternberg. However, the nurses were soon sent to various places around Manila to care for Navy patients at sites other than the Army hospital, including the Philippine Union College at Balintawak; Santa Scholastica, a former girl's music school; and the night club Jai Alai, which had been turned into a makeshift clinic. On December 24, all Army medical personnel (with 24 Army nurses, 25 Filipino nurses, and 1 Navy nurse—Ann Bernatitus) and patients were evacuated to Bataan, a mountainous peninsula that juts out into Manila Bay. The Navy medical personnel had no orders to evacuate, so they stayed in Manila, relocating from Union College to Santa Scholastica. The Navy nurses were captured on January 3, 1942, in Manila and were interred in Santo Tomas with the captured Army nurses and 3,800 foreign civilian men, women, and children. The navy nurses later moved to a camp at Los Banos in 1943, with 800 male internees. They were freed by the 11th Airborne Division on February 22, 1945.[45]

United States Navy Nurses at U.S. Naval Hospital, Philippines

Ann Bernatitus, LtJG   Laura Cobb, chief nurse
Mary Chapman, LtJG   Bertha Evans, LtJG
Helen Gorzelanski, LtJG   Mary Harrington, LtJG
Margaret Nash, LtJG   Goldie O'Haver, LtJG
Eldene Paige, LtJG   Susie Pitcher, LtJG
Dorothy Still, LtJG   C. Edwina Todd, LtJG[46]

Army nurses served in the Philippines at Sternberg General Hospital in Manila, at Fort Stotensberg near Clark Field, at Camp John Hay at Baguio, at Fort McKinley near Manila, and at Fort Mills on Corregidor Island in Manila Bay. There were 88 Army nurses, regular and reserve, stationed in the Philippines in early December 1941. The first two Army nurses surrendered to the Japanese shortly after Christmas day; they had been left behind near Baguio to care for women and children refugees. They were interred in the Baguio Internment Camp until they were moved to other camps in 1943.

United States Army Nurses

Second Lt. Ruby G. Bradley, Baguio; Santo Tomas
Second Lt. Beatrice E. Chambers, Baguio; Bilibid Military Prison[47]

The 14 Army nurses at Clark Field cared for critically wounded soldiers for weeks before evacuating to Sternberg in Manila. All but one Army nurse in the Philippines were evacuated to Corregidor or the Bataan peninsula by December 30, 1941. On April 9, 1942, the Bataan peninsula was surrendered to the Japanese, and those nurses had 15 minutes to evacuate to Corregidor, leaving the wounded and other medical personnel to the Japanese.

Not all of the nurses in the Philippines became POWs. Some were lucky enough to be evacuated. Eleven Army nurses and Navy nurse Ann Bernatitus evaded Japanese capture and escaped aboard the submarine USS *Spearfish* on May 2, 1942. On April 29, 1942, 20 Army nurses, along with some key officers and civilian women, were authorized to be evacuated to Australia on two of MacArthur's flying boats. Unfortunately, only one boat made it; the other experienced a casualty on Mindanao and could proceed no further. The 10 nurses on that aircraft became prisoners at the San Tomas Internment Camp when Mindanao fell on May 10, 1942.

The battle for the Philippines would soon end. Corregidor was surrendered on May 6, 1942. The nurses stayed on Corregidor tending over nine hundred wounded until June 25, when they were moved to Santo Tomas Internment Camp near Manila. Throughout their time as POWs, all of the prisoners suffered terribly from disease, lack of food, and brutality by their captors. The nurses continued to care for patients, and all the nurses managed to survive, though they were weak from hunger and disease.[48]

The 66 Army Nurse Corps POWs

Lt. Mina A. Aasen	Lt. Hattie R. Brantley
Lt. Earleen Allen	Lt. Minnie L. Breese
Lt. Louise M. Anschicks	Lt. Myra V. Burris
Lt. Phyllis J. Arnold	Lt. Helen Cassiani
Lt. Agnes Barre	Lt. Edith M. Corns
Lt. Clara Mae Bickford	Lt. Mildred Dalton
Lt. Earlyn Black	Captain Maude C. Davison, chief nurse
Lt. Ethel L. Blaine	Lt. Kathryn L. Dollason

Lt. Sallie P. Durrett
Lt. Bertha Dworsky
Lt. Dorcas E. Easterling
Lt. Magdalena Eckman
Lt. Eula R. Fails
Lt. Adele F. Foreman
Lt. Helen L. Gardner
Lt. Eleanor Mae Garen
Lt. Marcia L. Gates
Lt. Beulah M. Greenwalt
Lt. Alice J. Hahn
Lt. Helen M. Hennessey
Lt. Gwendolyn L. Henshaw
Lt. Verna V. Henson
Lt. Rosemary Hogan
Lt. Geneva Jenkins
Lt. Doris A. Kehoe
Lt. Imogene Kennedy
Lt. Blanche Kimball
Lt. Eleanor O. Lee
Lt. Frankie T. Lewey
Lt. Dorothy L. Ludlow
Lt. Winifred P. Madden
Lt. Inez V. McDonald
Lt. Letha McHale

Captain Gladys Ann Mealor, chief nurse
Lt. Mary Brown Menzie
Lt. Adolpha M. Meyer
Lt. Clara L. Mueller
Lt. Frances Louise Nash
Lt. Josephine May Nesbit
Lt. Mary J. Oberst
Lt. Eleanor O'Neill
Lt. Rita G. Palmer
Lt. Beulah M. Putnam
Lt. Mary J. Reppak
Lt. Rose F. Rieper
Lt. Dorothy Scholl
Lt. Edith E. Shacklette
Lt. Ruth M. Stoltz
Lt. Ethel M. Thor
Lt. Madeline M. Ullon
Lt. Evelyn B. Whitlow
Lt. Anna E. Williams
Lt. Maude Denson Williams, nurse-anesthetist
Lt. Edith M. Wimberly
Lt. Anne B. Wurts
Lt. Eunice F. Young
Lt. Alice M. Zwicker

All the nurses who were held in the Santo Tomas prison were rescued by the First U.S. Calvary Division on February 3, 1945. After they were liberated, all were promoted one grade in rank, outfitted with new uniforms, and then sent to San Francisco via Honolulu.[49]

During WWII, U.S. Army 2nd Lt. Reba Z. Whittle was a flight nurse on a C47 transport that was shot down near Aachen Germany behind enemy lines. She was held as a POW for four months at Stalag Luft 9C from September 1944 to January 1945. She worked in the Stalag's prison hospital with the lead British doctor.[50]

Persian Gulf War

The sexual assault of a POW is always a possibility, but the women POWs of WWII were apparently spared that humiliation, or at least it was not widely publicized. Rape is a weapon of war, of power, and men are not exempt from it, but this aspect is not widely discussed. However, when it comes to women, it is a primary concern. Two women were captured during the 1991 Persian Gulf War. Specialist 4 Melissa Rathbun-Nealy and Major Rhonda Cornum, an Army flight surgeon. Rathbun-Nealy was a 20-year-old Army truck driver. She was captured on January 30, 1991, when the heavy-duty truck she and Specialist David Lockett were driving wandered into a firefight and, in trying to retreat, became stuck in the sand. They were overrun by Iraqi troops. Both were wounded by enemy fire—she by a bullet and shrapnel in her arm, he by bullets in his chest. They were released in March 1991, and both stated they had been well treated. She insists she was not sexually assaulted, calling her captors gentlemen. The worst part of being a POW, she said, was the notoriety she gained as a result. A private person, she never did discuss her story with the mainstream media.[51]

Major Cornum, now a brigadier general, was captured in February during a rescue operation when the helicopter she was flying in, a UH-60 Black Hawk, was shot down during a firefight. Five of the eight crew members died in the crash; Cornum survived with a bullet wound in her shoulder, two broken arms, a crushed pinkie finger, numerous lacerations, and a torn knee ligament. She was taken prisoner by the elite Republican Guard, along with fellow crew member Sergeant Troy Dunlap. Loss of blood from the bullet wound made her weak, and with both arms broken, she could barely function. During one of the transits from one bunker to another, a guard molested her. Her screams of pain, however, kept him from raping her. She says, "We had heard the stories of what the Iraqi soldiers had done to women in Kuwait, so I had thought about the probability that I would be sexually abused if I were captured. I had never considered that I would be so badly injured, though. When I really was shot down, I was thinking of myself as a soldier, and a POW, and a severely injured person. I was not thinking of myself as a woman. I was amazed that this Iraqi soldier could only see me as a woman."[52]

Although Cornum was sexually assaulted, that information was not confirmed until just before her book, *She Went to War*, was released a year later. She did not want to make light of the assault, but she felt it was not the worst part of her imprisonment.

> "Since everything that happens to you as a prisoner of war is non-consensual, then the fact that one thing they did was non-consensual is not very relevant," she told the *Washington Post's* Allen. "So then you have to organize the bad things that can happen to you in some other hierarchy. My hierarchy was, is it going to make me stay here longer, is it life-threatening, is it disabling or is it excruciating. If it's none of those things, then it took on a fairly low level of significance.". . . Cornum insisted that women in the military should be judged on their own talents, and she dismissed those who would use her experience as an argument for keeping women out of jobs on the front lines. "Every 15 seconds in America, some woman is assaulted. Why are they worried about a woman getting assaulted once every 10 years in a war overseas? It's ridiculous," she told

Cathy Booth Thomas of *Time*. "Clearly it's an emotional argument they use . . . because they can't think of a rational one."[53]

Operation Iraqi Freedom

The military campaign against Iraq began in March 2003. Later that month, on March 20, a supply convoy began its journey into Iraq from Kuwait. The desert is not kind to motorized equipment, and many of the trucks broke down, causing delays. Privates First Class Jessica Lynch and Lori Piestewa were assigned to the 507th Maintenance Company deployed from Fort Bliss, Texas. Their part of the convoy was at the tail end, and they had not been able to keep up with the main convoy. When the truck Lynch was driving broke down, she was picked up by Piestewa, who was driving a Humvee. Their part of the convoy got lost, and on the morning of March 23 the stragglers wandered into Nasiriyah, a Saddam stronghold, where they were attacked. As Piestewa drove, the other three soldiers in the Humvee began shooting. However, Lynch did not fire a shot as her M-16 had jammed. In the harried attempt to backtrack to safety, the Humvee was hit with a rocket-powered grenade.

Piestewa, who survived the crash, died in an Iraqi hospital of massive head wounds. Lynch sustained numerous serious injuries. Her right arm was shattered, leaving her right hand almost useless. Her spine was fractured in two places, causing nerve damage and the inability to control her kidneys and bowels. Her left leg had broken in two places, and she had a compound fracture that damaged nerves, leaving her without feeling in that leg. She had also been a victim of anal assault before waking in the hospital. Lynch does not remember that. She was transferred to the General Hospital in Nasiriyah, where she was operated on and cared for before her rescue on April 1 by Special Forces.[54]

Specialist Shoshanna Johnson, also of the 507th, was in another part of the convoy. She was taken prisoner with four others after fighting until they were surrounded or wounded. Johnson had been shot in both ankles. She became the first African American female POW, although this undoubtedly gave her little comfort in the 22 days she was a prisoner. She and her comrades were rescued by the Marines on April 13.[55]

When one becomes a POW, there is of course fear of what one's captors will do. In her book, Cornum reports that her fellow male prisoners were beaten and physically treated much worse than she was. She felt that her molestation was less of an issue than that she was a senior officer who could not help her fellow prisoners. Military women do not want to be thought of as weak or emotionally vulnerable to the fear of sexual assault as a POW. They do not want to be thought of as victims. However, there comes a time when the harassment of everyday life in the military becomes too much. This will be discussed in the next chapter.

Notes

My thanks to Captain Barb for all of the great information on her Web page, "Military Women Veterans Yesterday–Today–Tomorrow," which can be accessed at http://userpages.aug.com/captbarb/index.html. I accessed her site many times for initial information before beginning more detailed research on the women listed on her site.

1. *Webster's Encyclopedic Unabridged Dictionary of the English Language* (New York: Gramercy Books, 1996), 895–896.

2. The Congressional Medal of Honor, http://www.medalofhonor.com/; Congressional Medal of Honor Society, http://www.cmohs.org/medal.htm.

3. Andrew Johnson, *President*, Home of Heros, "The Medal of Honor, DSC and Navy Cross To Women Heroes," http://www.homeofheroes.com/valor/09_women/b_awards_women.html.

4. American Association of University Women, St. Lawrence County, NY Branch. Women of Courage Profiles, "Mary Edwards Walker, Civil War Surgeon," http://www.northnet.org/stlawrenceaauw/walker.htm; Mary Edwards Walker's biography can be found in John Patrick Dever and Maria C. Dever, *Women and the Military* (Jefferson, NC: McFarland & Co., 1995) as well as the following Web sites: Women in History, "Mary Edwards Walker," http://www.lkwdpl.org/wihohio/walk-mar.htm; National Library of Medicine, "Dr. Mary Edwards Walker," http://www.nlm.nih.gov/changingthefaceofmedicine/physicians/biography_325.html; Wikipedia, "Mary Edwards Walker," http://en.wikipedia.org/wiki/Mary_Edwards_Walker.

5. This has been increasing since Desert Storm in 1991.

6. Home of Heroes, "Recipients of the Distinguished Service Cross," http://www.homeofheroes.com/distinguishedservicecross/index.html.

7. Lettie Gavin, *American Women in World War I: They also Served* (Niwot, CO: University Press of Colorado, 1997). Full-text citations for most DSC awardees can be found at Home of Heroes, "Military Medals and Awards," http://www.homeofheroes.com.

8. No other information was discovered regarding Emma Sloan's award. Gavin, *American Women in World War I*. Home of Heroes, "Women Awarded the Medal of Honor, Distinguished Service Cross, and Navy Cross," http://www.homeofheroes.com/valor/09_women/b_awards_women.html.

9. Naval Historical Center, "The Navy Cross Medal," http://www.history.navy.mil/medals/.

10. Home of Heroes, "The Medal of Honor, DSC and Navy Cross to Women Heroes," http://homeofheroes.com/valor/09_women/b_awards_women.html.

11. OSS was the precursor agency to the current Central Intelligence Agency.

12. Home of Heroes, "The Medal of Honor, DSC and Navy Cross to Women Heroes."

13. Ibid. "Recipients of the Distinguished Service Medal," http://homeofheroes.com/valor/02_awards/03_dsm.html.

14. Gavin, *American Women in World War I*, Appendix B.

15. Richard M. Prior and William Sanders Marble, "The Overlooked Heroines: Three Silver Star Nurses of World War I," *Military Medicine* (May 1, 2008).

16. Veteran Affairs Office of Lexington County, S.C., *Vet news*, "Women Medal Recipients-Military and Civilian," August 2005, 3–4, http://www.lex-co.com/depart ments/VeteransAffairs/Documents/VetNews200508.pdf.

17. Operation Iraqi Freedom, Official Web site of multinational force—Iraq, "Kentucky Guardsmen Decorated for Gallantry," press release, June 15, 2005, http://www.mnf-iraq.com/index.php?option=com_content&task=view&id=3850&Item id=21; "Distinguished Service: Nein Honored with Army's Second Highest Award," *The Bluegrass Guard* 11, no. 2 (June 2007): http://kynghistory.ky.gov/NR/rdonlyres/4D750AF5-B902-4870-BE88-06DAEF8A8ECA/0/bgg2007june.pdf.

18. Leo Shane III, "Female Soldier Awarded Silver Star," *Stars and Stripes*, June 18, 2005, http://www.stripes.com; Sgt. Sara Wood, USA, "Women Soldier Receives Silver Star for Valor in Iraq," *American Forces Press Service*, June 16, 2005, http://www.defense link.mil search engine. The Bronze Star is a U.S. Armed Forces individual military decoration that may be awarded for bravery, acts of merit, or meritorious service. When awarded for bravery, it is the fourth-highest combat award of the U.S. Armed Forces and the ninth-highest military award (including both combat and noncombat awards) in the order of precedence of U.S. military decorations. The Valor device (combat V) identifies the award as resulting from an act of combat heroism, http://en.wikipedia.org/wiki/Bronze_Star_Medal.

19. Janie Blankenship, "Woman Medic Earns Silver Star in Afghanistan," *VFW Magazine*, August 2008, www.vfw.org; Spec. Micah E. Clare, USA, "Face of Defense: Woman Soldier Receives Silver Star," *American Forces Press Service*, March 24, 2008, http://www.defenselink.mil search engine.

20. The American War Library, "Distinguished Flying Cross Display Recognition," http://www.amervets.com/replacement/dfc.htm#isr; The Distinguished Flying Cross Society, "DFC Citations: Amelia Earhart," http://www.dfcsociety.org/citation_detail. asp?ID=4944. Wilbur and Orville Wright were also honored with the award in 1928, also by an act of Congress.

21. Veteran Affairs Office of Lexington County, S.C., "Women Medal Recipients-Military and Civilian."

22. World War II Awards, "Distinguished Flying Cross. First Lt. Roberta Schil-bach Ross," http://www.ww2awards.com/award/241/R. Award of the Air Medal is primarily intended to recognize those personnel who are on current crew member or noncrew member flying status, which requires them to participate in aerial flight on a regular and frequent basis in the performance of their primary duties.

23. The Distinguished Flying Cross Society, "DFC Citations, Colonel Jackie Cochran," http://www.dfcsociety.org/citation_detail.asp?ID=4127.

24. Veteran Tributes, "Eileen Collins," http://www.veterantributes.org/Tribute Detail.asp?ID=238.

25. TSgt Jason Haag, "Wounded Warthog: An A-10 Thunderbolt II Pilot Safely Landed Her "Warthog" after it Sustained Significant Damage from Enemy Fire," *Combat Edge*, April 4, 2004, http://findarticles.com/p/articles/mi_m0JCA/is_11_12/ai_n6100282/.

26. *Army News Service*, "Pilot Earns Distinguished Flying Cross," November 2, 2006, http://www.defenselink.mil/home/faceofdefense/fod/2006-11/f20061103a.html.

27. National Archives, "A People at War, Women who Served: Annie G. Fox," http://www.archives.gov/exhibits/a_people_at_war/women_who_served/annie_g_fox.html.

28. The Florence Nightingale Medal is awarded by the International Red Cross and honors those persons who distinguish themselves in times of peace or war by exceptional courage and devotion to the wounded, sick, disabled, or civilian victims of a conflict or disaster and/or for exemplary services or a creative and pioneering spirit in the areas of public health or nursing education. The medal may be awarded posthumously if the prospective recipient has fallen in active service.

29. Arlington National Cemetery Web site, "Ruby Bradley, Colonel, U.S. Army," http://www.arlingtoncemetery.net/rbradley.htm.

30. Leo Shane III, "Female Soldier Awarded Silver Star," *Stars and Stripes*, June 18, 2005, http://www.stripes.com; Sgt. Sara Wood, USA, "Women Soldier Receives Silver Star for Valor in Iraq," *American Forces Press Service*, June 16, 2005, http://www.defenselink.mil search engine. The Bronze Star is a U.S. Armed Forces individual military decoration that may be awarded for bravery, acts of merit, or meritorious service. When awarded for bravery, it is the fourth-highest combat award of the U.S. Armed Forces and the ninth-highest military award (including both combat and noncombat awards) in the order of precedence of U.S. military decorations. The Valor device (combat V) identifies the award as resulting from an act of combat heroism, http://en.wikipedia.org/wiki/Bronze_Star_Medal.

31. Home of Heroes, "The Purple Heart, Our Nation's First Military Award," http://www.homeofheroes.com/medals/purple_heart/purple_heart.html.

32. National Archives, "A People at War, Women who Served: Annie G. Fox," http://www.archives.gov/exhibits/a_people_at_war/women_who_served/annie_g_fox.html.

33. Distinguished Women of Past and Present, www.distinguishedwomen.com/biographies/corbin.html; Encyclopedia Britannica, "Margaret Corbin," http://www.britannica.com/EBchecked/topic/137211/Margaret-Corbin; Encyclopedia Britannica, "Molly Pitcher," http://www.britannica.com/EBchecked/topic/462024/Molly-Pitcher; Elizabeth D. Leonard, *All the Daring of a Soldier: Women of the Civil War Armies* (New York: W.W. Norton, 1999).

34. Women in Military Service for America, *Resources: Historical Frequently Asked Questions*, http://www.womensmemorial.org/H&C/Resources/hfaq.html.

35. Leonard, *All the Daring of a Soldier*; Silvia Anne Sheafer, *Women in America's Wars* (Springfield, NJ: Enslow Publishers, 1996), 19–27. See also, DeAnne Blanton and Lauren M. Cook, *They Fought Like Demons: Women Soldiers in the American Civil War* (Baton Rouge, LA: Louisiana State University Press, 2002); Penny Colman, *Spies! Women in the Civil War* (Cincinnati, OH: Betterway Books, 1992); Laura Leedy Gansler, *The Mysterious Private Thompson: The Double Life of Sarah Emma Edmonds, Civil War Soldier* (New York: Free Press, 2005).

36. Encyclopedia Britannica, "Clara Maass, American Nurse," http://www.britannica.com/EBchecked/topic/353504/Clara-Maass#.

37. For a complete listing of all the awards and awardees, see Gavin, *American Women in World War I*, Appendix B.

38. See, for example, Evelyn M. Monahan and Rosemary Neidel-Greenlee, *And If I Perish: Frontline U.S. Army Nurses in World War II* (New York, Anchor Books, 2003); Brenda Moore, *To Serve My Country, To Serve My Race* (New York: New York University Press, 1996); Brenda Moore, *Serving Our Country: Japanese American Women in the Military during World War II* (Piscataway, NJ: Rutgers University Press, 2003).

39. Linda Witt, Judith Bellafaire, Britta Granrud, and Mary Jo Binker, *A Defense Weapon Known to Be of Value* (Lebanon, NH: University Press of New England, 2005); Mary T. Sarnecky, *A History of the Army Nurse Corps* (Philadelphia: University of Pennsylvania Press, 1999).

40. Army Medial Department Regiment, Ft. Sam Houston, TX, "Sharon Ann Lane," http://ameddregiment.amedd.army.mil/fshmuse/lane.htm.

41. The Cheney Award is an aviation award presented by the United States Air Force in memory of First Lt. William Cheney, who was killed in an air collision over Italy in 1918. It was established in 1927 and is awarded to an airman for an act of valor, extreme fortitude, or self-sacrifice in a humanitarian interest, performed in connection with aircraft, but not necessarily of a military nature, Wikipedia, "Cheney Award," http://en.wikipedia.org/wiki/Cheney_Award. Bethanne Kelly Patrick, "Operation Babylift Volunteer Became Last U.S. Nurse to Die in Vietnam," http://www.military.com/Content/MoreContent?file=ML_klinker_bkp; Allison Martine, "The Legacy of Operation Babylift," http://www.adoptvietnam.org/adoption/babylift.htm; U.S. Air Force Official Web site, "Information-Heritage-History person-Col Regina Aune," http://www.af.mil/information/heritage/person.asp?dec=&pid=123006467.

42. Arlington National Cemetery Web site, "Marie Therese Rossi Cayton," http://www.arlingtoncemetery.net/mariethe.htm.

43. Blanton and Cook, *They Fought Like Demons*; Colman, *Spies!*

44. The SS *Gripsholm* was a 1924 vintage ship built for the Swedish American Line that was chartered by the State Department and under the protection of the Red Cross from 1942–1946 to exchange POWs, diplomats, women, and children between the warfaring nations. A Tribute to the Swedish American Line, Exchange and Repatriation Voyages During WWII, http://www.salship.se/mercy.asp. Doris Sterner, *In and Out of Harm's Way: A History of the Navy Nurse Corps* (Seattle, WA: Peanut Butter Publishing, 1996), 131.

45. Dorothy Still Danner, *What a Way to Spend a War: Navy Nurse POWs in the Philippines* (Annapolis, MD: Naval Institute Press, 1995); Elizabeth M. Norman, *We Band of Angels* (New York: Random House, 1999), 277; Sterner, *In and Out of Harm's Way*, 112–116.

46. Sterner, *Navy Nurse Corps*, 110–111.

47. Mary T. Starnecky, *A History of the U.S. Army Nurse Corps* (Philadelphia: University of Pennsylvania Press, 1999), 187.

48. Ibid., 190–192.

49. Norman, *Band of Angels*, 279–281. There were other women held as prisoners as well—civilians with the Red Cross or other civilians living and working in the Philippines at the time of the invasion. See Norman for a full list. Sarnecky, *Army Nurse Corps*, 193–194.

50. The Wartime Memories Project-Stalag 9c POW Camp, "U.S. Army 2nd LT Reba Z Whittle," http://www.wartimememories.co.uk/pow/stalag9c.html#whittle.

51. The P.O.W. Network, "List of Names-Gulf War 1-Melissa Rathbun-Nealy," http://www.pownetwork.org/gulf/rd035.htm.

52. Rhonda Cornum, *She Went to War: The Rhonda Cornum Story* (Novato, CA: Presidio Press, 1992), 50.

53. Encyclopedia of World Biography, 2006 A-Ec, "Rhonda Cornum Biography," http://www.notablebiographies.com/newsmakers2/2006-A-Ec/Cornum-Rhonda. html.

54. Rick Bragg, *I Am a Soldier, Too: The Jessica Lynch Story* (New York: Knopf, 2003).

55. NationMaster Encyclopedia, "Shoshanna Johnson," http://www.nationmaster. com/encyclopedia/Shoshanna-Johnson.

CHAPTER 5

Gender, Sexuality, and Harassment

Just leave me alone and let me do my job!

—Anonymous female sergeant

I asked my class the other day, "Okay, who thinks sexual harassment is a good thing?" Not surprisingly, no one raised his or her hand. Yet it is a pervasive problem throughout our society and especially in the workplace. When asked why it was so pervasive, the students gave the common answer: "It's a power thing." But there was a lone voice who said, "Because they can get away with it." Wow.

There are many ways women can be made to feel unwelcome in an all-male or mostly male environment. These include structured discrimination, gender and sexual harassment, sexual assault, and rape. Most everyone understands that sexual harassment is a form of gender discrimination and that it is defined as "unwelcome sexual advances, requests for sexual favors, and other verbal or physical conduct of a sexual nature . . . when this conduct explicitly or implicitly affects an individual's employment, unreasonably interferes with an individual's work performance, or creates an intimidating, hostile, or offensive work environment."[1] A key aspect of this behavior is that the attention is *unwanted*. What becomes confusing and cause for angst among both men and women in the workplace is when flirting and teasing is consensual between one couple but unwanted attention when that same behavior is conducted by a third party. When that third party is rebuked, there may be resentment, hurt feelings, loss of face, or other humiliations that could make that person respond in an inappropriate or retaliatory manner. Inappropriate responses could include harassment or possibly spreading rumors of either sexually promiscuous behavior or homosexuality. These reactions are nurtured by heterosexual social norms that imply that women are supposed to welcome men's advances.

Sexual and gender harassment is pervasive in the workplace because it is tolerated. It is tolerated by the victims, who feel they must ignore it so as not to upset the workplace culture. It is tolerated by co-workers, who may not feel it is their place to intervene. It is tolerated by managers, who may feel that if the behavior is unacceptable to the victim, it is the victim's responsibility to report it or confront it. Unfortunately, tolerating the situation is condoning the behavior. Plus, the behavior may proceed on a continuum that starts at inappropriate comments or jokes, progresses to sexual misconduct, and ends at sexual assault and rape. Although the Defense Task Force on Sexual Harassment and Violence at the Service Academies (Defense Task Force) and the General Accounting Office (GAO) have both compiled reports on the prevalence of this behavior at the service academies, the Pentagon seems to ignore that sexual harassment is one side of the sexual assault problem.

In 2005, the Defense Task Force provided an assessment as to why there continued to be ongoing problems with these issues at the three service academies. They noted, "The existence of sexual harassment and assault is an inherent contradiction to the spirit of the Academies that strives to and succeeds in creating strong commitments to honor and service. This contradiction is a product of complex and dynamic factors that influence the attitudes and behaviors of cadets and midshipmen."[2]

There were eight factors that contributed to the ongoing problem of sexual harassment and assault at the service academies:

1. The lack of understanding of the value of women to the military
2. The impact of youth culture and the contribution of alcohol to sexually violent behavior
3. The highly regulated lives of cadets and midshipmen, the inability to grasp the reasoning behind some of the regulations, and the decision of some to ignore or disregard some less serious but unquestionably harassing behavior
4. The strong adherence to the honor concept[3] by cadets and midshipmen, but the failure of the codes to instill a basic regard for human dignity and respect
5. The value of peer loyalty over the obligation to report or stop harassing behavior
6. The fear of reporting sexually harassing behavior due to the backlash of peer isolation or retribution; a culture of "blaming the victim"
7. Abuse of the authority of cadets and midshipmen in positions of power
8. The devaluation of women due to the institutional limitations of career choice (women cannot be in direct ground combat occupations, Special Forces, or submarines), their minority status (15–17%) in a traditionally masculine environment, and the differing physical fitness standards between men and women[4]

Regardless of the causes, the bottom line is that cadets and midshipmen will eventually become officers in the military—leaders who will then be expected to uphold the "no tolerance for harassment" policy. And yet, if they do not understand it while in training, how will they respond when faced with it in the workplace? In the Navy, we like to say we train like we fight: there are no drills. Therefore, if officer candidates are not taken to task for their attitudes toward their female peers while at school, what makes anyone think their attitudes will change once they are in charge of troops or sailors? How will they be prepared to work with or lead women and uphold the standards of the military to treat everyone with respect and eradicate sexual harassment and assault?

The problem is obvious in the situation now facing the military services: seemingly uncontrollable sexual harassment and violence in the military, and a public outraged at the inability of the military to deal with it. The solution is equally clear: develop respect for human dignity, and leadership practices, in all echelons of leadership. This requires more than the lip service of zero tolerance that DoD has established. It requires leaders who are willing to make hard decisions about disciplining or discharging personnel who do not embody or embrace the concept that *readiness = respect*. It requires peers to tell their friends when their behavior or comments are inappropriate. It requires subordinates to *speak truth to power* when a supervisor is undermining stated DoD goals. It requires constant vigilance and holding people accountable for their actions. It does not require more research, studies, task forces, committees, or legislation.

Social Construction of Gender in the Military

The military is a gendered institution, which Joan Acker defines as an institution in which "gender is present in the processes, practices, images and ideologies, and distributions of power in the various sectors of social life."[5] She goes on to say that gendered institutions are "institutions historically developed by men, currently dominated by men, and symbolically interpreted from the standpoint of men in leading positions, both in the present and historically. These institutions have been defined by the absence of women." Acker concludes that despite the changes that have occurred in our society in regards to women's roles, both past and present, males still dominate the central institutions, of which the military is one.[6] There is little argument that this definition explains military culture in general and why assumptions of behavior based on gender continue.

When women compete with men in the public sector, it is with the intent of equality or performing to the current expectations of the job. This is seen as a neutral standard. But Acker states, "One conceptual mechanism is the positing of an abstract, general human being, individual or worker who apparently has no gender. On closer examination, that individual almost always has the social characteristics of men, but that fact is not noted."[7] Major General Jeanne Holm, in her history of women in the military, makes a statement about women's military integration that was referring to the WWII timeframe but can easily apply to today: "The women are expected to adjust and to conform to the rules laid down *by men for men.*"[8] The male standard is presumed to be the only acceptable standard.

The military serves society by providing the nation's security and ensuring the nation's security interests are upheld in the global context, with its primary emphasis being on combat performed by warriors. Traditionally, basic training has been seen as a rite of passage where boys are transformed into men. This is accomplished through socialization processes that include physical endurance and strength, discipline, conformity, competition, and aggression. In boot camp, men are trained to be warriors who eschewed and actively feared being labeled as "sissy," "girls," or any other number of derogatory female descriptions.[9] The warrior ideal is not only male, but *not* female.[10]

Roles for women are slowly changing as members of society recognize the inherent inequalities and seek change. The myth of separate spheres of work and family described by Rosabeth Moss Kanter[11] continues even as increasing numbers of women, especially married women, enter or remain in the workforce after childbirth. American women are rejecting the exclusive roles of wives and mothers as evidenced by the increasing numbers of women, both married and single, in the workplace. Some women work to help with the family economy; others are pursuing their own identity and career goals.[12] This is also the case with regard to military families.

However, in the military, this socially constructed myth remains the ideal. For the most part, the military is *manned* by heterosexual men, and the women take care of the family, following the soldier, sailor, airman, or marine wherever the military sends him. Attitudes are more difficult to change, even in the face of practical considerations. The historical and ongoing debates on the expansion of women's roles draw on traditional role paradigms and are a key in the fight against harassment and assault. Some men do not think women belong in the military and try to drive them out through other means. Only the strongest survive.

Masculinity in the Military

In the military, the epitome of the hegemonic male is the senior officer. At this level, decisions are made about policy, and the military hierarchy applies those policies. The military is a hierarchical system with two unequal groups— officers and enlisted personnel—and a system of ranks within each group. The institution maintains a system of inequality through the strata of rank. All enlisted personnel must defer to officers, and each rank must defer to the rank above him or her. This system inherently makes men, especially men at the lower ends of the ranks, feel powerless.

As in society, individual males in the military do not feel they have power unless they are very high in the chain of command. Michael Kimmel, a well-known sociologist, notes: "Manhood is equated with power—over women, over other men. Everywhere we look, we see the institutional expression of that power—in state and national legislatures, on the boards of directors of every major U.S. corporation or law firm and in every school and hospital administration." Men have power as a group and have been raised to believe they are entitled to feel that power; however, they do not feel powerful and, thus, feel frustrated and angry, especially when they see this entitlement being shared by women. "Men's feelings are not the feelings of the powerful, but of those who see themselves as powerless."[13] The military is the last bastion where men as individuals can feel powerful doing men's jobs. This manifests itself in the strongly felt attitudes that only men have the psychological drive, motivation, and physical strength required to be military warriors.

Competitiveness and aggression are the key marks of the military system. From a work perspective, the military is an up-or-out system: either you get promoted or you get out. This is much more stringent for officers than for enlisted personnel and adds pressure to compete favorably against your peers. For both officers and enlisted personnel, the competition between peers is manifest in annual evaluations that require rankings within groups once you reach a certain rank. These comparative rankings can and do affect promotions and opportunities to fill billets of greater responsibility. Nonetheless, the impact on male bonding and friendship is like being on a sports team—individual achievement is desired, yet in order to win you have to rely on your fellow teammates. Thus, the construction of hegemonic masculinity in the military is reinforced by those typically male traits that value competitiveness, loyalty, and team spirit in the workplace.

Since the military is also an internal labor force that hires for promotion from within, women are a small, but growing, minority at the higher ranks, but many more women as a percentage of the force are joining than ever before. Men still have most of the high-status (i.e., highest ranking) jobs, however. Even though women are becoming more fully vested in the military, there are still a few areas women have not been allowed to pursue: direct ground combat roles and service on submarines. While there are probably power relationships amongst men in the military, the primary recipients over whom men maintain their institutional and individual power are homosexuals and women. Inequality in opportunity is manifest in men's continued control of power at the highest echelons in the military and in Congress.

Structured Discrimination

There are three broad categories of military occupations and skills: professional, technical and support, and operational. The professional category includes the specialty areas of medics, corpsmen, nurses, medical doctors, dentists, medical service corps, chaplains, chaplain aides, paralegals, and judge advocate generals (lawyers). In the officer corps, there is little to no horizontal movement between the professional specialties until the most senior levels of command in the medical fields, when nurses, doctors, or even dentists can command a medical center. Professionals almost never laterally transfer to the operational or support communities.[14]

Technical and support positions include administration, training, personnel management, public affairs, supply, ordnance, communications, maintenance, transportation, logistics, intelligence, and noncombatant engineering. The vast majority of women in the military serve in these two specialty areas. It is rare, although possible, for officers in either the professional or support areas to be promoted to the highest military ranks—four-star general or admiral. This is because most of the jobs in that rank go to combatants.[15] In 2008, the first woman, General Ann Dunwoody, a logistician, was promoted to that rank.

The operational communities are perceived as the backbone of the military organization; these are the combat arms of the military, which are infantry, armor, and artillery in the Army and Marine Corps; surface, submarine, and aviator in the Navy; pilots and navigators in the Air Force, Army, and Marine Corps; combat engineers; electronic warfare officers; and all Special Forces. Women entered the operational communities in 1972 (aviation) and 1978 (shipboard duty), but it was not until 1993–1994 that women were authorized to serve in combatant surface ships and air combat units.[16] Women in the Army and Marine Corps continue to be precluded from serving in the combat communities of infantry, armor (tanks), and field artillery, and women in all branches are precluded from serving in the Special Forces. As a result, most women in the Army and Marine Corps find their structures of opportunity virtually halted at the two- or three-star level, and for enlisted women the senior enlisted advisor at a major combatant command. Women officers who entered the operational communities in the Navy and Air Force in the mid-1990s are still too junior to be eligible for promotion to general/flag officer (GFO) rank.

The support, technical, and medical occupations make up about 88 percent of the officer specialty areas, while the ground combat arms make up only 12 percent of the total officer occupations.[17] This tooth-to-tail ratio (12:88 or 1:7.33) is indicative of military culture in that it celebrates the combat arms as the most important, and most prestigious, aspect of the military, yet it requires more than seven people to support each ground combatant in his or her war-fighting efforts. Clearly, combat arms are the most advantaged in both the occupational opportunity and power structures in that most of the four-star positions in the Army and Marine Corps are held by those in the ground combat arms; in the Navy and Air Force, most four-star billets are held by aviators, surface ship officers, or submariners. Those who enter the combat arms have a clear opportunity to progress to the highest levels of the military, and women are excluded from pursuing many of those occupational specialties.

The Issue of Tokenism

Women who work in organizations where they are a small minority, under 20 percent of the workforce, are called token women, and they face several challenges not limited to work structure or requirements. In token situations, gender becomes an overriding issue in work and interpersonal relationships. Men may affirm their masculinity by discussing male concerns such as sports or by participating in gender displays. These displays include sexual language, jokes and teasing, conversations about sex, macho behavior, swearing, exaggerated displays of aggression, potency, and prowess-oriented war stories. While men may not be totally conscious of these behaviors, they do signify to women that they are outsiders. Regardless of a token's position in the organization, she most likely will have experienced many discriminatory or abusive situations. Adverse behaviors become less apparent as one becomes more senior, but women in leadership positions may face challenges to their authority, both from below in the form of passive-aggressive behavior or from above in the form of a lack of support or professional exclusion. Token women also may find themselves socially isolated or excluded from work-related social activities, such as golf outings or after-work happy hours.[18]

The high visibility of tokens creates performance pressures. They are seen as representatives of women as a group; when they make a mistake, it is highly visible and interpreted as a reason why women should be excluded from that workplace or occupational specialty. Tokens must put in extra effort to make their skills known and often have to prove their competence, sometimes repeatedly, as they move ahead in the organization. One reaction to this is for the woman to become an overachiever. This has the disadvantage of bringing more attention to the woman, which may have possible negative repercussions such as the woman becoming the subject of vicious rumors or feeling a lack of group support. A token's more common response is to try to blend in—adopting conservative dress, avoiding public events, working at home, keeping silent at meetings, and avoiding conflict, risk, and controversial situations. Often, she allows others to take credit for her accomplishments.[19] This situation reflects the traditional social norm that women should be the supporter not the supported.

Tokens may also be subject to professional isolation. This may consist of important information being purposefully withheld, managers being unwilling to critique performance constructively, or being excluded from participating in networking situations where socialization occurs and corporate politics are exposed. Women may also be subject to loyalty tests where they are pressured by the majority to turn against other women. Examples are sharing jokes at another woman's expense or avoiding networking and workplace friendships with other women in order to demonstrate their commitment to the dominant group.[20] Another hazard a woman might face if she becomes too friendly with other women in the workplace is being labeled a lesbian. In the military, this is grounds for discharge, and it is a common tool used to retaliate against a nonconforming woman.

A final challenge for tokens is that they may become entrenched in stereotypical roles and face erroneous assumptions about their abilities or status. This occurs when women workers are mistaken for wives or secretaries or are put in a role that limits their credibility. Kanter describes four such roles: mother, pet, seductress, and iron maiden. Mother is the stereotypical nurturer, disallowing any possibility for her to "make waves." Pet is the "little sister" who is incompetent or needs to be protected. The seductress' perceived sexuality blots out all other attributes, and the iron maiden—someone who stands up for herself—is sometimes forced to be colder and more distant than she otherwise would be.[21]

Women are forced to live up (or down) to those images and are not allowed to perform as individuals. The assigned roles are degrading and incompatible with the fulfillment of professional responsibilities. In addition, psychological and behavioral effects may manifest in a desire to withdraw, resulting in tokens becoming more isolated and perhaps jeopardizing the opportunities for other women by their failure to integrate.[22] Thus, along with the accepted structure of professional careers, the interpersonal problems of tokens, and the cultural expectations of the ideal worker, women's choices and opportunities are often limited.

Women in the military can be seen as double-deviants—first as women in a male-dominated environment, and second as seekers of accomplishments and rewards usually sought by men. Military women are highly visible in most occupational areas of the military because of their token numbers.[23] Women's visibility and distinction from men is heightened by the authorized, and sometimes mandatory, differences in uniforms, hair length, and authority to wear jewelry and makeup. This visibility emphasizes the differences between tokens and the majority and may make dominants fearful that tokens possess a competitive edge as a result, such as when a woman is touted for being "a first."

There is also a fear that the token will receive preferential treatment in assignments, leadership opportunities, evaluations, or training due to her increased visibility. On the other hand, a token loses her individuality and may be seen as a member of a stereotyped group expected to act in certain ways, subject to treatment as a generalized other. Visibility, isolation, and role stereotypes[24] are the bane of military women. Regardless of its recent ad campaign for "An Army of One," the military is still an institution and work environment that relies on teamwork and cooperation. It is also an institution in which tradition and routine are highly valued; change is initiated only through very hard lessons learned. Changes in institutional policies, group demographics, attitudes, and opportunities for peer support and networking are important for women's ability to succeed. Interpersonal processes and structural impediments that affect women's motivation and self-esteem reduce their effectiveness and are harmful to both the military and the individual.[25]

Sexual and Gender Harassment and Discrimination

Sexual harassment was defined earlier in this chapter. The key item in this definition is that it is focused on harassment toward an individual. Gender harassment is focused on women as a group—for example, stereotypical ideas about gender and women's abilities vis-à-vis men. Gender harassment is a form of sexual harassment that consists primarily of repeated comments, jokes, and innuendoes directed at a group because of their gender or sexual orientation. This behavior may or may not be aimed at eliciting sexual cooperation from those addressed, but it contaminates work environments. Gender harassment closely resembles racial and ethnic slurs in its ability to create an offensive and hostile work environment.[26]

In the military, gender harassment is often overlooked as a source of discrimination because it is so ubiquitous. Perpetrators cite their First Amendment rights of free speech and often label as "politically correct" those who try to hange attitudes and behaviors. Often comments are couched in the vernacular of truth, such as the verbalization that women could never perform as well as men in combat because of their relative lack of physical strength, emotional fortitude, or courage. Much of the rhetoric against increased roles for women in the military is based on gendered ideology, such as the myths that all men will protect women if women are in danger, that women need the protection of men, and that women would not be able to adequately cover for men in a combat situation. These types of comments tend to denigrate women as a group and perpetuate stereotypes. In addition, the continuous and relentless accumulation of insults and slights adds up to the feeling that women are not wanted in the organization. This reduces morale, which in turn reduces military effectiveness and productivity.

In her book *Power and Gender*, Rosemarie Skain defines and explains both sexual and gender harassment and its legal consequences. She notes that both are about power relationships, not sex, and that a vital relationship exists between sexual and gender harassment. Both are used to define women in a structurally inferior place and reinforce and perpetuate women's status as inferior to men. Thus, they are used to curtail women's ambitions[27] and discourage those who aspire to nontraditional roles in the military. They are inherently discriminatory in feel and in results.

One of the problems with reporting gender harassment is the perception that the victim is whining. The military prides itself with instilling "self-less service, courage, honor, respect, discipline, confidence, respect, [and] a willingness to go forward during the most difficult situations."[28] When a military service member comes forward with such a complaint, she is not seen as being strong, courageous, and respected. She, and others, may feel that being a victim is inconsistent with the military's definition of a good service member.[29] Thus, sexual and gender harassment not only reduces the victim's self-confidence, but it also undermines her motivation to remain in the military and do the best job possible.

Sexual Assault

Sexual assault and violence in the United States is a pervasive and sobering problem. According to the Rape, Abuse & Incest National Network (RAINN), 1 in 6 American women and 1 in 33 men have been victims of rape or attempted rape in their lifetime; 17.7 million American women and 2.78 million American men have been victims of attempted or completed rape. Every two minutes, someone is sexually assaulted somewhere in America. About 44 percent of rape victims are under age 18, and 80 percent are under age 30. In about two-thirds of all rape cases, the victim knows the assailant. According to a Department of Justice report "Sex Offenses and Offenders," there is a "remarkable similarity" among rapists: 99 in 100 are male, 6 in 10 are white, and the average age is early 30s. In the U.S., 60 percent of sexual assaults are not reported to the police, and only 6 percent of rapists will go to jail. Luckily, since 1993, sexual assault has fallen by more than 60 percent.[30]

Unfortunately, the military problem is greater, and the reports are not encouraging. In March 2009, Katie Couric did a CBS evening news report on sexual assault in the military. She reported that 1 in 3 military women would experience sexual assault while serving in the military. Yet even with these figures, it is a grossly under-reported crime. It is estimated that 80 percent of rapes in the military are never reported.[31] There are both psychological as well as physical reasons why victims are reluctant to report. Confidentiality and confidential counseling are necessary to ensure victims are provided the help they need without fear of public disclosure and the associated additional psychological trauma.[32]

Other reasons for failing to report include feared ostracism, harassment, or ridicule by peers. Additionally, as Couric reported, victims do not report assaults because they fear they will not be believed. Statistical results published by the Pentagon give a grim picture of the adjudication process of this crime. Of the 2,265 unrestricted sexual assault reports in FY 2008, 1,594 of the victims were service members (70%); 51.1 percent of the assaults were service member on service member and 29.8 percent were service member on nonservice member, thus 81 percent of the alleged assailants were service members. Of all investigations finalized for FY 08, 1,074 (50%) were found to be unsubstantiated, 136 (6%) were handled under civilian authority, and in 129 (6%) cases no perpetrator was identified. Of the 832 cases that were found to be substantiated, 317 (38%) went to courts-martial, 247 (30%) were given nonjudicial punishment, and other administrative actions and discharges were taken on 268 (32%) cases.[33]

In another CBS evening news report, national security correspondent David Martin reported on a VA study of one hundred and twenty-five thousand medical records of male and female war veterans. The study showed that one in seven female veterans of Iraq and Afghanistan who sought medical care from the VA reported sexual trauma—everything from harassment to rape. He also reported "that's just the tip of the iceberg, since the study covered only a fraction of the 870,000 veterans who have fought and no one who is still on active duty." These numbers impelled Representative Jane Harman (D-CA) to state, "Women serving in the military today are more likely to be raped by a fellow soldier than to be killed by enemy fire in Iraq."[34]

Sexual Assault Awareness and Prevention Programs

The military has finally come to the realization that sexual harassment and assault are as debilitating to readiness as racial discrimination and harassment. In a Secretary of Defense memo dated April 13, 2009, Secretary Gates states, "The Department of Defense has a no-tolerance policy toward sexual assault. This type of act not only does unconscionable harm to the victim; it destabilizes the workplace and threatens national security."[35] The no-tolerance policy is based on the recognition that the crime of sexual assault diminishes the Armed Forces' ability to function proficiently at all levels. Its impact is both immediate and long-lasting for individuals in the military and for the institution as a whole. Sexual assault negatively impacts a unit's mission in three ways: (1) The alleged perpetrators are often placed on administrative hold and therefore cannot deploy with their units; (2) victims may not be able to fulfill their duties or may otherwise have their ability to perform the mission compromised as a result of the traumatic events; and (3) the attention of the unit leadership shifts from the normal duties involved in maintaining readiness to addressing a victim's needs, investigating the alleged perpetration, and restoring the unit's cohesion and trust.[36]

The DoD has set up an organization called the Sexual Assault Prevention and Response Office (SAPRO). SAPRO has the responsibility of providing guidance and other information for victims of sexual assault, unit commanders, first responders, and others. It also addresses issues of confidentiality, reporting procedures, and other elements of DoD's sexual assault policy. Its web site offers training information, safety tips, resources, and links to related websites. SAPRO has three stated objectives: prevention through education and training, treatment and support of victims, and system accountability.[37]

In the past, it was up to the victim to report harassing behavior or assault. DoD has since refocused its efforts. As reported by *Navy Times*,[38] the Pentagon is pursuing a strategy of sexual assault prevention. The theme of the 2010 Sexual Assault Awareness Month is "Hurts One. Affects All . . . Preventing Sexual Assault Is Everyone's Duty." Messaging focused on sexual assault and mission readiness played a role in the 2009 campaign, represented by the strategically placed red dog tag logo with the words *Readiness = Respect*.[39] This prevention strategy is designed to empower service members to intervene in situations where possible sexual assaults may occur. The use of the buddy system—making friends and co-workers equally responsible for ending the unwanted behavior—is an integral part of this program.[40]

The Problems with Reporting

As reiterated in the Defense Task Force's report, the main problem with sexual harassment and sexual assault in the military is the ingrained idea that women do not equally contribute to the military mission and are not essential to the military. Since they are not authorized to participate in the ground combat arms, women are seen as inherently less valuable than men. There is also the belief that if a woman is sexually assaulted, it is partially her fault for putting herself in a position, in a majority male enclave, where she does not belong to begin with.[41] It goes back to the blame-the-victim mentality.

There is also an overriding perception that false sexual assault reports are common. The military does not have good statistics on the rates of false reports, and many times unsubstantiated reports are viewed as false. In other words the 50 percent of reports from 2008 deemed unsubstantiated could be understood to mean they are without validity. The problem with unsubstantiated reports is, of course, that it is usually a question of "he said she said," and unless the medical exam shows evidence of sexual trauma, no conclusion of rape can be made. Unfortunately, too many believe that unsubstantiated claims did not happen. The victim is seen as attempting to manipulate the system by deflecting other misconduct—such as underage drinking, fraternization, adultery, or other violations—when the assault occurred. Additionally, if victims have been involved in misconduct in conjunction with an assault, they may be reluctant to disclose the truth because they may feel guilty or believe they will be blamed, disbelieved, or will get into trouble. Disciplinary actions could be taken against a victim as well as any witnesses she might also unintentionally implicate. At times, victims may feel these minor misconducts are handled more severely than the sexual assault. However, such misconduct does not cause someone to be assaulted. It must be understood that a fear of repercussion and a reluctance to discuss the details of the assault can influence a victim's description of the rape, which can lead to false conclusions by the investigators.[42]

Another problem is the inconsistency of how sexual assault and rape cases are handled at individual commands. For example, in 2003 several women came forward to the Colorado Springs media with the revelation that they had been raped while cadets at the Air Force Academy, and that the administration did not take the allegations seriously. This eventually exploded into a full-fledged scandal when graduates from previous years reported similar experiences. As a result, a Congressional investigation was launched and a new leadership chain of command was installed at the school. The panel's report leaves no doubt that women cadets were not taken seriously when they reported sexual misconduct of their male peers. The allegations spanned a time frame of at least 10 years and possibly as far back as when women first entered the academy in 1976. The panel that reviewed the evidence came to the conclusion that there was a systemic acceptance of sexual assault at the academy and an institutional avoidance of responsibility.[43]

Probably one of the best parts of the SAPRO reporting procedure is the option of restricted or unrestricted reporting. A restricted report allows the victim to confidentially get the aid and medical treatment needed to deal with the assault but does not trigger an official investigation. An unrestricted report allows the victim to seek medical treatment but also triggers an official investigation. As is common in the civilian legal realm, in many instances the victim becomes revictimized during the investigation. The victim is often chastised for undermining the unit cohesion by reporting, and she is often vilified, ostracized, and accused of trying to ruin the perpetrator's career, although no one seems to view the perpetrator as violating unit cohesion by assaulting a fellow member.

The reaction of a commander to an allegation of sexual assault can also determine the probable outcome. In some cases, the actions taken against the alleged perpetrator in order to protect the victim can be seen as a guilty verdict before an investigation is concluded. While there is growing confidentiality of reporting for the victim, similar confidentiality for the accused is not common. Even if he is found not guilty, his reputation follows him.[44] If the victim and the perpetrator are in the same unit, separation of the two is a reasonable option but in many cases does not occur until the case is adjudicated, or it may not occur because of mission requirements: one or the other may have a specialty area vital to the command mission. This can cause undue stress for the victim, who may have to work for the alleged perpetrator.

There are many reasons why reporting sexual assault and rape does not accurately reflect the actual incidence of such crimes in the military and in the civilian community. The attitude that men can get away with such behavior by deflecting the guilt to the victim is pervasive. The victim is made to feel guilty for reporting, is blamed for allowing the act to happen, often loses the support of the command and her colleagues, and ultimately may feel her country betrayed her by victimizing her all over again.

Stephanie Sacks, a sexual assault therapist from Washington state, notes,

> For those who are sexually assaulted in the military, when the system betrays them, it often involves a betrayal at all levels. Their job and military career may be impacted; their peers, social support and positive co-worker relations suffer, their commander, military police and prosecutors may not respond effectively. Ultimately many feel like their country betrayed them. The quote "With great power comes great responsibility" seems especially appropriate in reference to sexual assault in the military. Clearly the military is a powerful system; as such it has a responsibility to protect those who serve in it so far as it is able. Those who join the military clearly recognize that it is dangerous and that there are risks. However, most imagine those risks would come from an outside "enemy." Unfortunately for many service members the greatest risk comes from the person serving next to them, above them or the system at large. Those who serve our country have the right to know that the system that works so hard to protect others is also protecting them from those within it.[45]

Congress has also taken steps to help those still in the military and veterans trying to use the VA system after discharge. Congresswoman Louise Slaughter (D-NY) has reintroduced the Military Domestic Violence and Sexual Assault Response Act (HR 840), which would enhance programs of prevention and deterrence, improve victims' services, and strengthen provisions for prosecution of assailants. It establishes a Victims' Advocate Office within the DoD, which would be responsible for assessing the sexual assault services currently provided. It calls for the employment of a sexual assault nurse examiner, psychiatrist, and clinical team at each DoD treatment facility. The bill would prohibit anyone from interfering with the reporting and investigation of sexual assault claims and would protect survivors from retaliation. The bill also directs a military commanding officer who receives a qualifying complaint alleging such violence to investigate and report it, so perhaps one day women will be confident their claims will be taken seriously and acted upon.[46]

The bill would also ensure that VA primary care providers receive training in the screening and referral of veterans who have suffered sexual trauma in the military. Luckily, some veteran's support groups are also lobbying Congress to take further action. Specifically, the Iraq and Afghanistan Veterans of America (IAVA) is using the Internet to get the word out about the lack of adequate care for female veterans. In a recent blog post, it reported on a recent GAO report that found that privacy standards for women veterans at VA facilities are not being met, comprehensive primary care is still not available for women veterans at all hospitals and clinics, and the VA still has shortages of qualified women's health and mental health care providers. They note, "This is absolutely unacceptable. The VA must work to ensure that women veterans receive the care they deserve. . . . Like their male peers, women veterans have shown incredible dedication and courage in defending their country. It's about time they get the same recognition and support."[47]

While a proactive strategy is a step in the right direction, the Pentagon's focus on eradicating sexual assault cannot be accomplished without also eradicating the acceptance of harassing behaviors as well. These are behaviors that in and of themselves seem innocent but that in fact contribute to a lack of professional demeanor and respect in the workplace. The call for co-workers to help prevent sexual assault can also be used to eradicate harassing behaviors. Intolerance of any type of harassment, discrimination, or assault must be embodied throughout the military organization for it to succeed. The culture needs to change—not an easy task, and one that must be led from the top and bought into at all levels of leadership in the military, from the lowest recruit to the most senior officer.

Some Military Women's Experiences with Harassment in the Military

I decided to do a small survey of military women to ask if they had ever experienced sexual harassment, how they felt about it, and what they did about it. In a snowball sample—contacting friends and friends of friends—I received 165 responses to a survey I posted on SurveyMonkey.com and sent to a network of military women. My intention was to see how tolerant military women were to what the civilian workplace perceives as harassment.

Responses came from all of the military services, but the majority of respondents were officers (83%). The respondents included 43 percent currently on active duty or active reserves and 47 percent retired. The remaining were veterans. About 28 percent reported they had never experienced unwelcome sexual advances, requests for sexual favors, or verbal or physical conduct of a sexual nature. The remaining experienced one or more of these events, although the majority (88%) indicated these behaviors were not explicitly or implicitly tied to continued employment, evaluations, or promotion opportunity. About 57 percent said the behavior did not interfere with work performance or create an intimidating atmosphere. Even though 43 percent said it did, only 26 percent of the respondents reported the behavior.

Some of the unreported harassing behaviors included inappropriate comments, either up front or so as to be overheard; posting nude photos in the workplace; showing pornographic movies during breaks; refusing to comply with an order; or overt ogling. Some survey comments included the following:

> They frequently made inappropriate comments about women and their bodies usually in a sexual way. Would also demean women in general and the boss would often refer to his wife as "the hog."

> For several years after I was commissioned, numerous Chiefs made unwanted passes at me when I was on travel, but I just walked away from each one. Annoying, but harmless.

> My CO made some sexually explicit comments just as a way of showing me who was boss. It was a power thing more than a sexual thing. . . . I just sucked it up and waited for my tour to end.

> The only weird thing I can remember was around the mid '90s following Tailhook and a couple of cases where Drill Sergeants had been caught having a variety of inappropriate relationships with female Privates, a number of the men in the unit got all hyper-sensitive like they were victims. They would proclaim that there was no way a woman could be "one of the boys" anymore, too risky. Things calmed down after awhile and the cohesion of the unit returned to normal, but the whole "poor me" thing was funny in a pathetic kind of way.

Many of the women who did not report the assault or harassment responded that they were unwilling to risk repercussions, that there was no procedure for reporting, or that they took care if it themselves.

> This was 1943; who would I report it to?

> No, there was no real chain of command for such things at the time. I served from 1967 to 1970.

To whom? Really, this was not an option in the 80s.

At the time (over 20 years ago) it was widely known that reporting something like that meant being ostracized and often an end to one's Navy career, neither of which I was willing to face.

I figured the perpetrators were quite drunk, and [they] backed off after a sustained period of rejection. I was unwilling to press charges. I chalked it up to alcohol and stupidity.

I would characterize my incidents as "casual" and not worth the time or effort to report it.

I handled it with the person directly.

While out at a unit function (involving alcohol) I (Private First Class) was told to report to my Sergeant's room when I returned to the barracks where he made some references to us engaging in some sexual acts. It was inappropriate and I told him that I wouldn't and he threatened to put me on extra duty or a working party if I refused. I did and eventually told him to f-off. I was wrong too but this was ridiculous.

Others who did make a report became disillusioned by the response.

To female boss who did nothing about it.

To my command, they did nothing and I didn't pursue it. Later on, after I'd left that command and their last evaluation of me would have effectively ended my career, I reported it to the district civil rights officer who helped me file the correct paperwork and subsequently aided me in getting the evaluations removed from my record.

The Marine Corps Inspector General's Office since it was a senior Marine officer. They "investigated" and found the charges baseless.

Supervisor. . . . I was told to "lighten up."

The first incident involved my XO, so I reported it to my CO. Basically nothing was done and excuses were made about the XO because he was "old Guard" and women in the military was a new concept to him and I needed to understand and ignore his behavior.

The stories of harassment and assault I received from this small survey were actually quite depressing, but it also shows how resilient women are to typical workplace harassment. When women were a minority in the military or in their units, the response was for them to ignore the abuse, decide it was not worth the trouble to report, or deal with it on their own. I also think many women ignore obtuse behavior because they believe reporting shows they cannot take care of themselves. Additionally, if a real threat of violence or quid pro quo sexual harassment[48] were to take place, their supervisors would be more inclined to believe them than if they reported every off-color remark or inappropriate behavior.

It is becoming clear that the DoD is embarrassed by the reports of harassment and assault on women in the military. Proactive support and education is a start, and DoD does these well, but it also takes the courage of co-workers and supervisors to halt the behavior at its source. Women will continue to join the military, do their jobs, and be successful even as they are fighting not only for our country but also to be seen as full members of the military community.

Notes

1. U.S. Equal Opportunity Employment Commission, "Sexual Harassment," http://www.eeoc.gov.

2. Defense Task Force on Sexual Harassment and Violence, "Report of the Defense Task Force on Sexual Harassment and Violence at the Service Academies" (Washington DC: Government Printing Office, June 2005), ES–1.

3. Honorable behavior and the value of trustworthiness in that a cadet or midshipman does not lie, cheat, or steal.

4. Defense Task Force on Sexual Harassment and Violence, "Report," 8–9.

5. Joan Acker, "Gendered Institutions: From Sex Roles to Gendered Institutions," *Contemporary Sociology* 21, no. 5 (1992), 565–569.

6. Ibid., 567.

7. Ibid., 568.

8. Jeanne Holm, *Women in the Military: An Unfinished Revolution*, rev. ed. (Novato, CA: Presidio Press, 1992), 104.

9. Mady Wechsler Segal, "Gender and the Military," in *Handbook of the Sociology of Gender*, ed. Janet Saltzman Chafetz (New York: Kluwer Academic/Plenum Publishers, 1999), 563–581.

10. Karen O. Dunivin, "Military Culture: Change and Continuity," *Armed Forces and Society* (Summer 1994), 531–547.

11. Rosabeth Moss Kanter, *Work and Family in the United States: A Critical Review and Agenda for Research and Policy* (New York: Russell Sage Foundation, 1977).

12. Suzanne M. Bianchi and Daphne Spain, "Women, Work, and Family in America," *Population Bulletin* 51, no. 3 (December 1996).

13. Michael Kimmel, "Masculinity as Homophobia: Fear, Shame, and Silence," in *Men and Masculinity: A Text Reader*, ed. Theodore Cohen (Wadsworth, 2001).

14. There are always exceptions—for example, the Army allowed nurse Clara Adams-Ender to transfer to the "line Army" when she took command of Ft. Belvoir,

Virginia, in 1991. Clara Adams-Ender with Blair S. Walker, *My Rise to the Stars: How a Sharecropper's Daughter Became an Army General* (Lake Ridge, VA: ACPE Associates, 2001), 231.

15. Margaret C. Harrell, Harry J. Thie, Peter Schirmer, and Kevin Brancato, *Aligning the Stars*, National Defense Research Institute, prepared for the Office of the Secretary of Defense (Santa Monica, CA: RAND, 2004), 5–7.

16. Jean Ebbert and Marie Beth Hall, *Crossed Currents: Navy Women in a Century of Change*, 3rd ed. (Washington, DC: Brassey's, 1999).

17. Bureau of Labor Statistics, "Job Opportunities in the Armed Services," *Occupational Outline Handbook, 2008–2009*, http://www.bls.gov/oco/ocos249.htm. Unfortunately, this statistic only includes ground combat as "combat arms" and includes shipboard and aviation occupations under "transportation occupations."

18. Rosabeth Moss Kanter, *Men and Women of the Corporation* (New York: Basic Books, 1977). Gender displays are "language or rituals so characteristic of one sex that they mark the workplace as belonging to that sex," Barbara Reskin and Irene Padavic, *Women and Men at Work* (Thousand Oaks, CA: Pine Forge Press, 1994), 11; Laura L. Miller, "Not Just Weapons of the Weak: Gender Harassment as a Form of Protest for Army Men," *Social Psychology Quarterly* 60 (1997): 32–51.

19. Kanter, *Men and Women*, 219–221.

20. Ibid., 226–229.

21. Ibid., 230–237.

22. Ibid.; Janice D. Yoder, "An Academic Woman as a Token: A Case Study," *Journal of Social Issues* 41, no. 4 (1985): 61–72.

23. Kanter, *Men and Women*, 225; Yoder, "An Academic Woman," 62. The token exception is the Nurse Corps, in which women are a substantial majority.

24. Susan D. Hosek, Peter Tiemeyer, Rebecca Kilburn, Debra A. Strong, Selika Ducksworth, and Reginald Ray, *Minority and Gender Differences in Officer Career Progression* (Santa Monica, CA: RAND, 2001); Kanter, *Men and Women*; Janice D. Yoder, Jerome Adams, and Howard T. Prince, "The Price of a Token," *Journal of Political and Military Sociology* 11 (Fall 1983): 327–328.

25. Hosek, Tiemeyer, Kilburn, Strong, Ducksworth, and Ray, "Minority and Gender Differences."

26. Student Judicial Affairs, Chico State University, CA, "Sexual Harassment," http://www.csuchico.edu/sjd/harassment/index.shtml.

27. Rosemaire Skain, *Power and Gender: Issues in Sexual Dominance and Harassment* (Jefferson, NC: McFarland, 1997).

28. Stephanie Sacks, "Sexual Assault and the Military: A Community Sexual Assault Program's Perspective," in *Connections: A Bi-Annual Publication of the Washington Coalition of Sexual Assault Programs: Military Culture and Sexual Assault Victims* (Fall/Winter 2005), 19, http://www.wcsap.org/advocacy/connections.htm.

29. Ibid., 17–20.

30. Bureau of Justice Statistics, "Sex Offenses and Offenders," http://www.ojp.usdoj.gov/bjs/pub/pdf/soo.pdf; RAINN, "Who Are the Victims? Breakdown by Gender and Age," http://www.rainn.org/get-information/statistics/sexual-assault-victims.

31. Katie Couric, "Sexual Assault Permeates U.S. Armed Forces," CBS News, http://www.cbsnews.com/stories/2009/03/17/eveningnews/main4872713.shtml.

32. Defense Task Force on Sexual Harassment and Violence, "Report."

33. Couric, "Sexual Assault"; Defense Task Force on Sexual Harassment and Violence, "Report"; Department of Defense, "Department of Defense FY08 Report on Sexual Assault in the Military, March 2009," http://www.sapr.mil./Contents/Re sourcesReports/AnnualReports/DoD_FY08_Annual_Report.pdf.

34. David Martin, "Alarming Sexual Assault Rate Found among Vets," CBS News, October 28, 2008, http://www.cbsnews.com/stories/2008/10/28/eveningnews/.

35. Robert M. Gates, "Sexual Assault Awareness Month—April 2009," memorandum for secretaries of the military departments, April 13, 2009, http://www.sapr.mil/contents/SAAM/Awardee_Program_final.pdf.

36. DoD Sexual Assault Prevention and Response 2010 Sexual Assault Awareness Month Campaign Announcement, http://www.sapr.mil./Contents/SAAM/2010/2010_CAMPAIGN_INFO_FOR_SARCS.pdf.

37. Department of Defense, Sexual Assault Prevention and Response, "About SAPRO" http://www.sapr.mil/.

38. William H. McMichael, "DoD Hopes Troop Intervention Will Reduce Sexual Assaults," *Navy Times*, April 20, 2009, 24.

39. DoD Sexual Assault Prevention and Response 2010 Sexual Assault Awareness Month Campaign Announcement.

40. See the SAPRO Web site for "My Duty" videos and other information at http://www.sapr.mil.

41. Sacks, "Sexual Assault and the Military."

42. Ibid.

43. Tillie K. Fowler, Chair, *Report of the Panel to Review Sexual Misconduct Allegations at the U.S. Air Force Academy* (Washington, DC: Tillie K. Fowler, September 2003).

44. I say *he* because 99 percent of perpetrators are male, for both male and female rape victims.

45. Sacks, "Sexual Assault and the Military," 20.

46. Kim Gandy, "Stop Rape and Assault, and That's an Order!" April 6, 2009, http://www.now.org/news/note/040609.html.

47. Paul Rieckhoff, "GAO: VA Failing to Serve our Women Warriors," July 17, 2009, http://iava.org/blog/gao-va-failing-serve-our-women-warriors.

48. For example, quid pro quo sexual harassment ("this for that") could include a situation in which your boss threatens you with the loss of a job benefit, or actually changes your working conditions, because you will not submit to his sexual demands. U.S. Law.com "Quid Pro Quo Sexual Harassment," http://www.uslaw.com/library/article/bshQuidProQuo.html.

CHAPTER 6

Balancing Life in the Military

The nature of military life and the personal sacrifices involved in pursuing a military career can appear to conflict with women's family roles. The family is generally thought to be greedier for women than for men, and if women are also in the workforce then there may be competition between work and family for both participation and loyalty.[1] This is especially true of women in a highly masculine organization like the military. As more women enter the military, there will be more dual-military couples who must balance deployment schedules and family life. Society's shift in attitudes toward divorce and unwed motherhood has resulted in more single-parent families headed by either males or females. These changing demographics have resulted in increased support to military families, rules that demand military personnel have dependent care plans for turning over the care of their children to someone else when they deploy, and the recognition that the spouse's morale and well-being affect the motivation and performance of the military member.[2]

The worry about work and family balance for military women was not an issue prior to 1975, when women were systematically discharged if they got pregnant, if they married a man with children, or if they adopted. Back then, the military had little interest in keeping women satisfied, as there were plenty of men to fill the ranks. However, with the decision to go to an all-volunteer force in 1973, the military found it no longer had the manpower it needed to sustain a large standing army and Cold War–era operations. Suddenly, women and minorities found they would get equal pay for equal work, plus numerous benefits, by joining the military. And they did so in droves. In 1973, women represented less than 1 percent of the total force. By 1980, this had risen to 8 percent, and it currently stands at about 15 percent.[3]

Because of the masculine nature of the institution, as well as its overall conservatism that values traditional and normative roles, women struggle to have a fulfilling personal life while pursuing a military career. A fulfilling personal life consists of graduating from high school or college, getting a job, finding a partner, getting married, having kids, buying a house, saving money, going on vacations, planning for retirement, and enjoying the grandkids. Of course, not everyone has these particular goals. Many people never get married, or if they do get married, they do not have children. Many people, men and women, marry later in life and decide they are too old to have children. But work, for women, has become as much of a social obligation and expectation as it is for men. Women comprise approximately 46.5 percent of the total workforce, and that number is expected to rise to 47 percent by 2016.[4] The military will probably never see a percentage of women in its workforce equivalent to the civilian sector, and this chapter examines some of the reasons.

Military Socialization

The military requires instant obedience to orders, especially in times of war or other emergency situations. Additionally, there is an institutional mindset that must be developed in order for military personnel to willingly go into harm's way and do their job. Most people are not raised to either of these standards, so the military must use varying tactics to get service members to adhere to these requirements. Enlisted personnel attend recruit training, otherwise known as boot camp. Officers go through a variety of different training venues—the most well known are ROTC, the federal service academies (Military Academy at West Point; Naval, Air Force, and Coast Guard Academies), and Officer Candidate School. All these venues have the same purpose: to provide a basic military indoctrination that makes military personnel out of civilians.[5] This is accomplished through both physical demands and educational courses.

Since the military's core activity is *combat*, military culture is defined and depicted by a "combat, masculine-warrior (CMW) paradigm."[6] Thus, the purpose of recruit and officer training is to instill these warrior values and develop military members willing and able to fight for our country. The problem with the CMW paradigm is, of course, that women are not men and, barring a sex-change operation, will never be men. Thus, they are automatically outside the norm and must accommodate to the required standards and culture. The military has not changed its culture as a result of the increase of women in its ranks; however, it has become more inclusive and tolerant of the improvements diversity can make in its mission effectiveness.

Men and women, in general, go through the same recruit and officer training, though this was not always the case. The current exception is that there is separate recruit training for enlisted men going into combat ground forces in the Army and Marine Corps.[7] However, there are differential physical fitness standards based on gender and age, which some men have used to isolate and exclude women from full acceptance.[8] Nevertheless, women do have a place in the military and are needed in the current Middle East conflicts, both as warriors and as women.

Recruit training is of varying lengths, depending on the branch of service. After boot camp, there may or may not be follow-on formal training for specific occupations. In some cases, military members are expected to learn via on-the-job training, or OJT. This is primarily reserved for nontechnical and unskilled jobs, which are becoming more rare in the increasingly complicated arms profession.

Although not meant to be a screening process, recruit and officer training do weed out those who cannot or will not adjust to the military lifestyle and expectations. The primary screening happens before entry into boot camp, when educational, physical, mental, age, and legal requirements are validated. For example, there are minimum and maximum age, height, and weight limits, as well as certain educational requirements, such as a high school diploma or GED for enlisted personnel and a bachelor's degree for officers. A battery of tests must be taken, and passed, before being eligible for military duty, along with a medical exam that screens for certain diseases, eyesight and hearing requirements, and that the individual has all of his or her fingers and toes. There are also disqualifiers for felony and some misdemeanor arrests, as well as screens for alcohol and drug abuse. The military is not an equal-opportunity employer!

A Job in the Military

Once women make it through their initial military indoctrination, several structural impediments can prematurely derail the pursuit of a military career. The gendered work structure of the military requires individuals who are committed to a career at the expense of their family and other obligations. The ideals of service to country and devotion to duty are the patriotic calls to arms that inspire organizational commitment and the willingness to give one's life for one's country, if need be. Women pursuing a military career must confront this work ethic. If they devote too much time to their family, they violate the work devotion schema; if they delegate too many of their family responsibilities, they violate the family devotion schema.[9] Military women thus find themselves in a position where hard choices about work and family must be made. Thus, work-family conflict seems inevitable.

Military service has been linked to both the responsibilities of citizenship and the transition of boys to men.[10] The fact that boys, but still not girls, must register for selective service when they turn 18 is a relic of a past when military service was an expectation, not a choice. Today, with the AVF, draft registration is an anachronism. The chance of the United States initiating a draft short of the threat of World War III is nil, yet Congress seem loathe to stop selective service registration and certainly does not want to make women militarily responsible. The military's policy of excluding women from direct ground combat (infantry, tanks, field artillery, and Special Forces) is partial justification for this reasoning. However, the result is that our country is telling young women that the military is a man's job and that they are not needed for our country's defense.

Not surprisingly, then, the propensity for women to join the military is very low. Only about 6 percent of high school senior girls indicate a propensity to enlist, and less than half of them actually do, according to studies conducted by David R. Segal.[11] The overall enlistment trend, for both high school boys and girls, is in a long-term decline. Yet women do join, both in the enlisted ranks and as officers, and they are in all the military branches, though in varying percentages dependent on occupational opportunities. For example, the Air Force has the highest percentage of women, at 19.6 percent, and it also has the greatest job opportunities for women, with 99 percent of its jobs, both combat and support, open to women. The Marine Corps, in contrast, has the lowest percentage of women in its force—6.3 percent—and also has the lowest job placement opportunities, at 62 percent, because of ground combat exclusion policies.[12]

Additionally, women are drawn to occupations that are historically women's work, such as nursing, physician's aides (i.e., corpsmen or medics), and other health care occupations (40.8%); or administrative, supply, and logistics (21.1%). In an effort to even out the workforce, women are being pushed into nontraditional jobs, such as maintenance (11.2%) and tactical operations (12.2%), and their numbers are slowly rising in those fields[13] even with the exclusionary restrictions currently in place. Nevertheless, women are enjoying unprecedented opportunities to excel and have viable careers in the military, albeit not without several hurdles.

Working an Executive Schedule

For the most part, college-educated women in the civilian workforce find themselves in elite jobs that require an executive schedule. For example, a lawyer's or executive's schedule requires an ideal worker who must perform superlatively and be able to do it for 50 to 70 or even more hours a week. For academics or managers, jobs may require relocation when opportunities for advancement arise. This also affects workers who do not have elite jobs; Americans work more overtime now than at any time since WWII.[14] This type of work schedule makes it difficult for women to compete unless they are childless or have a partner who deals almost exclusively with the domestic responsibilities. The assumption is that the ideal worker has few responsibilities for child rearing or housework and is supported by a spouse with domestic responsibilities—a "flow of family work," which "most men enjoy but most women do not."[15]

This gendered phenomenon is reiterated in the many studies on the division of labor in the household. For example, both Julie Brines and Veronica J. Tichenor[16] found that even when women were the primary breadwinners in the family, and even if the husband was out of work, the wives still did the majority of the domestic chores. Mary Blair-Loy,[17] in her study of women executives, also found some semblance of traditional gender roles in the management of their households. She found that even when elite women executives hired out family work to full-time nannies and housekeepers, they, not their husbands, retained ultimate responsibility for their children's care.

In contrast to civilian work norms, the military requires the ideal worker norm for nearly all of its workers, whether enlisted or officer, male or female, married or single, parenting or not. There is a distinct, unstated norm that either you are single, with no ties to keep you from working as long as needed, or you have a spouse at home who will care for your family while you work. There is an old cliché that says, "If the Army (or Navy or . . .) wanted you to have a wife, it would have issued you one!" This sentiment is apparent in the demands the military makes on its workers, which are discussed in the following sections. It is precisely because of these demands, and the expectation that the military is your number one priority, that fewer women participate.

The Nature of Work in the Military

The military makes a number of demands on its personnel and family members that differentiate it from most work organizations. These include geographic mobility, family separations, residence in foreign countries, and normative constraints on both the family and the service member. Probably the greatest demand on a military member is the risk of death or injury.[18] The ongoing operations in Iraq and Afghanistan, and the media attention on the casualties and deaths, bring this home daily to both the American public and the service members' families. Since the invasion of Iraq in March 2003, more than 4,200 U.S. service members have been killed, including 118 women. More than 31,000 have been wounded, about half of whom were seriously wounded and unable to return to duty within 72 hours.[19] One of the arguments against women in combat during the 1992 Presidential Commission on the Assignment of Women was the possibility of the death of a mother, leaving an orphaned child.[20] Women themselves might also think of this possibility and decide to delay or forego parenthood while in the military.

For women, normative constraints play a huge part in the childbearing decision. While having a family and a military career are not seen as mutually exclusive for women, the military does encourage women to plan their child-bearing to coincide with duty assignments that do not require them to deploy. Even when pregnant in a nondeployable unit, women face negative attitudes from both co-workers and supervisors. In a recent Navy study, this was true for both enlisted and officers before and after giving birth.[21] Women who want a military career care about their professional reputations. They sometimes even turn on other women who may show weakness or excessive femininity in order to boost their standing with their peers and supervisors.[22] Pregnancy is the ultimate form of femininity and is seen by some members as incompatible with military duty, regardless of occupation or duty station. Thus, women who want to make a career out of the military, especially officers and senior enlisted,[23] either delay or deny childbearing.

Periodic deployments may inhibit couple formation or put undue stress on a relationship. This is especially true for members deployed in a combat zone, such as Iraq or Afghanistan. While deployments were limited to about 6 months before those operations began, since the war these limits have been extended for certain units for up to 18 months. There are two schools of thought here. Mady W. Segal[24] has made the case that periodic deployments can keep the romance in a relationship. But she also notes that deployments and other separations are exceedingly stressful. The stage in one's life at the time of separation is also salient. A single person might cherish the chance to visit foreign countries and travel. A young married couple may have a difficult time, especially if it is their first long separation.[25] As one ages, the separation may not seem as tragic, but I know from personal experience that separations are never easy, nor do they get easier no matter how many you go through.

While men seem to have no problem asking women to wait for them, it appears to be a gender-role reversal for women to ask the same of an unmarried boyfriend. It can be especially stressful for a dual-military couple if both deploy on opposing schedules. While short separations may indeed keep the romance in a relationship, extended separations tend to push people apart. Separations interfere with partner communication and relationships, cause feelings of resentment and abandonment, and in general cause distress for everybody concerned.[26] There is also the risk of infidelity, further inhibiting or destroying a solid marital union.

Relocation can be a relationship inhibitor for an unmarried military career woman. If she begins a relationship with a military member, one or the other of them will have to relocate at some point. If they are married, they can try to negotiate a move to the same general area. If they are not married, they will be assigned according to the needs of the military. If a woman were having a relationship with someone not in the military who had his own stable career, he most likely would not want to move. While military men in a civilian relationship also face this dilemma, it is more common for women to follow their hearts than for men to pick up and move for a woman. Living apart from a loved one, just as in a deployment situation, does not engender increased closeness.

The military requires long hours of work. This is true whether the unit is deployed or not. There may be times when a member must stay away for one or more nights during a training mission or real emergency. It is not unusual for officers and senior enlisted personnel to work 12-to-14-hour days, including weekends. Senior officers work even more hours per week, not unlike civilian CEOs. This type of schedule makes it difficult to both start and maintain a relationship. In this situation, women may think having a child would be counterproductive, as someone else would have to raise the child.

The overall requirements of the military lifestyle make it more difficult for women to marry and have children. This is because of the combination of several factors, including a concern for career development; the difficulty in starting or maintaining a relationship due to long work hours, deployments, or relocation; and the near impossibility of being an ideal worker while also being a parent without the same flow of family support that men usually enjoy.

The Life Course and Family Experiences of Women in the Military

In a gendered institution such as the military,[27] experiences through the life course are different for women than for men. Especially relevant are the issues of raising children, managing career and family, dealing with marital problems, and transitioning into retirement. This is because in our society, the norm of domesticity and parental care is primarily thought to be the responsibility of women.[28]

For some personnel, the military can be considered a "two-person single career," described by Hanna Papanek as "the combination of formal and informal institutional demands which is placed on both members of a married couple of whom only the man is employed by the institution,"[29] presupposing a wife at home who takes care of family responsibilities and supports her husband in his job by acting as social chair. While this scenario is true for many executive-level occupations in the United States, and was a pattern expected of the wives of the officer corps of the military, it is becoming less so as more women achieve executive positions in both the civilian and military workplaces. The duties of the military wife, especially the CO's wife, included hosting or attending social events, taking care of the house and family, volunteering at the local base charity or thrift shop, and taking care of enlisted wives' issues when the men were away.

The increased numbers of women officers at higher echelons of the military, and of women in general, have helped to eliminate these spousal expectations. For example, as of 2002 in the highest flag and general officer ranks, women are more likely to be single (36.4%) than men (2.8%).[30] If women commanders are not married, the traditional duties of the CO's wife may fall to the spouse of a junior male officer, to another member of the crew, or to a volunteer command ombudsman. If she is married, her husband rarely takes on the duties of CO's wife, nor is he expected to. In recent years, many of these social expectations have been dropped, which has benefited the male officers, too. However, much of the informal support provided to the families of deployed military members still falls to those who remain at home. They have to support each other. Plus, the commanding officer is still expected to provide support for the families, even if he or she has no volunteer spouse at home to provide it. It is a conundrum. In general, there are differences in the military work requirements on the life course depending on gender and rank.

Marriage and Family Demographics

In the United States, there is a general trend in recent years toward postponed marriage with a resultant delay in childbearing. Young people today seem to prefer to complete college and settle into the labor market before starting a family.[31] This solves the work-family balance issue in the short-term, but eventually decisions will need to be made about whether to get married and/or have children.

Women and men delay marriage for several reasons. When people marry later in life, they can attend school longer before they enter the labor force and live independently. Women who marry later are less likely to divorce but are more apt to have a child out of wedlock. There is also a higher propensity for people never to marry. According to Daphne Spain and Suzanne Bianchi,[32] the proportion of women in their early 20s who had never married doubled between 1950 and 1990, from one-third to two-thirds, while the proportion of never-married women in their late 20s almost tripled during this same period, from 13 percent to 32 percent. This same trend toward later marriage were similarly dramatic for men. Women in the military, especially women officers, forego marriage at a greater rate than their civilian counterparts. If they do marry, they are more likely to remain childless or have fewer children than their civilian peers.[33] What is it about this particular occupation that contributes to this reaction in women?

Marriage

Marriage in the military differs by rank and gender. Traditionally, marriage was limited to mid-to-senior-grade male officers and senior enlisted noncommissioned officers, all of whom had civilian wives. Marriage in the junior ranks of both officers and enlisted personnel was rare, primarily due to the low pay and the requirement to live in the barracks or bachelor officer's quarters. With the advent of a professional volunteer force, marriage in the mid-grade enlisted

Table 6.1 Percent of Married and Single Personnel on Active Duty by Pay Grade[1]

Rank	Married	Single
E1–E4	31.8%	68.2%
E5–E6	69.5%	30.5%
E7–E9	85.3%	14.7%
Total Enlisted	**52.3%**	**47.7%**
W1–W5	83.1%	16.9%
O1–O3	57.1%	42.9%
O4–O6	87.3%	12.7%
O7–O10	97.0%	3.0%
Total Officer	**69.4%**	**30.6%**

[1]ICF International, *Profile of the Military Community: DoD 2006 Demographics* (Washington, DC: Office of the Deputy Under Secretary of Defense, Military Community and Family Policy, 2007), 29, https://cs.mhf.dod.mil/content/dav/mhf/QOL-Library/PDF/MHF/QOL%20Resources/Reports/2006%20Demographics%20Report.pdf.

ranks has become more commonplace, and pay and benefit policies have changed to reflect that reality. Table 6.1 shows the percent of married active duty personnel for FY 2006.[34]

While less than a third of the entry level (E1–E4) enlisted force is married (31.8%), this number more than doubles for mid-grade (E5–E6) to 69.5 percent and increases at the highest enlisted ranks to 85.3 percent. For officers, because they are generally older when they commission out of college, this number is slightly higher at 57.1 percent for junior officers (O1–O3), 87.3 percent for mid-level officers (O4–O6), and 97.0 percent for flag and general officers (O7–O10). The mean age of married enlisted personnel is 30.1, while the mean age of married officers is 36.6.[35] All of these statistics are consistent with the life course trend that those 35 and older are more likely to be married than younger cohorts.[36]

However, a pattern emerges when broken out by gender, with women overall less likely to be married than men, both in the military and in the civilian workforce (see Table 6.2). When compared to civilian college graduates, male military officers are more likely to be married than their civilian peers, while college women in the workforce are more likely to be married than military women. A possible explanation for this is that there is a tradition for male officers to be married and that the military culture promotes and rewards marriage, especially in the senior officer ranks where there is an expectation of a dual-person career.[37] In the highest flag and general officer ranks, men are more likely than women to be married and have children (55.4% for men and 21.2% for women).[38] As Joan Williams points out, the requirements of an ideal worker

Table 6.2 Percent of Married Active Duty by Gender and Rank and Civilian Comparison Group[1]

Gender	Enlisted	Married Civilians in Labor Force	Officers	Civilian College Grads	Total DoD
Male	53.5%	59.5%	72.5%	63.9%	56.5%
Female	44.9%	53.4%	52.6%	59.9%	46.1%
Total	52.3%	56.7%	69.4%	61.9%	55.0%

[1]Department of Defense, Office of the Under Secretary of Defense, Personnel, and Readiness, *Population Representation in the Military Services, FY 2006* (Washington, DC: Author, 2008), 27, 28, and 39, http://www.defenselink.mil/prhome/poprep2007/index.html.

norm and the executive schedule make it much more difficult for women to aspire to the highest offices if they are married or have children.[39]

In general, men are much more likely to be married than women, and officers are more likely to be married than enlisted, with women in both categories less likely to be married than their male peers. This is consistent with what Spain and Bianchi[40] found—that labor force participation and higher earnings are correlated with delayed marriage for women. Also, as discussed previously, there are both societal and institutional work barriers for women to be married and have children. Women who desire the flexibility to balance work and family are less likely to seek jobs from employers that require an ideal worker because of the social expectations of her as the primary caregiver.

This is validated by another statistic. While 41.5 percent of women officers are likely to be single with no children, only 23.6 percent of male officers are. The numbers for enlisted male and female are about the same at 44.3 percent and 46.3 percent, respectively. Married military women are also less likely to have children. Only 25 percent of married military men, both enlisted and officer, did not have children, compared to a childlessness rate of over 51 percent for married women officers and 47.6 percent for married enlisted women.[41] One begins to wonder if this is the price women must pay to have a career in an organization like the military. Almost half of enlisted women and two-fifths of women officers have forgone marriage, and about half of the women who have gotten married have not had children.

Junior Enlisted Families

Junior enlisted families have unique family issues. Enlisted men in the military have a tendency to marry at an earlier age than their civilian counterparts. This is likely because of imminent separations due to deployment or wartime taskings but may also be due to the benefits obtained when married: the allowances for moving a family, additional pay for family needs, and family medical and dental benefits. Junior enlisted personnel also start families sooner compared to their civilian peers, who often pursue their education and employment and defer marriage and family until their mid-to-late 20s. Some of the issues associated with early marriage are immaturity and inexperience in dealing with some of the unique stressors of military life on family, marriage, and child-rearing.[42] There are also financial strains, as these people are at the bottom of the pay scale. Even with the increases in military compensation over the past 25 years, the pay at these lower ranks is not meant to be a family wage. Spouse employment may also be an issue. Many spouses are young and inexperienced, and women who live in or near a military community have higher unemployment rates and lower wages.[43]

Separations in this life phase may be especially stressful, especially if the civilian wife is secluded in off-base housing or half a continent away from her parental home with little to no informal social or family support. New marriages are fragile and may not survive separation. If there are young children in the family, the lack of social support can make the separation unbearable. Relocation to an overseas assignment may also become an issue. While a young couple with no children may relish the adventure, one with small children may find it too difficult to deal with facing language, cultural, social barriers on their own.[44] Others may prefer to take assignments overseas while their children are young so they do not have to worry about the quality of the schools. Couples with older children may be concerned with the quality of the schools, the type and expense of after-school programs, and lack of spousal employment opportunities. On the other hand, couples with older children have an opportunity to give their children a more varied life experience by living overseas.[45]

Although the United States has reduced the number of military personnel stationed overseas in Europe and Asia, there are still a substantial number of military personnel and their families who live overseas, especially in Germany, Korea, and Japan. The social, language, and cultural barriers are difficult even for mature and experienced personnel, especially if it is their first time living so far away from home. A more pressing issue for military families is the increase in the number of unaccompanied tours, especially to the Middle East. These types of separations, especially with the increased risk of death or injury, challenge many military families, but junior enlisted families are especially hard hit.

Dual-Military Couples

A dual-military couple refers to an active duty member who is married to another active duty member or reservist. About 12.4 percent of married couples in the military are dual military. The majority (83.1%) are enlisted, which makes sense as 85 percent of military members are enlisted.[46] The percentage

Table 6.3   Active Duty Dual-Military Marriages by Service Branch[1]

Gender	Army	Navy	Marine Corps	Air Force	Total DoD
Male	5.0%	5.5%	5.0%	13.5%	7.4%
Female	37.3%	46.5%	63.6%	59.1%	49.0%
Total	8.7%	9.9%	8.3%	21.2%	12.4%

[1]Department of Defense, Office of the Under Secretary of Defense, Personnel, and Readiness, *Population Representation in the Military Services*, FY 2006 (Washington, DC: Author, 2008), 27, 28, and 39, http://www.defenselink.mil/prhome/poprep2007/index.html.

of women in dual-military marriages is higher than for men, of course, because there are fewer women in the military. About 49 percent of married women are in dual-military marriages compared to 7.4 percent of men. These percentages vary greatly by branch of service, however, with the Army having the lowest percentage of women in these marriages—37.3 percent—and the Marine Corps having the highest percentage—63.6 percent. Table 6.3 shows the percentage of active duty members in dual-military marriages, by service branch. Note that the Marine Corps has the lowest percentage of women in its force but the highest percentage of women in dual-military marriages.[47]

There is a lessening trend for dual-military couples to be childless—from 61 percent in 1990 to 58.6 percent in 2006.[48] According to research conducted by Claudia Goldin,[49] there is an increasing trend for career women to have both a career and family simultaneously for cohorts who graduated from college between 1980 and 1990. The ability to balance work and family in a dual-military marriage requires planning, patience, and a very good dependent care plan.

Some of the problems with dual-military marriages include double the separations as well as differences in duty stations, including being separated geographically by continents. The trend is growing for dual-military couples to be stationed together; in 2002, 35 percent were not jointly assigned, but by 2006, only 12 percent were not jointly assigned.[50] This trend is a positive step in the quality of life for these couples. Dual-military couples with children also may face issues similar to those experienced by single parents when one spouse is deployed, and child care issues may flare up if both parents have to work late or are unexpectedly deployed. While most dual-service couples are in the same branch of service, there are also inter-service couples, which heightens the chance of geographic separation.[51]

Civilian Spouses of Military Women

A growing trend is for military women to be married to a civilian spouse (22.8%).[52] A male spouse will have many of the same difficulties as civilian wives in terms of finding and keeping a good paying job and the normative behavior requirements. In addition, these token males can be isolated and marginalized, not only by a system that is not prepared to support a dependent male spouse, but also by other military members—especially wives, who may feel threatened.[53] A number of these civilian husbands are former military and may have an easier time navigating the military bureaucracy,[54] as well as have their own retirement income to ease the financial strain.

Pregnancy

Pregnancy can be a very trying time for a woman in the military. While child bearing in general is being delayed, there are still mothers in the military, both married (22.4%) and unmarried (11.4%).[55] Point-in-time enlisted pregnancy rates in the Navy indicate that in 2001, 10 percent of E2 to E4 were pregnant, 12 percent of E5 to E6 were pregnant, and 2 percent of E7 to E9 were pregnant.[56] E2 to E4 would correlate to an age of between 18 and 22, while women ranked E5 and E6 could be as young as 22 up to retirement age (38 to 48). Pregnancy is seen as a detriment to a person's career because of the implication that the military is no longer the primary commitment in one's life.[57]

Pregnancy in the military is also a concern due to the possible impact on a unit's manning. If a woman is on a ship or deployable unit, she will be transferred until after giving birth. This has implications for mission effectiveness. In addition, women are given several weeks of paid convalescent leave after giving birth. This can be combined, with the approval of the command, with regular leave up to a total of three months. This is a wonderful benefit for a military mother, but it does place an extra burden on her co-workers, who have to take on her job responsibilities. There are no temporary replacements for people on leave.[58]

Additionally, pregnant women may experience isolation and other negative attitudes (being avoided or ignored or treated with less respect) from both their co-workers and supervisors.[59] This has implications for a woman's career, as supervisors might (consciously or not) grade a woman lower while or after she is pregnant. This is especially a concern if the weight gained during the woman's pregnancy has not been lost within six months of giving birth. This could even result in discharge if the woman remains outside the military's physical fitness guidelines.[60] It is no wonder that many women have opted out of having children while in the military.

Parenting

While the trend of marriage in the military is increasing, there has been a subsequent downward trend in parenting. In 1995, 42.5 percent of the force was married with children, but in 2006 this decreased to 37.8 percent. This down-ward trend is a result of a decrease in the number of non–dual-military couples with children, since that demographic is the largest percentage of married couples in the military. Simultaneously, there has also been a downward trend in single parenting, from a high of 6.4 percent in 2001 to 5.2 percent in 2006.[61]

Parenting while in the military is difficult for many of the reasons already given. The military parent works long and sometimes unpredictable hours. There are many and long separation periods, and the deployed parent may not be available to see the birth of his child or get to know the child until almost a toddler. Geographic mobility may force a family to move to a different location every two or three years, requiring the children to attend many different schools. Also, there is always the fear and risk of injury or death of the military parent. The parent who remains home is in essence a single parent for the duration of the deployment. This may cause problems with spousal employment due to child care issues, children's health issues, and the general coping skills of both the parent and child.[62]

For dual-military parents, there may be the risk of both parents deploying at the same time. This was a very common occurrence during Operations Desert Shield/Desert Storm in 1990–1991. Military parents must ensure they have a dependent care plan so they know their children are being taken care of. Likewise, single military parents must also have a dependent care plan. The plan must make provisions for both short-term absences—such as for school or training—and long-term absences such as deployment. The failure to produce a family care plan may result in disciplinary action and/or separation from the military.[63]

Divorce is the single most common reason for most military members to become single parents with custody. While women have a higher proportion of single parenthood than men in the military, the total number of single fathers is higher. At the end of 2006, there were 48,762 single fathers as compared to 22,834 single mothers.[64]

Regardless of how one becomes a single parent, there are unique work–family balance issues to address. Just like in the civilian labor force, single parents need convenient, affordable, and dependable child care when their children are young. They may need it not only during the day but on nights and weekends as well, and sometimes they may need it overnight. Once children are school age, they still may need supervision during evening and other hours. While the military does have on-base child care facilities on a sliding-fee scale, they usually are not open past six in the evening or on weekends unless for special occasions as directed by the base commander. Also, if the family does not live near the base, on-base facilities might be inconvenient, or the facility might not have any available slots.[65] However, the military does have a referral service to help military members find off-base child care as needed.[66]

Single parents may also be stigmatized by their peers and supervisors, who think they are not as committed to the military due to their family situation. Military members are socialized to put service before self.[67] This is a dilemma for single parents, especially women, who want to remain in the military due to the pay and benefits they receive yet have no co-parent to rely on when there are work-family conflicts.[68] Single parents also can be socially isolated, as they may be separated from friends and family and have little to no down time. When they deploy, most women rely on their mothers to watch their children while most fathers rely on their ex-spouse,[69] though this can cause other issues with work-family balance as grandparents increasingly work outside the home.[70] Deploying dual-military and single parents who must rely on nonmilitary caregivers—who may not be familiar with the military system—can have problems if the child has to move away from his home of record, as there may be issues of accessibility for health care and other services.[71] As children grow, the caretaking issue works itself out, but at each change of duty station, some of the same issues must be faced again and again. As such, deployments are a stressful time for all members of the family.

Divorce

With increased separations due to the war in the Middle East, there has been some speculation that divorce in the military is on the rise. However, according to the 2006 *DoD Demographics* report, rates were at 1.7 percent for officers and 3.5 percent for enlisted in 1996, went down to 1.4 percent for officers and 2.9 percent for enlisted in 2000, and are back up again to 1.9 percent for officers and 3.7 percent for enlisted personnel in 2006. The conflicts in Iraq and Afghanistan do not appear to have made a difference in these statistical trends. However, these statistics only show the number of divorces of people who remained on active duty.[72] They do not take into account the divorce rates of people who left active duty and then divorced. So the record is necessarily skewed.

For a military woman undergoing a divorce, there is one advantage—she still has a job, with equal pay and good benefits. However, with children involved, there is the issue of custody. The laws and regulations are too numerous to delve into in this book, but divorce while in the military can become convoluted because of both state and federal jurisdiction. Cases regarding custody rights, alimony, child care, and other such issues can be overridden by federal jurisdiction; however, if the service member is deployed, the case may not necessarily wait until he or she returns.

Blended Families

Many single parents marry or remarry. This results in blended families, which have their own unique issues and problems. Because of the stress associated with the demands of the military and the demands of a new family, many of these marriages fail. Separations, geographic mobility, and/or living overseas all have an impact on the family depending on the stage of the life course. This may be especially true if the new family is also new to the military lifestyle.[73]

Elder Care

As in the civilian sector, military members are part of the sandwich generation. Women are more likely to care for a parent, and women who have delayed childbearing are especially vulnerable to the emotional and economic demands of both aging parents and young children. The lower fertility rate of baby boomers also means there are fewer siblings to help take up the slack. While men have these same issues, they are more likely to provide financial assistance rather than participate in caregiving.[74]

In the military, there is a growing responsibility to care for adult dependents. Although the gender of the caregivers is not known, they are included in all ranks, as shown in Table 6.4. The ages of these adult dependents range from 23 to over 63, but the majority are female and over age 50 (73.5%).[75] Caution must be exercised when viewing these statistics, however, because this only shows those adults who have been claimed as dependents by the active duty sponsor. There are probably many other elder caregivers who have not claimed their adult charges as dependents. According to this table, the only group that appears exempt from eldercare responsibilities are senior officers—admirals and generals (GFOs) in pay grades O7 to O10. I can only provide an

Table 6.4   Age and Gender of Adult Dependents by Active Duty Sponsor Pay Grade[1]

Sponsor Pay Grade	Ages 23–40		Ages 41–50		Ages 51–62		Ages 63 and Older		Total	
	M	F	M	F	M	F	M	F	M	F
O1–O3	0	0	3	56	49	391	85	264	137	711
O4–O6	0	0	1	1	22	167	84	422	107	590
O7–O10	0	0	0	0	0	0	2	6	2	6
W1–W5	0	0	3	10	11	114	26	125	40	249
E1–E4	1	24	31	306	60	359	36	65	128	754
E5–E6	1	4	29	529	227	1720	267	858	524	3111
E7–E9	0	1	5	28	58	708	227	884	290	1621
Subtotal	2	29	72	930	427	3,459	727	2,624	1,228	7,042
Total	31		1,002		3,886		3,351		8,270	

[1]Department of Defense, Office of the Under Secretary of Defense, Personnel, and Readiness, *Population Representation in the Military Services*, FY 2006 (Washington, DC: Author, 2008), 27, 28, and 39, http://www.defenselink.mil/prhome/poprep2007/index.html.

educated speculation that the reason is that there are few officers at those pay grades (less than one thousand), and those officers who were required to provide dependent care as senior officers probably retired if those responsibilities continued, since the work schedule for GFOs increases dramatically once selected to those executive ranks.

As in other families, military members may be living far from their families when these issues arise. This might also mean that the closest relative is an aunt or uncle, niece or nephew, grandparent, or cousin. Elder care may not necessarily be limited to one's parents, especially if the cared-for relative's parents or children live some distance away. The increase in childless couples may eventually mean an increase in extended family members responsible for their care.[76]

Extended Caregiving

For all issues of extended caregiving, the military is not liable under the Family and Medical Leave Act (FMLA). If a service member has an issue with the illness of a spouse, parent, or child, there are provisions for humanitarian transfer for up to six months. If the member is sick, a finite amount of medical leave can be used. In these situations, the member retains all pay and benefits. However, if the situation has not improved in the allotted time, the member may face discharge. This can be especially heartbreaking if the member is close to the retirement requirement of 20 years but cannot work it out.

Separation and Retention

Military personnel have several points in their careers when they must decide whether to stay or go. Retention is a combination of both promotion selection and individual decisions. Decision points come in two-to-four-year increments, depending on the branch of service and the promotion point reached. The first decision point is after initial service obligation, usually 4–8 years of active service. Ninety-five percent of all female officers stay to this point. Several retention and promotion points occur in the next 8 to 10 years.[77] One of the reasons women officers resign from the military is due to the perceived conflict between work and family.

In a 2004 study of women Air Force and Marine Corps officers, Adrienne Evertson and Amy Nesbit found that, "The appeal of the military for women contributes to their work ethic and attitude of being a top performer. This same attitude spills over into their role as mother and wife, wanting to be a top performer at home as well. Unfortunately, the women interviewed said that it is not possible to do so all the time. At one point or another, something has to give because otherwise, it is one person trying to do two full-time jobs. The women know they have chosen to have the family but also want the career and their dedication to both exceeds their abilities."[78]

One option to alleviate this conflict is for women to join the reserve force of their respective service. The reserve forces are a part-time force that trains one weekend a month and two weeks each year. During national emergencies, however, they can be called upon to deploy outside of their home of residence, causing issues quite similar to their active-component peers. In general, though, the reserve force is a good option for women who want to focus on family while maintaining ties with the military.[79]

Marriage appears to have a different effect on retention for men than women officers. Married men were more likely to stay in the service and be promoted than single men, while the opposite appears true for women. Additionally, married women officers with children tend to resign at a higher rate than their male peers.[80] There are several possible explanations. It may be due to the higher income level of the marriage that would allow women to stay home; the perception that, as educated women, they would be able to find a job outside the military with similar pay and benefits; or that married male officers tend to have a supportive civilian spouse to manage the household.

Retention for enlisted women does not appear to follow the same trend; enlisted women's retention is within two percentage points of the retention for men.[81] In general, since enlisted personnel are younger, they are less likely to be married than officers.

Retirement

After a minimum of 20 years of service, active duty military members are authorized to transfer to the reserve (retired) force. Depending on the amount of time spent in the military, one can get a minimum of 50 percent of active duty pay up to 75 percent of active duty pay (if the member stays for 30 years). Military members who retire are at various stages of the life course, depending on when they came into the military. Some are eligible to retire as early as age 38; some stay until age 57 or longer (flag and general officers can stay up to 35 years, or age 60). Some still have small children, while some have already seen their children off to college. For some people, the transition to civilian life can be stressful. They may have spent a lifetime in the military environment and have few civilian relationships. Some members may become depressed with the change and especially the loss of status. In most cases, the retiree will start a second career.[82]

There are a number of transitions a military member must make in order to successfully change roles. There are issues of employment, both for self and spouse; where to relocate; ensuring an adequate financial situation; and changes in one's status as well as changes within the family. Many women take advantage of the financial and other benefits to start families after retirement. All these issues take adequate planning and communication within the family.[83] While retirement planning is not unique to military members, it happens at a younger age and requires many decisions about lifestyle and where to settle, and as a result has become an industry unto itself.

Conclusion

The military is an occupation in which women find they must change their personal desires to conform to the military lifestyle. Women in the military, both officer and enlisted, tend to delay both marriage and child rearing. More women in the military are childless and single than in the civilian sector. Career women, especially, may delay family until after they leave the service or retire.

The military is also an institution in which the life course and family experiences differ for people of different rank and gender. Younger enlisted families have a more difficult time than junior officer families, who are older, perhaps better educated, and have more financial stability. Mid-career members, both officer and enlisted, tend to be family oriented, but the majority are men; only about half of active duty military women are married and only a quarter have children.

Additionally, women face unique challenges when they become pregnant while in the military. Since women are still the primary caregivers in our society, those expectations are magnified in a military system geared toward the tradition of the male breadwinner and the stay-at-home wife and mother. Attitudes are changing as more women enter the military, but the gendered male norms are still the standard.

One of the benefits of a military career is the generous retirement system, which includes a cash retainer plus access to many other benefits including medical and dental programs and access to military bases, which have many facilities such as stores, gyms, and theaters. For women in the military, these benefits can outweigh some of the gendered disadvantages and may be seen as a very attractive option compared to the jobs and opportunities available in the civilian workplace.

Notes

1. Mady Wechsler Segal, "The Military and the Family as Greedy Institutions," *Armed Forces and Society* 13, no. 1 (1986): 9–38.

2. Mady Wechsler Segal and David R. Segal, "Military Sociology," in *International Military and Defense Encyclopedia*, ed. Trevor N. Dupuy (Washington, DC: Pergamon-Brassey's, 1993).

3. Lory Manning, *Women in the Military: Where They Stand*, 6th ed. (Washington, DC: Women's Research and Education Institute, 2008).

4. Department of Labor, Women's Bureau, "Quick Stats on Women Workers 2008," May 12, 2009, http://www.dol.gov/wb/stats/main.htm.

5. Presidential Commission on the Assignment of Women in the Armed Forces, "Report to the President," November 15, 1992, 9.

6. As of this writing, the United States is on a wartime training and deployment schedule, but even in peacetime, the main training focus of the military is combat and combat support. Karen O. Dunivin, "Military Culture: Change and Continuity," *Armed Forces and Society* (Summer 1994): 531–547.

7. Presidential Commission, "Report."

8. See Carol Cohn, "How Can She Claim Equal Rights When She Doesn't Have to Do as Many Push-Ups as I Do?" *Men and Masculinities* 3, no. 2 (October, 2000): 131–151.

9. Mary Blair-Loy, *Competing Devotions: Career and Family among Women Executives* (Cambridge, MA: Harvard University Press, 2003).

10. David R. Segal, *Recruiting for Uncle Sam: Citizenship and Military Manpower Policy* (Lawrence: University Press of Kansas, 1989).

11. David R. Segal, "The Propensity to Enlist in the United States Military," October 1, 1998, http://web.mit.edu/ssp/seminars/wed_archives_98fall/segal.htm.

12. Manning, *Women in the Military*.

13. Ibid.

14. Joan Williams, *Unbending Gender: Why Family and Work Conflict and What to Do about It* (Oxford: Oxford University Press, 2000), 71.

15. Ibid., 24.

16. Julie Brines, "Economic Dependency, Gender, and Division of Labor at Home," *American Journal of Sociology* (1994): 103–652; Veronica J. Tichenor, "Status and Income as Gendered Resources: The Case of Marital Power," *Journal of Marriage and the Family* 61 (1999): 638–650.

17. Blair-Loy, *Competing Devotions*.

18. Segal, "The Military and the Family."

19. Iraq Coalition Casualty Count, as of November 20, 2009, http://icasualties.org/oif/. Wounded not reported by gender.

20. No mention was made of the possible death of the father, which could also leave an orphaned child. Mimi Finch, "Women in Combat: One Commissioner Reports," *Minerva* 12, no. 1 (1994): 1–12.

21. Zannette A. Uriell, *Pregnancy and Parenthood: Results of the 2001 Survey* (Millington, TN: Navy Personnel Research, Studies, and Technology Department, Navy Personnel Command, 2004).

22. Rosabeth Moss Kanter, *Work and the Family in the United States: A Critical Review and Agenda for Research and Policy* (New York: Russell Sage Foundation, 1977).

23. Uriell, *Pregnancy and Parenthood*.

24. Mady Wechsler Segal, "The Nature of Work and Family Linkages: A Theoretical Perspective," chapter 1 in *The Organization Family*, ed. Gary L. Bowen and Dennis K. Orthner (New York: Praeger, 1989).

25. Segal, "The Military and the Family."

26. Ibid., 20–21.

27. Joan Acker, "Gendered Institutions: From Sex Roles to Gendered Institutions," *Contemporary Sociology* 21, no. 5 (1992): 565–569.

28. Williams, *Unbending Gender*.

29. Hanna Papanek, "Men, Women, and Work: Reflections on the Two-Person Career," *American Journal of Sociology* 78, no. 4 (1973): 852–872.

30. Defense Manpower Data Center (DMDC), "Marital Status of Active Duty Members as of December 31, 2002" (unpublished data received October 2003 from DMDC).

31. Suzanne M. Bianchi and Lynne M. Casper, "American Families," *Population Bulletin* 55, no. 4 (Washington DC: Population Reference Bureau, 2000).

32. Daphne Spain and Suzanne Bianchi, *Balancing Act: Motherhood, Marriage, and Employment among American Women* (New York: Russell Sage, 1996), 27.

33. Mady Wechsler Segal, "Gender and the Military," in *Handbook of the Sociology of Gender,* ed. Janet Saltzman Chafetz (New York: Kluwer, 1999), 563–581.

34. As of September 30, 2006.

35. Military Homefront, Reports homepage. *Profile of the Military Community: DoD 2006 Demographics*, 31, http://www.militaryhomefront.dod.mil/portal/page/mhf/MHF/MHF_DETAIL_0?current_id=20.20.60.70.0.0.0.0.0.

36. Spain and Bianchi, *Balancing Act*.

37. Papanek, "Men, Women, and Work."

38. DMDC, "Marital Status."

39. Williams, *Unbending Gender*.

40. Spain and Bianchi, *Balancing Act*, 28.

41. DMDC, "Marital Status."

42. James A. Martin and Peggy McClure, "Today's Active Duty Military Family: The Evolving Challenges of Military Family Life," chapter 1 in *The Military Family*, ed. James A. Martin, Leona N. Rosen, and Linette R. Sparacino (Westport, CT: Praeger, 2000).

43. Brad Booth, William Falk, David R. Segal, and Mady Wechsler Segal, "The Impact of Military Presence in Local Labor Markets on the Employment of Women," *Gender and Society* 14 (1998): 318–332.

44. Segal, "The Nature of Work."

45. Ibid.

46. Military Homefront, *Profile*, 33, 34.

47. Ibid., 34.

48. Ibid., 45.

49. Claudia Goldin, "The Long Road to the Fast Track: Career and Family," *The Annals of the American Academy (AAPSS)* 596 (November 2004): 20–35.

50. Defense Data Manpower Center and Service's Human Resource Staffs and Commands, *Annual Report on Status of Female Members of the Armed Forces of the United States, FY 2002–2006* (Washington, DC: Department of Defense Office of Personnel and Readiness, Military Personnel Policy, 2007). Presented in chart format by Defense Department Advisory Committee on Women in the Services (DACOWITS), 7.

51. Mady W. Segal and David R. Segal, "Implications for Military Families of Changes in the Armed Forces of the United States," in *Handbook of the Sociology of the Military*, ed. Giuseppe Caforio (New York: Kluwer Academic, 2003), 225–233.

52. DMDC, "Marital Status."

53. Martin and McClure, "Today's Active Duty."

54. Segal and Segal, "Implications for Military Families."

55. DMDC, "Marital Status."

56. Uriell, *Pregnancy and Parenthood.*

57. Segal, "The Military and the Family."

58. Federico E. Garcia, *Women at Sea: Unplanned Losses and Accession Planning* (Alexandria, VA: Center for Naval Analysis, 1999).

59. Uriell, *Pregnancy and Parenthood.*

60. Department of Defense, "DoD Physical Fitness and Body Fat Programs Procedures," *Department of Defense Instruction 1308.3*, November 5, 2002, http://www.dtic.mil/whs/directives/corres/pdf/130803p.pdf.

61. Military Homefront, *Profile*, 56.

62. Brad Booth, Mady Wechsler Segal, and D. Bruce Bell, with James A. Martin, Morten G. Ender, David E. Rohall, and John Nelson, *What We Know About Army Families: 2007 Update* (Alexandria VA: ICF International, 2007).

63. Department of Defense, "Subject: Family Care Plans," *Department of Defense Instruction 1342.19*, July 13, 1992, http://www.dtic.mil/whs/directives/corres/pdf/134219p.pdf.

64. Military Homefront, *Profile.*

65. David S. Wolpert, James A. Martin, Lea M. Dougherty, Barbara Janofsky Rudin, and Susan Kerner-Hoeg, "The Special Case of the Young Enlisted Family," chapter 3 in *The Military Family*, ed. James A. Martin, Leona N. Rosen, and Linette R. Sparacino (Westport, CT: Praeger, 2000).

66. Nancy Duff Campbell, Judith C. Appelbaum, Karin Martinson, and Emily Martin, *Be All That We Can Be* (Washington, DC: National Women's Law Center, 2000).

67. Martin and McClure, "Today's Active Duty," 15.

68. Segal, "The Military and the Family."

69. Uriell, *Pregnancy and Parenthood.*

70. Spain and Bianchi, *Balancing Act.*

71. Segal and Segal, "Implications for Military Families."

72. Military Homefront, *Profile*, 36.

73. Martin and McClure, "Today's Active Duty."

74. Spain and Bianchi, *Balancing Act.*

75. Military Homefront, *Profile*, 54.

76. Jody Heymann, *The Widening Gap: Why America's Working Families Are in Jeopardy and What Can Be Done about It* (New York: Basic Books, 2000).

77. Office of the Under Secretary of Defense Personnel and Readiness, "Career Progression of Minority and Women Officers" (Washington, DC: Author, 1998).

78. Adrienne Evertson and Amy Nesbit, *The Glass Ceiling Effect and Its Impact on Mid-Level Female Officer Career Progression in the United States Marine Corps and Air Force* (Monterey, CA: Naval Post-Graduate School, 2004), 115.

79. See Darlene M. Iskra, *Breaking Through the Brass Ceiling: Strategies of Success for Elite Military Women* (Saarbrücken, Germany: VDM Verlag Dr. Müller Aktieng-esellschaft & Co. KG, 2008).

80. Laura S. Jeffrey, "Women in Uniform: Should You Stay or Go?" *Military Times*, October 1, 2007, http://www.militarytimesedge.com/advancement/military-career-advancement/edge_women_inuniform_122808/1/.

81. U.S. Government Accountability Office, "Military Personnel: Reporting Additional Servicemember Demographics Could Enhance Congressional Oversight" (Washington, DC: Author, 2005).

82. David S. Wolpert, "Military Retirement and the Transition to Civilian Life," chapter 7 in *The Military Family*, ed. James A. Martin, Leona N. Rosen, and Linette R. Sparacino (Westport, CN: Praeger, 2000). Reserve and Guard retirees have different retirement benefits, and generally must wait until age 60 to receive them.

83. Ibid.

Epilogue

The evolution of the participation of women in the military has not taken a linear path. In some cases it has taken a few steps backward before proceeding to new roles and ideologies about women. Women participated in WWI, but their service was virtually unknown until Dorothy and Carl J. Schneider wrote their well-researched book *Into the Breach* in 1991.

Women's service in WWII was also relegated to anonymous history until the 1970s after the start of the AVF, when interest in women's participation increased. In 1982, General Jeanne Holm published a seminal work called *Women in the Military: An Unfinished Revolution.* It was revised in 1992 and covered the entire history of women in the military through the Persian Gulf War of 1991. It stopped short of covering the women in combat debates of 1993–1994 and the women in submarine debates in 1999–2000. This book discusses those eras, but its purpose is to provide an overview rather than delve deeply into any of the issues.

Since the 1980s, books about women in the military have blossomed. Many books delve into a singular subject, like women in aviation or nursing, scandals like Tailhook, or a single service branch, like the Women's Army Corps. Many women, particularly those of the WWII era, have written autobiographies about their experiences. There is a dearth of information about women in the Korean War and the Vietnam War because the number of women in the military during those periods was very small—less than 1 percent of the force, and their roles were limited. Witt and colleagues' work, *A Defense Weapon Known to Be of Value,* is one of the few comprehensive looks at women's participation in the Korean War. Only a handful more have been written about women in Vietnam. The annotated bibliography at the end of this book gives both a selected review of the books I have used in this research as well as web sites where bibliographies can be found online.

Slowly, researchers are finding information in the archives or by conducting individual interviews, and more stories are being told. Nursing and nurse's stories appear to have a larger presence in the researched material, probably because women have been in military nursing since nursing began. In recent years, women who have served in Iraq and Afghanistan have written about their experiences. This does not just include military women, but imbedded journalists and reporters as well.

This book has hopefully served as an introduction to the varied and numerous histories of women in the military, as well as a synopsis of the service of women from all walks of life who have participated in our country's armed forces. Each woman, in her own way, has contributed to the overall success women have brought to the military.

As discussed in this book, there are still four main issues women must face before being fully vested in the military. The first, and most important, is that the sexual harassment and sexual assault of women in the military must end. Most of the perpetrators are not strangers; they are service women's superiors, peers, shipmates, classmates, acquaintances, and other people with whom they work. Why is it so prevalent? I have tried to show that it is a combination of women's socialization to "not make waves" and ignore it, as well as some men's beliefs that they have an inherent right to bully others. It is pervasive because onlookers do not challenge those assumptions when a co-worker is being harassed. It is easier to look the other way. The Pentagon's Sexual Assault Awareness campaign that calls for friends to watch out for each other is a start, but service members must also rise to the challenge and let the harassers know that their behavior is unacceptable. This takes lots of courage. Commanders need to hold people accountable. Accountability needs to go all the way up the chain of command. The lesson of Tailhook is that senior officers are not immune to failing to assert their leadership in tough situations.

The second issue that needs to be resolved is women in combat and collocation. The Lioness program requires women to collocate with combat troops. They are a needed and useful tool, but were sent in initially without adequate training or record documentation. This is being addressed by some members of the House through attempted legislation to help solve the problem; but awareness of women's contributions is a key factor. Women get self-defense training, but in many cases they must act offensively. The integration of combat training in boot camp and advanced military training must be accomplished so that women and men can learn to work together when the bullets start flying. Segregated and inadequate training in offensive tactics for women only serves to reiterate to men that women cannot hack combat. It is a structural and training issue. Women are fighting and dying in combat, and not just the women in the Lioness program. DoD policies need to catch up with reality. The current situation only makes it more dangerous for both men and women.

Third is the issue of women on submarines. It is being revisited, and it appears that the Navy is "moving forward"[1] on the plan to integrate the larger Trident class submarines with women officers in 2011. However, the arguments against women in submarines have not substantially changed since I studied this issue for my master's thesis.[2] I found the arguments groundless. Women are serving on submarines in several other countries, including Canada, Great Britain, and Australia. The tight quarters and lack of privacy can be overcome (think of astronauts in a space shuttle). The habitability standards may need to be changed for women on submarines, just as they are modified for the men who serve on them. As one young woman wrote in response to an article against women in submarines, "Women are superior to men for submerged operations. They're physically smaller, take up less space, breathe less air, and eat less food. They have better social skills and tolerate close quarters better, and they are physiologically tougher and have better endurance for the environment. All submariners should be female."[3]

Finally, the military services should make it easier for women to have both careers and families. The current military career projection does not allow for time off, like a sabbatical, to step back from work for a while and concentrate on other things. The Coast Guard has had a program for years that allows members to leave the service and then return at a later time. The Navy just this year started a pilot program wherein members apply to take up to three years off to pursue other goals. It is hoped this program will be extremely successful and will prove to not adversely affect a future career.

In a recent speech by First Lady Michelle Obama to a collected group of veterans, mostly women, she told of women's fight to be included in the military and to overcome the barriers that were put up just because of their gender. She said: "[We] can look to the example of women like Amy Krueger, who lost her life in the unthinkable violence at Fort Hood two weeks ago. Amy had enlisted in the Army after the September 11th attacks. And when her mother told her that she couldn't take on Osama bin Laden all by herself, Amy replied, simply: 'Watch me.' She said, 'Watch me.' And I think that more than anything, that phrase 'watch me' sums up the spirit of our women in uniform throughout our history. When others doubted you, or dismissed you, or questioned whether you could endure the training or complete the mission—that was your response: 'Watch me.' Right? Watch me succeed. Watch me risk everything I have for the country I love. Watch me do my part to protect this nation and protect this union. Watch me."[4]

With an all-volunteer force, it is incumbent upon the military to utilize the best people for the task, regardless of gender or sexuality. In many cases, the best man for the job is a woman. Just because it has never been done does not automatically mean it will be unsuccessful. It may not be done in the exact same way, but it may be done more effectively and more efficiently. Military women around the world can now proudly say, "Watch me," and people will listen.

Notes

1. On November 19, 2009, I was able to speak directly to CNO Admiral Gary Roughead, and he assured me that the proposal to put women on submarines was now a plan that was "moving forward."

2. Darlene Marie Iskra, "Women in Submarines: Have the Arguments about Expanding Women's Sea Going Roles in the U.S. Navy Changed Over Time?" (unpublished master's thesis, University of Maryland College Park, 2003). A portion of that research was published as Darlene M. Iskra, "Attitudes toward Expanding Roles for Navy Women at Sea: Results of a Content Analysis," *Armed Forces and Society* 33, no. 2 (January 2007): 203–223.

3. Melissa Tyson, rebuttal to "Women Should Not Serve in Submarines," *U.S. Naval Institute Proceedings* (July 2000).

4. Michelle Obama, "Remarks By the First Lady at Tea for Military Women," White House, November 18, 2009 www.whitehouse.gov/the-press-office/remarks-first-lady-tea-military-women.

Important Policy Decisions, Court Cases, and Legislation for Military Women

Executive Order 10240, Signed by President Truman on April 27, 1951

Permitted the services to terminate, regardless of rank, grade, or length of service, women's service under the following conditions:

Is the parent, by birth or adoption, of a minor child (under 18)

Has custody of a minor child

Is the stepparent of a minor child and the child is within the household more than 30 days a year

Is pregnant

Or, while serving, has given birth to a living child

Z-Gram 116, Equal Rights and Opportunities for Women, August 7, 1972

Then Chief of Naval Operations Admiral Elmo Zumwalt expanded roles for Navy women, enabling them to become naval aviators flying noncombatant aircraft. Also opened NROTC (Naval ROTC) units to women, allowed women in all of the staff corps, instigated a pilot program for women at sea, allowed for the selection of women to the Joint War Colleges, and opened more billets for women.

Court Cases

Crawford v. Cushman, 531 F.2d 1114 (February 23, 1976)

The Second Circuit Court held that the Marine Corps regulation requiring the discharge of a female Marine as soon as pregnancy was discovered violated the Fifth Amendment in that no other temporary disability forced mandatory discharge. Although this did not rescind Executive Order 10240, the DoD later came out and forbade the mandatory separation of mothers.

Frontiero v. Richardson, 341 F. Supp. 201 (May 14, 1973)

Supreme Court decision declared it unconstitutional to require a female member of the military to prove a civilian spouse or dependent children were dependent upon her for support unless the same rules were applied to male members.

Owens v. Brown, 455 F. Supp. 291 (1978)

Class-action suit filed against the Navy for discrimination in that women could not serve on ships. Judge John Sirica ruled Title 10, section 6015, unconstitutional in that it did not provide equal protection under the law as guaranteed by the Fifth Amendment. Though this did not force the Navy to send women to sea, it was the impetus for the modification of the law.

Rostker v. Goldberg, 453 U.S. 57 (1981)

Supreme Court decision that draft registration that excluded women was constitutional in that the draft selected men for combat positions whereas women were excluded from serving in those positions.

Legislation

Public Law 241, Naval Act of 1916

Authorized that "all persons who may be capable of performing special useful service for coastal defense" could be enrolled in the Naval Coast Defense Reserve Force. Secretary of the Navy Josephus Daniels used the language to enlist women in the Yeoman (F) and Woman Marines for service during WWI.

Public Law 77–554, Act to Establish the Women's Army Auxiliary Corps, May 1942

Established the Women's Army Auxiliary Corps (WAAC) on May 15, 1942, as an auxiliary corps without full military status.

Public Law 77–689, Women's Reserve of the Navy, July 30, 1942

Established the Navy, Marine Corps, and Coast Guard reserves for women (WAVES, Women Marines, and SPARS, respectively) for the duration of WWII plus six months.

Public Law 78–110, July 1, 1943

Established the WAC, as a separate corps within the Army, with full military status.

Public Law 78–441, September 1944

Allowed WAVES, SPARS, and Women Marines to be assigned to Hawaii and Alaska.

Public Law 80–36, Army-Navy Nurse Act of 1947, April 16, 1947

Established a permanent nurse corps in both the Army and the Navy and authorized a Women's Medical Specialist Corps in the Army.

Public Law 80–625, Women's Armed Services Integration Act of 1948

Allowed for the permanent assignment of women to the armed forces but severely restricted their assignment, numbers, promotion opportunity, and military benefits.

Public Law 84–585, June 1956

Removed the 20-percent limitation on the number of women at the O-4 officer level.

Public Law 90–130, 1967

Removed percentage restrictions on women's ranks and numbers established by the original 1948 legislation; allowed women to hold permanent rank as captains in the Navy and colonels in the other services; and allowed women to become admirals or generals.

Public Law 94–106, DoD National Defense Authorization Act of 1976

Allowed women to be enrolled in the Federal Service Academies starting in 1976.

Public Law 95–202, GI Bill Improvement Act of 1977, November 23, 1977

Authorized veteran's status for WASP and American Merchant Marine in Oceangoing Service of WWII.

Public Law 102–190, 1992–1993 Defense Authorization Act, December 5, 1991

Authorized women to fly in combat aviation.

Public Law 103–160, Department of Defense Appropriation Authorization Act of 1994, November 30, 1993

Authorized women to serve in combat ships.

Public Law 106–398, Floyd D. Spence National Defense Authorization Act for Fiscal Year 2001, October 2000

A provision in the bill requires the DoD to give a 30-day notification of any change to the Navy's submarine assignment policy for women, virtually halting any momentum on changing this status.

Public Law 107–304, Bob Stump National Defense Authorization Act For Fiscal Year 2003, December 2, 2003

An amendment to this bill prohibits the DoD to require or encourage military women to wear an abaya while performing duties in Saudi Arabia.

Public Law 111–40, A Bill to Award a Congressional Gold Medal to the Women Airforce Service Pilots ("WASP") July 1, 2009

Sponsored by Senator Kay Bailey Hutchinson (R-Tx), 75 other Senate sponsors, and 335 House sponsors, this bill authorizes the award of the Congressional Gold Medal for surviving WASP pilots, recognizing their achievement as the first military aviators and their sacrifice during WWII.

The Uniform Code of Military Justice (UCMJ): Articles Relating to Sexual Harassment

The following table shows types of sexual harassment and the violation of the UCMJ relating to the conduct.

If the sexual harasser:	He or she may be found guilty of:	In violation of USMJ article:
Influences or offers to influence the career, salary, or job of another in exchange for sexual favors	Extortion	Article 127
Makes threats to elicit sexual favors	Communicating a threat	Article 134
Offers rewards or demands for sexual favors	Bribery and graft	Article 134
Makes sexual comments	Indecent, insulting, or obscene language or conduct prejudicial to good order and discipline	Article 134
Makes sexual comments	Provoking speech or gestures or disrespect	Articles 89, 91, and 117
Makes sexual contact	Assault Assault and battery Indecent liberties with a female Rape	Article 128 Article 128 Article 134 Article 120
Engages in sexual harassment to the detriment of job performance	Dereliction of duty	Article 92
Is an officer	Conduct unbecoming an officer	Article 133
Is commanding officer	Wrong committed by the commanding officer	Article 138

United States Marine Corps, Marine Corps University, "Sexual Harassment," in *User's Guide to Marine Corps Values*, http://www.cpp.usmc.mil/schools/corporals/website/Guided%20Discussions/Chap%2009%20Sexual%20Harassment.pdf.

Ships Named for Women

Of the thousands of ships that have served in the United States military, very few have been named for women. The primary type of ship named for women were U.S. Army hospital ships (USAHS), and the women for whom they were named were all nurses, due to their courage and sacrifice during wartime. Other ship types included Army transport ship (USATs), tug boats, and other auxiliary (i.e. noncombatant) ships.

Only two Navy combatant ships were named for women, the USS *Higbee* (DD-806) and the USS *Hopper* (DDG-70).

The women for whom these ships were named serve as role models for military personnel to emulate. May they and their sacrifices never be forgotten.

Army Ships

USAHS *Emily H. M. Weder*, May 24, 1944, hospital ship.[1] Major Weder, ANC, entered the Army Nurse Corps in 1918 and died at Walter Reed General Hospital in 1943. She had been chief operating room nurse at Letterman and Walter Reed General Hospitals. Her last tour of duty was in the Ninth Corps Area,[2] where she was in charge of recruiting reserve nurses and assigning and supervising nursing services at all the station hospitals in that area. Weder's obituary in the *American Journal of Nursing* called her "one of the most widely known and sincerely loved women in the Corps."[3]

USAHS *Blanche F. Sigman*, May 29, 1944, hospital ship. First Lt. Blanche F. Sigman, ANC, was the chief nurse of the 95th Evacuation Hospital, a unit situated under canvas at Nettuno, Italy, during the bitter and bloody fight for the Anzio beachhead. On February 7, 1944, Sigman and her colleagues, First Lt. Carrie Sheetz, Second Lt. Marjorie G. Morrow, and Red Cross nurse Esther Richards, were hit by enemy fire when a German bomber, with a British fighter in hot pursuit, jettisoned its payload of bombs over the hospital. All four nurses perished. The ship was later decommissioned as a hospital ship and became a troop transport ship.[4]

USAHS *Ernestine A. Koranda,* December 11, 1944, hospital ship. Second Lieutenant Koranda was stationed at Townsville, Queensland, Australia, in March 1942, at the 12th Station Hospital. She noted they "did what they could to treat the wounded coming in from New Guinea and other Pacific Islands." On December 19, 1943, she boarded a plane for a thousand-mile trip to Sydney, Australia, where she planned to wed her fiancé, Bob Middleton. Only an hour into the trip, the plane developed engine trouble and crashed. There were no survivors. Although originally buried in Australia, her remains were returned to the United States after the war, and she was buried with military honors at Wadena Cemetery, in Wadena, Minnesota. Lt. Koranda is on the *Honor List of Dead and Missing* issued by the War Department in 1946.[5]

USAHS *Frances Y. Slanger,* February 13, 1945, U.S. Army hospital ship with the largest patient capacity to date (1,628 patients). Second Lieutenant Slanger of the 45th Field Hospital was the only Army nurse to be killed by enemy action on the drive from Normandy to the Rhine. She was killed October 21, 1944, when her tent was struck by a German shell. She died of abdominal wounds two hours later.[6]

USAHS *Aleda E. Lutz,* February 13, 1945, hospital ship. Lieutenant Lutz, ANC, was killed when her homebound plane crashed into a mountain near Marseilles, France. Lutz had recorded 814 hours in the air when the C-47 hospital plane evacuating 15 wounded soldiers from the battlefront near Lyons, Italy, crashed, killing all aboard. Aleda E. Lutz is one of the most celebrated female war heroes of WWII. As a First Lieutenant Army flight nurse, she flew 196 missions evacuating over thirty-five hundred men. She also logged the most flight hours of any flight nurse. She earned six battle stars before her death, and she was recorded as the first military woman to die in a combat zone in WWII. Lutz was awarded the Air Medal four times, the Oak Leaf Cluster, the Red Cross Medal, and the Purple Heart. She was also the first woman awarded the Distinguished Flying Cross in a world war, our nation's second highest military honor. It was awarded posthumously.[7]

Navy Ships

USS *Pocahontas* (YT-266), 1942, harbor tug. Three other navy ships also carried this name—a screw steamer in 1852, an oceangoing tug (AT-18), and a German ship seized and used as a troop transport during WWI (ID-3044). Pocahontas is, of course, a figure beloved in American colonial history—the wife of Virginia tobacco grower John Rolfe and daughter of Algonquin chief Powhatan.[8]

USS *Dorothea L. Dix* (AP-67), 1942, transport. Dorothea Dix (1802–1887) is best known for her work as a social reformer, crusading for proper conditions for the treatment of the "insane." During the Civil War, she was appointed superintendent of Union army nurses and was fair in her nursing of both Union and Confederate soldiers.

USS *Elizabeth C. Stanton* (AP-69), 1942, the lead transport in a new class of transport ships built during WWII. Elizabeth C. Stanton (1815–1902) was an abolitionist, a suffragist, and an early proponent of women's rights. A controversial figure for her time, she did not support the 14th and 15th Amendments to the constitution giving African American men legal rights, insisting that the rights should be extended to women, black and white, as well. This caused a rift within the women's rights movement that was not fully resolved for many years.

USS *Florence Nightingale* (AP-70), 1942, transport. Florence Nightingale (1820–1910) was an early nursing pioneer and is most famous for her work during the Crimean War (1853–1856). After hearing reports of the horrible conditions for wounded soldiers, she and a staff of 38 women volunteer nurses arrived early in November 1854 to a makeshift military hospital in Scutari, near modern day Istanbul, Turkey. There were few medicines, neglected hygiene, and mass infections, many of which were fatal. Ten times more soldiers died from illnesses such as typhus, typhoid, cholera, and dysentery than from battle wounds. Fatalities were high due to overcrowding, the hospital's defective sewers, and the lack of ventilation. Florence insisted on adequate lighting, diet, hygiene, and activity, and although she and her team did what they could to improve cleanliness and hygiene, conditions were not fully corrected until the British government sent a sanitary commission to build proper sewage facilities and improve ventilation. It is directly through her thorough observations that the association between sanitary conditions and healing became recognized and established. She continued work in this area throughout her career, reducing deaths by disease through attention to the sanitary conditions required in military and civilian hospital settings.

USS *Lyon* (AP-71), 1942, transport. Mary Lyon (1797–1849) was an early pioneer in women's education, first establishing the Wheaton Female Seminary (now Wheaton College) and two years later was the founder and first president of Mt. Holyoke Female Seminary (now Mt. Holyoke College), both in Massachusetts. For more than 150 years, Mt. Holyoke has empowered women for serious intellectual pursuits, public leadership, and service to humanity as its founder envisioned.[9]

USS *Susan B. Anthony* (AP-72), 1942–1944, a transport ship that participated in the allied invasions of North Africa and Normandy and was sunk by a German mine on June 7, 1944, although no lives were lost. Susan B. Anthony was an early suffragist and a leader in the struggle for women's rights, especially voting rights.

USS *Sacagawea* (YT-326), a harbor tug that served in Charleston harbor from 1942 to 1945. Sacagawea was an interpreter on the Lewis and Clark expedition of 1802–1806.

USNS *Sacagawea* (T-AKE-2), 2000. She is the second of a new class of replenishment ships, 1 of 40 replenishment ships in the Naval Fleet Auxiliary Force.

USS *Watseka* (YT-387), a 1944 harbor tug named for a Potawatomi woman who was born in Illinois. A city in eastern Illinois is also named in her honor.

USS *Higbee* (DD-806), 1945, a Gearing-class destroyer named for Lenah S. Higbee, superintendent of Navy Nurse Corps 1911–1922. *Higbee* was the first ship laid down, christened, and commissioned for a woman who had served in the U.S. Navy and the first so named to see combat.

USS *Hopper* (DDG-70), 1996. Built and commissioned at Bath Iron Works in Bath, Maine, the Arleigh Burke–class guided-missile destroyer is named for Rear Admiral Grace Murray Hopper, a computer technology pioneer who led the Navy into the digital age.

USS *Roosevelt* (DDG-80), 1996, explicitly named for both Franklin Delano Roosevelt, the 32nd president of the United States, and First Lady Eleanor Roosevelt.

USNS *Mary Sears* (T-AGS-65), an oceanographic survey ship, launched in October 2000 and still active as of 2007. She was named for Commander Mary Sears, United States Navy Reserve (USNR), an oceanographer closely involved in the development of Woods Hole Oceanographic Institution.[10]

USNS *Amelia Earhart* (T-AKE-6), a sister ship of *Sacagawea* launched in 2008. Amelia Earhart was an early pioneer in aviation.

Coast Guard

USCGC *Harriet Lane* (WMEC 903), 1984, homeported in Portsmouth, Virginia. She was the second Coast Guard ship to be named for Harriet Lane. The first was a revenue cutter that served from 1858–1867. Harriet Rebecca Lane Johnston (May 9, 1830–July 3, 1903) was niece to perpetual bachelor James Buchanan and acted as first lady of the United States from 1857 to 1861.[11]

USCGC *Stratton* (WMSL-752), keel laid in 2009, expected completion 2011. Named after Dorothy C. Stratton, Purdue University's first full-time dean of women. She was also the head of the SPARS, the women's Coast Guard reserve, during WWII. The ship's sponsor is First Lady Michelle Obama.[12]

Notes

1. Information in this section adapted from Global Security, "USAHS U.S. Army Hospital Ships," http://www.globalsecurity.org/military/systems/ship/usahs.htm.

2. Ninth Corps Area was headquartered at the Presidio in San Francisco and was responsible for the states of Arizona, California, Idaho, Montana, Nevada, Oregon, Utah, and Washington.

3. Obituaries, *American Journal of Nursing* 43, no. 10 (1943): 967.

4. Mary Sarnecky, *A History of the U.S. Army Nurse Corps* (Philadelphia: University of Pennsylvania Press, 1999), 225–226; Mary Sarnecky, "1901–2001: A Century of Heroism," *Army Magazine* (2001), http://www3.ausa.org/webpub/DeptArmyMagazine.nsf/byid/CCRN-6CCRVE.

5. South Dakota Casualties of World War II, South Dakota Community Foundation, "Fallen Sons and Daughters: Alphabetical listing ,Ernestine Mae Koranda," http://www.state.sd.us/military/VetAffairs/sdwwiimemorial/.

6. Sarnecky, *A History*, 239–240.

7. U.S. Army Medical Department, Office of Medical History, Army Nurse Corps History, "Highlights in the History of the Army Nurse Corps, 2001," http://history.amedd.army.mil/ancwebsite/append.htm; The Michigan Women's Hall of Fame, http://hall.michiganwomenshalloffame.org/.

8. Wikipedia, "Military Ships Named for Women," http://en.wikipedia.org/wiki/List_of_U.S._military_vessels_named_after_women.

9. National Women's Hall of Fame, "Mary Lyons," http://www.greatwomen.org/women.php?action=viewone&id=102.

10. Military Sealift Command, Ship Inventory, S- Mary Sears, USNS, http://www.msc.navy.mil/inventory/citations/marysears.htm.

11. United States Coast Guard, Atlantic Area Cutters, Harriet Lane, (WMEC-903), http://www.uscg.mil/lantarea/cgcHarrietLane/default.asp.

12. United States Coast Guard, History, Personnel, Women in the Coast Guard, Captain Dorothy Stratton, http://www.uscg.mil/History/people/DStrattonBio.asp.

General and Flag Officer Firsts

General and Flag Officer Firsts

	General/ Admiral O10	Lt. General/ Vice Admiral O9	Major General (MG)/ Rear Admiral O8	Brig. General/ Rear Admiral Lower Half O7
Army	General Ann Dunwoody 2009	Lt. Gen. Claudia Kennedy 1997	MG Mary E. Clarke 1978	BG Elizabeth Hoisington, WAC 1970
Army Nurse	X	X	MG Nancy R. Adams, ANC 1997	BG Anna May Hays, ANC 1970
Army Reserve	X	X	MG Celia Adolphi 1999	BG Dorothy Pocklington, ANC 1989
Navy	X	VADM Pat Tracey 1996	RADM Fran McKee 1983	RDML Fran McKee 1976
Navy Nurse	X	X	RADM Frances Shea, NC 1983	RDML Alene Duerk, NC 1972
Navy Reserve	X	X	RADM Karen Harmeyer, NC 2001	RDML Grace Hopper 1983
Marine Corps	X	Lt. Gen. Carol Mutter 1996	MG Carol Mutter 1994	BG Margaret Brewer 1978

(*Continued*)

General and Flag Officer Firsts (*Continued*)

	General/ Admiral O10	Lt. General/ Vice Admiral O9	Major General (MG)/ Rear Admiral O8	Brig. General/ Rear Admiral Lower Half O7
Marine Reserve	X	X	BG Tracy Garrett 2009	BG Tracy Garrett 2007
Air Force	X	Lt. Gen. Leslie F. Kenne 1999	MG Jeanne Holm 1973	BG Jeanne Holm 1971
Air Force Nurse	X	X	MG Melissa Rank, NC 2005	BG Ann Hoefly, NC 1971
Air Force Reserve	X	X	MG Nora A. Astafan 1993	BG Frances Mossman 1983
Coast Guard	X	VADM Vivian Crea 2006	RADM Vivian Crea 2003	RDML Vivian Crea 2000
Coast Guard Reserve	X	X	RADM Mary O'Donnell	RDML Mary O'Donnell 1999
Army National Guard	X	X	MG Marianne Mathewson-Chapman, ANC 2000	BG Sharon Vander Zyl, ANC 1992
Air National Guard	X	X	BG Roberta Mills, AFNC 1994	BG Roberta Mills, AFNC 1992

Source: Darlene M. Iskra, *Breaking through the Brass Ceiling: Strategies of Success for Elite Military Women* (Saarbrücken, Germany: VDM Verlag Dr. Müller Aktiengesellschaft & Co. KG, 2008); Library of Congress, Researchers, Federal Research Division, Heritage Calendars 1997–2002, http://www.loc.gov/rr/frd/Heritage-Calendars/home.html.

Chronology

1776   Hannah Thomas took over as keeper of Gurnet Point Light, near Plymouth, Massachusetts, when her husband joined the Army to fight in the Revolutionary War. Lighthouses were an important navigational aid for ships, and the keepers were the historical predecessors of our modern-day Coast Guard.

1779   Margaret Corbin became the first woman in the United States to receive a pension from Congress for her injuries due to military service.

1828–1947   Two researchers, Mary Louise Clifford and J. Candace Clifford, found the names of 138 women who were employed as lighthouse keepers during these years. The majority were the wives or daughters of keepers or other employees who died on the job.

1861–1865   Trained women nurses served in the civil war either working alone, as Clara Barton, or as contract nurses, such as Dr. Mary Walker.

1865   Surgeon Mary Walker was awarded the Medal of Honor—the first and only woman, so far, to be so honored.

1898   Spanish-American War. Army contract nurses served with the Army. After the war, about two hundred contract nurses voluntarily remained in service.

1901   Founding of the Army Nurse Corps by the Army Reorganization Act of 1901. The corps was women only, and the nurses had no military rank. Dita H. Kinney became its first superintendent and served until 1909.

1908   Founding of the Navy Nurse Corps with Esther Voorhees Hasson as superintendent, originally overseeing a corps of only 20 women (called "The Sacred 20") that eventually increased to 110 by 1912. She served until 1911.

1916   The Naval Reserve Act of 1916 allowed for the enlistment of qualified "persons" for service. Secretary of the Navy Josephus Daniels took advantage of this wording to allow the enlistment of women into the Navy and Marine Corps during WWI.

1917   On March 19, the Navy authorized the enlistment of women as Yeomen (F) and Woman Marines. Over 11,000 naval reserve and 305 marine women served in the United States during WWI. Pvt. Opha Mae Johnson became the first woman to enlist in the Marine Corps Reserve August 13, 1918. Most of these women Marines, referred to as Marinettes, freed male Marines from clerical billets at Headquarters Marine Corps, enabling them to fight in France. Others filled jobs at recruiting stations across the country. Although women did not have the right to vote, they were willing and able to serve their country. They were recruited to "Free a Man to Fight." When the armistice was signed on November 11, 1918, the women were no longer needed and all were separated from service by June 30, 1919.

1918   Army nurses Beatrice M. MacDonald and Helen McClelland each received the Distinguished Service Cross for service in Belgium during WWI.

1920   Law authorizing relative rank for Army nurses was signed by President Woodrow Wilson on May 28. Highest rank achievable was major, for the superintendent of the Nurse Corps; captain for assistant superintendents; first lieutenant for chief nurses; and second lieutenant for all other nurses. It also prescribed that nurses would be subordinate to medical officers in matters of medical and sanitary matters. Major Julia Stimson was the first superintendent of the Army Nurse Corps to wear that rank. Navy nurses were not included in this legislation.

Army General Orders Number 49 defined the rights and privileges associated with relative rank. It stated that Army nurses would be accorded the precedence, respect, titles, rank insignia, and protection in their relative rank as those of commissioned officers. But it denied them the right of command and did not pay them equally to the corresponding rank of male officers.

USS *Relief*, a hospital ship, was commissioned on December 28. Navy nurses are permanently assigned to a ship for the first time. The chief nurse of the ship was J. Beatrice Bowman, one of the

	original Sacred 20, who later served as the third superintendent of the Navy Nurse Corps from 1922–1935.
1926	Bill authorizing regular retirement for Army and Navy nurses after 30 years of service, or at 20 years on reaching the age of 50, became law on May 13. In 1928, a death benefit was granted to survivors of nurses who died on active duty. And in 1930, nurses disabled in the line of duty were granted disability benefits.
1941–1945	WWII: Some four hundred thousand women served their country in uniform during the war. They served in all combat theaters and worked in all jobs except combat jobs at sea, in the air, or on land. This did not, however, preclude them from being killed or captured by the enemy.
1941	Five Navy nurses became Japanese POWs after the fall of Guam in December; they were repatriated in August 1942.
1942	Public Law 554 established the Women's Army Auxiliary Corps (WAAC) on May 15 as an auxiliary corps without full military status. Mrs. Oveta Culp Hobby was sworn in as the first director.

The 77th Congress authorized relative rank for the Navy Nurse Corps, 22 years after its authorization for Army nurses. Highest rank achievable was similar to that of Army nurses: lieutenant commander for the superintendent of the Nurse Corps, lieutenant for assistant superintendents, lieutenant junior grade for chief nurses, and ensigns for all other nurses. It also prescribed that nurses would be subordinate to medical and dental officers in medical and sanitary matters. At that time, the superintendent of the Navy Nurse Corps was Lieutenant Commander Sue Dauser.

Public Law 689 (Naval Reserve Act of 1938) was amended and established the Women's Reserve of the Navy—unofficially known as WAVES, Women Accepted for Volunteer Emergency Service—on July 30, with Mildred McAfee, commissioned as a lieutenant commander, as director. This same legislation also established the Marine Corps Women's Reserve, with Major Ruth Cheney Streeter as director. Four months later, the Coast Guard Reserve was established, with Dorothy Stratton, commissioned as a lieutenant commander, as director. They used the acronym SPAR, from the Coast Guard motto "Semper Paratus—Always Ready." The women in these services had full military status, including equal pay for equal rank, unlike the Army and Navy Nurse Corps or the WAACs.

In September, the Army Air Force established the Women's Auxiliary Ferrying Squadron (WAFS), with Nancy Harkness Love as director, under the auspices of the civil service. Almost simultaneously, the Women's Flying Training Detachment (WFTD) was established under the directorship of Jackie Cochran.

The first two African American WAAC companies completed basic training at Fort Des Moines, Iowa.

1943   Conversion of WAAC to Women's Army Corps (WAC). This was accomplished to help the Army compete for personnel with the other services, whose full military benefits could not be matched by WAAC.

In July, the WAFS and the WFTD were merged to become the Women Airforce Service Pilots (WASP) under the directorship of Jackie Cochran, with Nancy Harkness Love as executive officer.

LtJG Vera Hamerschlag, United States Coast Guard (USCG), took command of the Chatham, Massachusetts, Loran monitoring station, in which 11 other SPARS served. At the time, the existence of the navigation system was highly classified.

Minnie Spotted Wolf, Native American Blackfoot, became first Native American woman in the Marine Corps.

1944   LtJG Harriet Ida Pickens and Ensign Frances E. Wills, the USN, became the first African American women commissioned into the Navy. Female Navy officers were not segregated because their numbers were so few.

1946   Secretary of the Navy ordered all naval ratings opened to all sailors regardless of race. For the first time, black women were able to enlist in the Navy and were integrated into the WAVES assignment system.

1947   Army-Navy Nurse Act established Army and Navy Nurse Corps as permanent staff corps of the branches and integrated nurses into the officer ranks of those two services, with full military privileges.

1948   Air Force established as a separate branch, derived from the Army Air Corps. Women were fully integrated with the exception of the ability to fly aircraft, one of the main missions of the Air Force.

Women's Armed Services Integration Act established the right of women to serve in the regular active peacetime forces of the armed services.

However, within the law, Title 10, USC 6015, prohibited Navy women from serving in naval vessels other than hospital ships and transports, as well as aircraft engaged in combat missions.

Title 10, USC 8549, prohibited women in the Air Force from serving on military aircraft engaged in combat missions.

Mary Agnes Hallaren, USA, became the first female regular Army officer as the director of the WAC. She was an early pioneer in the call for full integration of women into the army.

1949   The Air Force Nurse Corps was established.

1950   In August, for the first time in history, the women reserves were mobilized for the Korean War, where the number of women Marines on active duty reached peak strength of 2,787. Like the women of two previous wars, they stepped into stateside jobs and freed male Marines for combat duty.

The first direct commissions into the WAC were offered to women college graduates.

1951   Defense Advisory Committee on Women in the Armed Services (DACOWITS) was established. This committee proved to be a strong and powerful supporter of women. Ironically, this same year, Executive Order 10240 authorizes the service branches to discharge any women who becomes pregnant or becomes a parent by adoption or by marriage to a single father.

1952   Navy women were accepted for commission in the Medical Service Corps.

Ceremony at the White House commemorated the first issue of U.S. Postal Service stamp honoring women in the military.

1953   Female hospital corpsmen began serving on hospital ships and transports. Prior to this, the only women assigned to ships were nurses.

1960   National Aeronautics and Space Administration (NASA) selected and tested 25 women for the space program; 13 passed all the same tests and requirements of the male astronauts, but they never made it into space. Those women were Jerrie Cobb, Bernice Steadman, Janey Hart, Jerri Truhill, Rhea Woltman, Sarah Ratley, Jan and Marion Dietrich, Myrtle Cagle, Irene Leverton, Gene Nora Jessen, Jean Hixson, and Wally Funk. Of this group, only Jerrie Cobb successfully completed all three phases of testing. However, all passed the same tests and requirement that the Mercury 7 men did.

Chief Master Sgt. Grace Peterson, USAF, became the first female chief master sergeant. At the time of her promotion, Peterson was the first sergeant of a four-hundred-person Women in the Air Force (WAF) squadron at McGuire Air Force Base, New Jersey.

1967   Public Law 90–130 amended Title 10 USC equalizing promotion and retirement rules for male and female officers. This law removed several restrictions on the career opportunities for military women, particularly the ceilings on promotion. This opened positions for women to general and flag ranks and removed the 2-percent ceiling for women on active duty.

              March 18: Master Sergeant Barbara J. Dulinsky, USMC, who had volunteered for duty in Vietnam, reported to the Military Assistance Command in Saigon—the first woman Marine ordered to a combat zone. A total of 28 enlisted women and 8 women officers served in Vietnam.

1968   Sergeant Major Yzetta Nelson, USA, became the first woman promoted to command sergeant major.

1969   The Air Force opened ROTC to women.

1970   The Army promoted both Anna Mae Hays, chief of the Army Nurse Corps, and Elizabeth Hoisington, director of WAC, to brigadier general.

1971   The Air Force promoted both Jeanne Holm, director of WAF, and E. Ann Hoefly, chief of the Air Force Nurse Corps, to brigadier general.

1972   Equal Rights Amendment was passed by Congress and ushers in many changes in both civil and military law and policies in anticipation of its ratification by the states.

              Army and Navy opened ROTC to women.

              The Navy promoted Alene B. Duerk, chief of the Navy Nurse Corps, to rear admiral.

              Frontiero v. Richardson Supreme Court decision struck down as unconstitutional differences in dependent's benefits between male and female service members. Prior to this ruling, a woman could not claim her husband as a military dependent unless he was unable to work and depended on her for his livelihood.

              The Navy opened additional occupational fields to women, such as intelligence, cryptology, public affairs, and maintenance; began assigning women other than nurses to the hospital ship USS *Sanctuary;* opened the Chaplain Corps and Civil Engineering Corps to women; and authorized Pilot Program Scholarships for women who committed to serving four years of active duty.

1973   End of the draft and beginning of the AVF. Congress authorized legislation ending the women's reserve as a separate entity in the Coast Guard, allowing women to serve on active duty in both the regular and reserve components. This same year, the

Coast Guard opened officer candidate school to women, becoming the first service to do so.

Navy women became eligible for duty in noncombatant aircraft. The Navy accepts its first female chaplain, Lt. Florence Dianna Pohlman. Lt. Pohlman is the first female chaplain in any service.

The Army authorized WAC enlistees to enter parachute rigger training.

1974   A Navy woman, Lt. Barbara Allen Rainey, became the first woman pilot in the military in February. She was also the first woman jet pilot in the Navy. She was killed in an aircraft crash in 1982 while performing her duties as a flight instructor

Army women became eligible for duty in noncombatant aircraft. The Army's first female military pilot was Second Lt. Sally D. Woolfolk, who received her wings to fly UH-1 Huey helicopters on June 4.

Congress reduced the minimum enlistment age for women to coincide with men.

1975   The Army authorized the admission of women to Army Officer Candidate School (OCS) training at Ft. Benning, Georgia.

The Coast Guard announced it would accept female applicants for the Coast Guard Academy class entering July 1976. The women would receive the same training as the male cadets, including going to sea aboard the training barque *Eagle*.

In October, President Gerald Ford signed legislation authorizing women's admission to the Federal Service Academies: the Military Academy at West Point, the Naval Academy in Annapolis, and the Air Force Academy in Colorado Springs.

The Secretary of Defense ended the involuntary discharge of pregnant women and mothers from the military.

Donna M. Tobias was the first woman to become a U.S. Navy Deep Sea Diver. She worked on search and salvage operations, underwater repairs of surface ships and submarines, and on the conversion of two barges into diving and salvage liftcraft. She also served as a submarine escape instructor, hyperbaric chamber operator, and a SCUBA instructor at a Navy SCUBA diving school. In the late 1970s she participated in leading-edge hyperbaric treatments for medical purposes and the evaluation of one-person portable recompression chambers.

1976   The Navy promoted its first line officer, Fran McGee, to rear admiral.

Navy women attended Aviation OCS.

The first classes of women reported to the Coast Guard, naval, military, and air force academies.

1977   Sergeant Cheryl Sterns, United States Army Reserve (USAR), became the first woman member of the Army's Golden Knights parachute team. Sgt. Sterns goes on to hold the most women's skydiving championships and world records and is entered in the *Guinness Book of World Records* for completing the most parachute jumps in 24 hours at 352 jumps.

Air Force women became eligible for duty in noncombatant aircraft.

The Coast Guard assigned women to shipboard duty. The high-endurance Coast Guard cutters *Morgenthau* and *Gallatin* were selected to receive 10 enlisted women and 2 female officers each.

Ensign Janna Lambine, USCG, became the first woman helicopter pilot in the Coast Guard.

Army Combat Exclusion Policy kept women out of specialties or units that involve direct combat.

In November, Congress passed PL 95–202, authorizing veteran status for WASPs.

1978   The Coast Guard removed all assignment restrictions based on gender. All billets and occupations are open to qualified women.

In *Owens v. Brown*, probably the most important decision affecting women in the Navy, District Judge John Sirica, U.S. District Court for the District of Columbia, ruled that Title 10, USC 6015, was unconstitutional. The attorney who pursued the class-action suit was Ruth Bader Ginsberg. Both Sirica and Ginsberg would later serve on the U.S. Supreme Court.

As part of the FY 1979 Defense Authorization Act, Title 10, USC 6015, was amended to allow the assignment of women to noncombatant ships and temporary duty to any ship not expected to perform a combat mission.

Colonel Margaret Brewer, United States Marine Corps (USMC), became the first woman appointed to brigadier general in the Marine Corps.

The first enlisted women, one from each of the five Armed Services, debut as members of the White House Honor Guard. Three of the five were Army Specialist 4 (SP/4) Christine Crews, Air Force Sergeant Elizabeth Foreman, and Navy Seaman Catherine Behnke.

The Navy introduces a new warfare community, special operations officer. These officers have three specialty areas—diving and salvage, explosive ordnance disposal (EOD), and expendable ordnance management. Women are authorized to compete for this specialty area.

1979   LtJG Beverly Kelley, USCG, became the first women to command a U.S. military vessel—the USCGC *Cape Newhagen*, a 14-person, 95-foot patrol boat operating out of Maui, Hawaii—on April 1, 1979. Kelley was one of the first women officers assigned to the Coast Guard cutter *Morgenthau*.

Naval Flight Officer program opened to women.

Lt. and naval reservist Donna Lynn Spruill became the first woman Naval aviator to obtain carrier qualification on board the USS *Independence* (CVN 40) in a fixed-wing aircraft. She later became a pilot for Delta airlines.

The Marine Corps assigned women as embassy guards.

Brigadier General (BG) Hazel W. Johnson, USA, became the first African American woman general officer upon becoming chief of the Army Nurse Corps.

Ensign Susan Trukken, USN, became the first woman special operations officer, a navy diving and salvage specialist. She eventually qualifies as a saturation diver, the first woman to do so.

Ensign Susan Fitzgerald, USN, became the first women to qualify as an EOD officer in the Navy.

1980   Roberta "Bobbi" McIntyre, USN, became the first woman to obtain surface warfare officer (SWO) qualification in January.

Defense Officer Personnel Management Act (DOPMA) was signed and abolished a separate personnel system for women officers in the Army, Navy, and Marine Corps, equalizing those branch personnel procedures with men in the armed services. The unfortunate repercussion was that women now competed with men for jobs and promotions but were handicapped by restrictions on assignment to certain occupations and billets, thus reducing, rather than improving, their promotion opportunities.

Sgt. Maj. Eleanor L. Judge, who enlisted in the Marine Corps in 1949, was appointed as the sergeant major of Marine Corps Base Camp Pendleton. This feat made her the first female Marine to be appointed to this post.

1981   In *Rostker v. Goldberg,* the Supreme Court upheld the constitutionality of excluding women from the draft and selective service registration. The reasoning behind this ruling was that the draft was to conscript men for combat duty; since women could not serve in combat, there was no discrimination in their exclusion.

1982   The Navy authorized women pilots for the jet pipeline and to become "carrier qualified."

1983   Public Law 98–160 was passed, establishing the Secretary of Veterans Affairs Advisory Committee on Women Veterans.

The Army put Direct Combat Probability Coding (DCPC) into effect, mirroring the Air Force's and Navy's interpretation of the combat exclusion laws. This policy is tested later in the year during Operation Urgent Fury. Despite numerous occasions in which support personnel directly come in contact with the enemy, the Army continues to officially stand by this policy.

Lt. Colleen Nevius, USN, became the first woman to graduate from the Navy's Test Pilot School at Patuxent River Naval Air Station, Maryland. Her graduation was understood to open many other doors for women aviators—including selection as astronauts, since this was a NASA requirement at the time.

In October, integrated Army units deployed to Grenada on Operation Urgent Fury. About 170 female soldiers served in the operation including military police, helicopter pilots, crew chiefs, maintenance personnel, intelligence specialists, truck drivers, and medical personnel.

1984   All Navy Operational Air Reconnaissance (VP) squadrons opened to women.

The Navy commissioned its first ship designed and built from the ground up as a gender-neutral platform—the USS *Safeguard* ARS-50, a salvage ship. Four ships were eventually commissioned in this class, including USS *Grasp,* USS *Salvor,* and USS *Grapple.* About 25 percent of the approximately 90-person crew included women sailors and officers.

1985   The House of Representatives approved HR 1378, granting federal land at Arlington Cemetery for a memorial to women in military service. The Women in Military Service for America (WIMSA) memorial opened in 1997.

1986   Lt. Susan Cowan, USN, a special operations officer (diver), became the first woman assigned as XO afloat, aboard the USS

Quapaw (ATF 110). Lt. Cowan was in the first class of women at the Naval Academy, graduating in 1980.

1987   In order to help retain women surface warfare officers, who found their career paths stymied after their initial sea tours on board noncombatant and mostly non-seagoing tenders (AR, AD, AS), the Navy opened billets on 17 replenishment ships and 3 maritime prepositioning ships.

1988   The Navy opened 24 Combat Logistics Force ships to women.

Senior Chief Boatswain's Mate Diane Bucci, USCG, became the first enlisted woman to command afloat when she became officer in charge of the tugboat, USCGC *Capstan*. USCGC *Capstan* patrolled the upper Potomac River and Chesapeake Bay conducting search and rescue, law enforcement, aids to navigation, and environmental protection missions.

Commander (CDR) Debra Guernes, USN, became the first woman selected for command at sea. One of the first women surface warfare officers, she took command of USS *Cimarron* (AO 177) in 1991.

Lieutenant Commander (LCDR) Kathryn Sullivan, USNR, was the first woman selected to be a Navy astronaut. She earned her PhD in geology from Dalhousie University in 1978. The first American woman to walk in space, Dr. Sullivan is a veteran of three shuttle missions with over 532 hours in space. She is a 2004 inductee to the Astronaut Hall of Fame as well as a 2008 inductee into the Women Divers Hall of Fame. She is a captain (O6) oceanography officer in the naval reserve for the National Oceanic and Atmospheric Administration (NOAA).

Capt. Jacquelyn S. "Jackie" Parker, United States Air Force Reserve (USAFR), was the first woman Air Force pilot to attend U.S. Air Force Test Pilot School at Edwards Air Force Base, California. In addition to a number of other firsts, in 1994 the New York Air National Guard offered her a slot in F-16s, and she became the first women to qualify as a combat pilot in that airframe.

1989   During the invasion of Panama in Operation Just Cause, Captain Linda Bray USA, of the 519th MP Battalion, led a platoon of military police in an attack against a Panamanian Defense Forces compound near Panama City. Almost 800 women participated, constituting about 4 percent of the total force. At least 150 were in combat areas, some coming under enemy fire and some returning fire. Bray became a celebrity after leading her unit in capturing a concealed weapons storage location in a half-hour firefight. Controversy ensued due to the combat exclusion policy, and the Pentagon played down her story. Facing persistent harassment after the episode, Bray left the Army in 1991.

Cadet Kristin Baker became the first woman brigade commander and captain of the West Point Corps of Cadets at the U.S. Military -Academy.

Aviation Machinist's Mate Airman Apprentice Joni Navarez, USN, became the first woman sailor to graduate from the Rescue Swimmer School.

1990   The military had been gearing up for Operation Desert Storm in the Persian Gulf since August; almost forty-one thousand women deploy.

Commander Rosemary Mariner, USN, became the first women aviator to command a navy aircraft squadron (VAQ-34). Mariner was with the first group of women to go to flight school in 1973, was the first military woman to fly a tactical jet (A-4 Skyhawk), and was an avid advocate for equal rights for women in the military even while she was still serving.

In December, LCDR Darlene M. Iskra, USN, a navy diver, is the first woman to command a commissioned naval vessel when she takes over as commanding officer of USS *Opportune* (ARS-41) in Naples harbor. Her ship also served during Operation Desert Storm in the eastern Mediterranean.

1991   During Operation Desert Storm, 15 women are killed and 2 are taken as POWs. One of the prisoners, Major Rhonda Cornum, USAF, a flight surgeon, would eventually be promoted to brigadier general.

Lt. Pamela Davis Dorman, USN, became the first female chaplain deployed to a war zone with the U.S. Marine Corps.

The Kennedy-Roth Amendment to the 1991 Defense Authorization Act repealed the provisions of Title 10, USC 8549, allowing women to serve aboard combat aircraft engaged in combat missions.

Midshipman Julianne Gallina was the first woman to be named brigade commander, U.S. Naval Academy.

1992   LCDR Barbara Scholley, USN, a navy diver, became the first woman to assume command of a Reserve ship, USS *Bolster* (ARS-38). Scholley went on to have an important career as a salvage diver, overseeing the recovery of the turret of the USS

Monitor a historic civil war wreck as the Navy's on-scene commander in 2002.

BG Carol A. Mutter USMC, became the first woman to assume command of a Fleet Marine Force unit when she assumed command of the Third Force Service Support Group in Okinawa.

1993   Secretary of Defense Les Aspin ordered all the service branches to open combat aviation to women; he directed the Navy to draft legislation to repeal the combat ship exclusion, Title 10, USC 6015, and directed the Army and the Marine Corps to review their billet structure with an eye toward opening more assignments to women.

The Navy opened enlisted aircrew positions in shore-based combat squadrons; Second, Third, and Seventh Fleet Afloat Staffs; and afloat on Oilers (AO), Ammunition Ships (AOE), Landing Craft Carriers (LCC), and Food Stores (AFS) ships.

A transition board approved 17 female naval aviators for transition to combat aircraft. The first two women who reported to Tactical Electronic Warfare Squadron 130 were Lt. Shannon Workman, USN, pilot, and Lt. Terry Bradford USN, naval flight officer (NFO). Lt. Workman became the first woman pilot to qualify for night landing on a carrier and subsequently became the first woman combat pilot to successfully pass fleet carrier qualifications in the EA-6B Prowler.

In May, the Air Force announced all aircraft assignments were open to women.

Congress repealed Title 10, USC 6015, in the FY 94 Defense Authorization Bill, opening most naval vessels to women. Submarines and smaller patrol ships remained closed due to space constraints.

CDR Jane Odea, CDR Lin Hutton, CDR Rosemary Mariner USN, and Naval Reserve CDR Joellen Oslund were the first women aviators selected for promotion to captain.

Lt. Col. Patricia Fornes, USAF, became the first woman to command a combat squadron upon taking over the 740th Missile Squadron, Minot Air Force Base, North Dakota.

Sheila Widnall was named Secretary of the Air Force during the Clinton Administration, the first and only woman to be so named to this date.

Senior Chief Mary Bonnin, USN, became the first (and so far only) woman to qualify as Master Diver in the U.S. Navy.

1994   In February, the Navy notified Congress that all aviation squadrons, the Naval Construction Force "Seabees," and all classes of ships with the exception of submarines, mine counter measure ships (MCM), coastal mine hunters (MHC), and coastal patrol craft (PC) were open to women.

The U.S. Naval Academy revised the service selection policy and, for the first time, women midshipmen were required to select warfare specialties under the same guidance as men. On service-selection day, 63 women midshipmen chose surface warfare for their future career.

USS *Dwight D. Eisenhower* (CVN 69) became the Navy's first integrated combatant and deployed to the Persian Gulf with a mixed gender crew. Sixty-three women received permanent assignment orders to the ship; Radioman First Class Terry Pelletier, USN, was the first to receive her orders. The first two Navy women F/A-18 pilots flew combat missions from the USS *Eisenhower* as they enforced the no-fly zone over southern Iraq.

Major Jackie Parker became the first woman Air National Guard F-16 combat pilot. First Lt. Jeannie Flynn became the first USAF female F-15E combat pilot.

Petty Officer Margaret Cooper, USN, the first woman underwater "Seabee," graduated with honors from Underwater Seabee Navy Dive School.

BG Mutter, USMC, became the first woman major general in the Marine Corps and the most senior woman on active duty in the Armed Forces.

1995   LCDR Mary Townsend-Manning, USN, became the first woman to complete submarine engineering duty officer qualifications and became eligible to wear "dolphins."

CAPT Lin V. Hutton, USN, became the first woman to assume command of a Naval Air Station, NAS Key West.

USS *Benfold* (DDG 65) was delivered as the first combat ship to be built, keel up, with habitability modifications necessary for full gender integration.

Major Sarah M. Deal became the Marine Corps' first woman pilot. She flies the CH-53E Super Stallion, the military's largest helicopter.

Colonel Eileen Collins, USAF, became the first woman pilot of a space shuttle, Discovery (February 3–11, 1995), on the first flight of the new joint Russian-American Space Program. Mission highlights included the rendezvous with the Russian Space

Station Mir, the operation of Spacehab, the deployment and retrieval of an astronomy satellite, and a space walk.

1996   The USS *Hopper* (DDG 70) was commissioned and named for Rear Admiral (RDML) Grace Murray Hopper, a leading pioneer in the field of computer technology. USS *Hopper* is the first warship since WWII, and the second in the Navy's history, to be named for a woman from the Navy's ranks.

LtJG Erica Niedermeier, USN, ordnance officer, was one of two officers who supervised the strike team on USS *Laboon* (DDG-58) that fired eight Tomahawk cruise missiles at Iraq as part of the joint service strike against Saddam Hussein. She is one of 22 women assigned to the ship's crew of 340. The missile strikes were the first time female sailors took part in combat operations since the Navy opened warship assignments to women in 1994.

CAPT Roseanne Milroy, Nurse Corps, Navy (NC), USNR, became the first Nurse Corps officer to command a fleet hospital—the Naval Reserve Fleet Hospital 23 in Minneapolis, Minnesota.

CAPT Bonnie B. Potter, Medical Corps (MC), USN, became the first female physician in the Navy, Army, or Air Force to be selected for flag rank.

Vice Admiral (VADM) Pat Tracey, USN, was the first woman in the military promoted to three stars, thus becoming the senior woman in the military.

Lt. Gen. Mutter made history again when she became the first female Marine to wear three stars.

1997   RADM Bonnie Potter, MC, USN, became the first woman to assume command of National Naval Medical Center Bethesda.

Female Marines begin attending Marine Combat Training, allowing them the same combat training opportunities as men.

COL Maureen LeBoeuf, USA, was appointed professor and head of the department of physical education at the U.S. Military Academy, the first woman named head of an academic department and "Master of the Sword."

Lt. Gen. Claudia Kennedy, USA, an intelligence officer, became the Army's first female three-star general.

Sgt. Heather Johnson, USA, became the first woman to stand watch at the Tomb of the Unknowns, Arlington National Cemetery.

1998   Five female surface warfare officers were selected to command combatant ships; CDR Maureen Farren, USN, was the first woman to command a surface combatant, USS *Mt. Vernon* (LSD 39) in June.

CDR Kathleen McGrath, USN, assumed command of USS *Jarrett* (FFG 33) in December.

CAPT Deborah Loewer, USN, was the first woman selected for a major afloat command; she assumed command of USS *Camden* (AOE 2) in December. Loewer went on to become the Navy's first warfare-qualified female rear admiral in 2003. She retired in 2006.

Lt. Kendra Williams, USN, F/A-18 pilot, was credited as the first female pilot to launch missiles in combat. She was flying in support of Operation Desert Fox.

1999   In March, CDR Michelle Howard, USN, assumed command of USS *Rushmore* (LSD 47). She was the first African American woman to assume command of a surface combatant. A 1982 Naval Academy graduate, Howard was the first woman graduate selected for RDML, in 2008.

MHC- and MCM-class ships were opened to female officers and enlisted. *Cormorant* and *Kingfisher* were the first to receive enlisted women.

Colonel Eileen Collins, USAF, was the first woman shuttle commander, of STS-93 *Columbia* (July 23–27, 1999). STS-93 deployed the Chandra X-Ray Observatory; the telescope has enabled scientists to study exotic phenomena such as exploding stars, quasars, and black holes.

Lt. Gen. Leslie F. Kenne, USAF, became the Air Force's first female three-star general. For the first time in history, all of the DoD services have women at this rank.

2000   Tech. Sgt. Jeanne M. Vogt, USAF, became the first enlisted female to ever receive the Cheney Award. She is credited with saving a woman who suffered a seizure while aboard a civilian aircraft.

Three Navy women divers were inducted into the inaugural Women Divers Hall of Fame; CAPT Marie E. Knafelc, Medical Corps, Diving Medical Officer; CAPT Karin Lynn, Civil Engineer Officer; CAPT Bobbie Scholley, Deep Sea Diving Officer.

2002   Master Chief Jacqueline DiRosa, USN, became the first female force master chief for the Bureau of Medicine and Surgery.

Major Martha McSally, USAF, successfully spearhead legislation that prohibits military women from wearing the abaya and by default the burka, in Muslim countries.

2003   Navy opened Sea Operational Detachments to women.

Master Chief Beth Lambert, USN, became the first female command master chief of an aircraft carrier, USS *Theodore Roosevelt* (CVN 71). She was one of the Navy's first female aviation structural mechanics, the first woman named Sailor of the Year, a member of the first class of female chiefs to deploy on an aircraft carrier, and, perhaps most significant, the first female to serve aboard a carrier as command master chief—the highest-ranking enlisted sailor onboard.

2004   The commanding officer billet aboard Coastal Patrolcraft (PC) opens to female officers.

Army BG Rebecca Halstead (USMA '81) became the first woman graduate of any federal service academy to attain the rank of general officer. Before the end of the year, BG Anne Macdonald (USMA '80) became the second.

Command Sergeant Major Cynthia Pritchett, USA, was named as the Army's first and only female command sergeant major of a sub-unified combatant command, serving as the principle enlisted advisor to Lt. Gen. David Barno for Combined Forces Command—Afghanistan from May 9, 2004, to April 5, 2006.

2005   Lt. Marissa McClure, USN, reported as the first female CO of a PC.

RDML Wendi Carpenter, USN, became the second female warfare-qualified flag officer and the first female aviator of that rank.

2006   Master Chief Jacqueline DiRosa, USN, became the first female fleet master chief at U.S. Fleet Forces Command, Norfolk, Virginia.

VADM Vivian Crea, USCG, became the first Coast Guard three-star admiral. Assigned as deputy commandant of the Coast Guard, she became the first woman to reach that position.

Mass Communication Specialist MC1(SW) Jackey Bratt, USN, became the first female combat photographer to be awarded the Bronze Star for her service in Iraq at the Navy Expeditionary Combat Command.

Capt. Nicole Malachowski, USAF, became the first female Thunderbird pilot. The Thunderbirds are the Air Force's air demonstration squadron.

2007   In January, Sgt. Maj. Barbara J. Titus, USMC, became the first female sergeant major of Marine Corps Installations West, a command overseeing seven installations west of the Mississippi River.

2008   General Ann Dunwoody, USA, a logistics specialist, became the first female four-star General officer in the military.

Maj. Jennifer Grieves, USMC, became the first female pilot of Marine One, the president's helicopter. On her last duty day, in July 2009, she made history again by convening the first all-female flight crew for President Obama. Maj. Grieves was the pilot, Maj. Jennifer Marino of Palisade, Colorado, was the copilot, and Sgt. Rachael A. Sherman of Traverse City, Michigan, was crew chief.

2009   WASP were awarded the Congressional Gold Medal.

Women have done some amazing things and have come a long way since the Army and Navy Nurse Corps were considered, in the hierarchy of the military, beneath Army mules. Military women have proven their worth to the military over and over again. They join when they are needed, they join to pursue the same goals as men, and they join because they are patriotic citizens. Even though there are still structural limitations to their service, women continue to pursue their dreams, work hard toward their goals, and provide a needed service to our country. We should salute each and every one.

Annotated Bibliography

General

DePauw, Linda Grant. *Battle Cries and Lullabies: Women in War from Pre-History to the Present*. Norman: University of Oklahoma Press, 1998. A historically researched book that covers women in war throughout history. Well written, it provides a historical context for the current debates about women's roles in the military, particularly women in combat. This book shows that women have participated in warfare from the earliest available historical accounts.

DePauw, Linda Grant. *Seafaring Women*. Boston, MA: Houghton Mifflin, 1982. A historical look at seagoing women, including some of the lore regarding women at sea and stories of women pirates, whalers, traders, and others.

Deborah G. Douglas, *American Women and Flight Since 1940*. Lexington: University Press of Kentucky, 2004. A historical look at women in aviation, both military and civilian, during WWII and the second half of the 20th century. This book has some very good information about the women in civilian aviation organizations, women in the aviation industry, the WASPs, the demobilization after the war, how the women's movement affected women in aviation and in space, and a look at the possibilities for the future of women in aviation.

Ebbert, Jean, and Mary-Beth Hall. *Crossed Currents: Navy Women in a Century of Change*, 3rd ed. Washington, DC: Brassey's, 1999. The history of women in the Navy, from the Yeoman (F) in WWI through the changes that occurred with women in combat ships in the mid-to-late 1990s.

Ebbert, Jean, and Mary-Beth Hall. *The First, the Few, the Forgotten: Navy and Marine Corps Women in World War I*. Annapolis, MD: Naval Institute Press, 2002. This book takes a specific look at the service of women in the Navy and Marine Corps during WWI, exploring the diversity of military duties the women performed, as well as documenting the various policies and challenges the women faced.

Feinman, Ilene Rose. *Citizenship Rites: Feminist Soldiers and Feminist Antimilitarists*. New York: New York University Press, 2000. The feminist perspective on citizenship, women's rights, and women in the military.

Franke, Linda Bird. *Ground Zero: The Gender Wars in the Military.* New York: Simon & Schuster, 1997. Though somewhat dated, Franke provides an analysis of some of the issues regarding women in the military in the 1990s, including pregnancy, family issues, women in combat, Tailhook, sexual harassment, and women at the service academies.

Fraser, Antonia. *The Warrior Queens.* New York: Alfred A. Knopf, 1989. A must read for women who enjoy history, this highly researched book reads like a historical novel. Women have truly been a part of history through the ages, but their accomplishments have been devalued and forgotten. This book brings the glorious history of women in the military to life.

Gavin, Lettie. *American Women in World War 1: They Also Served.* Niwot, CO: University Press of Colorado, 1997. A complete and well-researched book about all of the different groups of American women who went overseas to France, Belgium, and Britain during WWI. The book also includes a list of all the women who were injured or killed, noncombat deaths, and all the decorations received.

Harrell, Margaret, and Laura Miller. *New Opportunities for Military Women: Effects upon Readiness, Cohesion, and Morale.* Santa Monica, CA: RAND, 1997. Empirically researched report on whether women adversely affect military readiness. Findings indicate they do not, but there are concerns with double standards and physical strength requirements.

Haynsworth, Leslie, and David Toomey. *Amelia Earhart's Daughters: The Wild and Glorious Story of American Women Aviators from World War II to the Dawn of the Space Age.* New York: William Morrow, 1998. Stories of female aviators, from the early days of WWII as ferry pilots to the recent contributions of our female astronauts.

Herbert, Melissa S. *Camouflage Isn't Only for Combat.* New York: New York University Press, 1998. A study of how military women negotiate their gender in the masculine workplace through various gendered behaviors and appearances.

Holm, Jeanne. *Women in the Military: An Unfinished Revolution.* Rev. ed. Novato, CA: Presidio Press, 1992. A thoroughly researched book on the history of American women in the military from the American Revolution until the end of the Gulf War in 1991. This book is the first source to read prior to any deeper research on military women.

Honey, Maureen. *Creating Rosie the Riveter: Class, Gender, and Propaganda during World War II.* Amherst: University of Massachusetts Press, 1984. A study of how the government used the media to rally women to step up as industrial workers, volunteers, and military members during WWII. This includes the related propaganda campaign to get women back into homes after the war. Discusses issues of women and work, race, and the normative middle-class values of America.

Iskra, Darlene M. *Breaking through the Brass Ceiling: Strategies of Success for Elite Military Women.* Saarbrücken, Germany: VDM Verlag Dr. Müller Aktiengesellschaft & Co. KG, 2008. This book is an academic study of women general and flag officers (GFO) in all five of the armed services, whether retired, reserve, or on active duty. It discusses what it takes to become a GFO in terms of jobs, attitudes, and work and family balance.

Kerber, Linda K. *No Constitutional Right to be Ladies: Women and the Obligations of Citizenship*. New York: Hill and Wang, 1998. A thoroughly researched work discussing the rights and obligations of citizenship and the long, slow road of women's citizenship status—from coverture to service in the military and everything in between.

Manning, Lory. *Women in the Military: Where they Stand*. 6th ed. Washington, DC: Women's Research and Education Institute, 2008. A small pamphlet that gives demographic information on women in the military, both current and historically.

Moore, Brenda. *To Serve My Country, To Serve My Race*. New York: New York University Press, 1996. The history of the only female African American unit to deploy to Europe in WWII, it is also a treatise on the history of African American service during and after the war. It discusses issues such as training, integration, morale, unit cohesion, sexuality, and death. Excellent research on an important part of Army history.

Moore, Brenda. *Serving Our Country: Japanese American Women in the Military during World War II*. New Brunswick, NJ: Rutgers University Press, 2003. Catalogues the participation of Nisei women and their service as WACs and in the Army Medical Corps during WWII. Includes pre- and post-history and places it in a historical sociological context.

Morden, Bettie J. *The Women's Army Corps 1945–1978*. Washington, DC: United States Army Center for Military History, 1989. Provides the history of the WAC, from Victory over Japan (VJ) Day in 1945 and the quest for permanent status from 1945 to 1948 until 1978, when Congress disbanded the WAC and gender integrated the Army.

Norman, Elizabeth M. *We Band of Angels: The Untold Story of American Nurses Trapped on Bataan by the Japanese*. New York: Random House, 1999. This volume covers the WWII history of the Army and Navy nurses who were POWs under the Japanese in the Philippines.

Sarnecky, Mary T. *A History of the U.S. Army Nurse Corps*. Philadelphia: University of Pennsylvania Press, 1999. This historical account begins with women's service as nurses in the Revolutionary War and continues through the Vietnam Era. However, it particularly focuses on nursing in WWII.

Smolenski, Mary C., Donald G. Smith, Jr., and James S. Nanney. *A Fit, Fighting Force: The Air Force Nursing Services Chronology*. Washington, DC: Office of the Air Force Surgeon General, 2005. Chronology of the history of Air Force nursing from 1948 to 2005. Available online at http://www.airforcehistory.hq.af.mil/Publications/fulltext/NursePamforWeb.pdf.

Sterner, Doris M. *In and Out of Harm's Way: A History of the Navy Nurse Corps*. Seattle, WA: Peanut Butter Publishing, 1996. Sterner writes this history in chronological order by what occurred during the service of each of the Navy's superintendents of nursing—from 1798, before being officially sanctioned, and then from 1908 through 1996.

Verges, Marianne. *On Silver Wings: The Women Airforce Service Pilots of World War II 1942–1944*. New York: Ballentine Books, 1991. An historical look at the pioneering women who flew for the U.S. military in WWII—not as military personnel, but as civilians, without any of the benefits associated with being members of the military. They came from all walks of life and faced the same dangers as men while ferrying planes, towing targets, testing new aircraft, and performing many other noncombatant flying duties. Using private papers, personal interviews, and government files, Verges documents the adventurous women who volunteered to serve their country and their fight for veteran's status, which was granted in 1977.

Weitekamp, Margaret A. *Right Stuff, Wrong Sex: America's First Women in Space Program.* Baltimore, MD: The Johns Hopkins University Press, 2004. This is a well-researched book on the history of women's aviation from the 1940s and Jackie Cochran, through the training of the Mercury 13 women who were preparing along with John Glenn and the other Mercury astronauts to go into space, and the disappointing decision to discharge them out of the program.

Zimmerman, Jean. *Tailspin: Women at War in the Wake of Tailhook.* New York: Doubleday, 1995. This is a complete account of the scandal of Tailhook 1992, including an analysis of what contributed to the scandal and the fallout affecting the Navy as a result of the scandal. Much better reading than the actual Tailhook report, it provides background information and a look into the lives of the victims and the perpetrators.

Biographies

Adams-Ender, Clara, with Blair S. Walker. *My Rise to the Stars: How a Sharecropper's Daughter Became an Army General.* Lake Ridge, VA: CAPE Associates, 2001. General Adams-Ender is one of the few African Americans in the general officer ranks, male or female. She has written a delightful book about her life, her Army career as a nurse, and her realization that she had the "right stuff" to be a general but that a little politicking along the way would not hurt.

Barkalow, Carol, with Andrea Raab. *In the Men's House.* New York: Poseidon Press, 1990. One of the first women to graduate from West Point in the class of 1980, Barkalow documents the challenges the first classes faced, as well as her first few years in the Army. Barkalow made the Army a career, retiring as a colonel; this is the first part of her story.

Collins, Winifred Quick, with Herbert M. Levine. *More than a Uniform: A Navy Woman in a Navy Man's World.* Denton: University of North Texas Press, 1997. The autobiography of a woman who joined the Navy during WWII and her progression through the ranks until her retirement as a captain. If she had been a man, she would have been an admiral.

Cornum, Rhonda, as told to Peter Copeland. *She Went to War: The Rhonda Cornum Story.* Novato, CA: Presidio Press, 1992. The story of Cornum's life before, during, and after her time as a POW during Operation Desert Storm.

Cummings, Missy. *Hornet's Nest: The Experiences of One of the Navy's First Female Fighter Pilots.* San Jose, CA: Writer's Showcase, 1999. The autobiography of one of the first female fighter pilots in the military and her struggle for acceptance and credibility in the male fighter pilot fraternity.

Danner, Dorothy Still. *What a Way to Spend a War: Navy Nurse POWs in the Philippines*. Annapolis, MD: Naval Institute Press, 1995. The personal story of survival of the Navy nurses at Los Banos prison in the Philippines during WWII.

Dever, John P., and Maria C. Dever. *Women and the Military*. Jefferson, NC: McFarland, 1995. Selected biographies of women who served in the world's militaries from ancient times through wars and other conflicts until 1995. It also includes biographies of women who aided the military, such as Marie Curie (WWI) and Julia Child (who served in the OSS during WWII). Inclusion criteria included women "firsts"; women who had unusual experiences while in the military, such as Rhonda Cornum, a POW during the Gulf War of 1991 (Desert Storm); women who served as role models; and women who endured extraordinary prejudice. The biographies are primarily of American women, but there are also biographies of women who served in or aided other countries.

Disher, Sharon Hanley. *First Class: Women Join the Ranks at the Naval Academy*. Annapolis, MD: Naval Institute Press, 1998. The story of the struggles women endured to integrate the U.S. Naval Academy in the late 1970s.

Freedman, Dan, and Jacqueline Rhoads, eds. *Nurses in Vietnam: The Forgotten Veterans*. Austin, TX: Texas Monthly Press, 1987. This volume highlights the biographies of nine nurses who served in Vietnam between 1965 and 1971. Eight to ten thousand women served in Vietnam, the vast majority of them nurses, and eight women died. The stories run the gamut from frontline medical stations to rear-echelon rehabilitation hospitals.

Hancock, Joy Bright. *Lady in the Navy: A Personal Reminiscence*. Annapolis, MD: Naval Institute Press, 1972. Captain Joy Bright Hancock enlisted as a Yeoman (F) in WWI, worked for the Navy's Bureau of Aeronautics between the wars, and rejoined the Navy during WWII. During her second go-round, she was an officer, and she eventually became a Navy captain. As the assistant chief of Naval personnel for women, she was instrumental in the fight to make women a permanent part of the armed forces.

Holmstedt, Kirsten. *Band of Sisters: American Women at War in Iraq*. Mechanicsburg, PA: Stackpole Books, 2007. The stories of 12 women who served in Iraq, from pilots to gunners to nurses. The women are in combat; the women are warriors. Why does policy still preventing women from doing all they can do and being all they can be?

Hovis, Bobbi. *Station Hospital Saigon: A Navy Nurse in Vietnam 1963–1964*. Annapolis, MD: Naval Institute Press, 1992. Written by one of the four nurses tasked with converting a dilapidated apartment building into a hospital in just four days, this story is a rare look into the Vietnam War in the early days of the conflict.

Kennedy, Claudia J., with Malcolm McConnell. *Generally Speaking: A Memoir by the First Woman Promoted to Three-Star General in the United States Army*. New York: Warner Books, 2001. An excellent autobiography that highlights the general's early career, the challenges she faced and how she managed them, and her leadership philosophy. Written in an informative yet advisory tone, she manages to tell young officers what it takes to become a three-star general in the Army.

Ruff, Cheryl Lynn, and K. Sue Roper. *Ruff's War: A Navy Nurse on the Frontline in Iraq*. Annapolis, MD: Naval Institute Press, 2005. This book was written by a navy nurse, since retired, about her participation as a nurse anesthetist in a surgical company behind the frontline First Marine Expeditionary Force at the start of the war in Iraq in 2003. The story is reminiscent of an old episode of *MASH*, with helicopters bringing in wounded to the doctors and nurses waiting to provide care at the front lines. The teams had to make life-or-death decisions, often in terrible weather and unsanitary conditions. It provides a stark image of war and the amazing efforts needed to save lives.

Spears, Sally. *Call Sign Revlon: The Life and Death of Navy Fighter Pilot Kara Hultgreen*. Annapolis, MD: Naval Institute Press, 1998. The death of Kara Hultgreen in 1994 started a concerted effort by naval aviators to argue that women did not have the ability to fly fighter aircraft. Misinformation about her flying abilities was leaked to the press and to opponents of women in combat. Trying to set the record straight, this book is an account of Hultgreen and her short military career by a biased observer—her mother. However, she does a very good job of presenting her case using empirical evidence, such as her daughter's training records; journals; and interviews with friends, colleagues, and commanding officers to provide a real look at the woman whose death caused so much controversy.

Van Devanter, Lynda, with Christopher Morgan. *Home before Morning: The Story of an Army Nurse in Vietnam*. New York: Beaufort Books, 1983. One of the first books to come out in the wake of the Vietnam War, this is a story not just of Van Devanter's time in Vietnam but of the aftermath when she returned home: lack of understanding by her friends and family, divorce, and depression.

Williams, Kathleen Broome. *Improbable Warriors: Women Scientists and the U.S. Navy in World War II*. Annapolis, MD: Naval Institute Press, 2001. Williams traces the history of four women scientists who worked for the Navy during WWII: Mary Sears, oceanographer; Florence van Straten, meteorologist; Grace Murray Hopper, computer scientist; and Mina Spiegel Rees, science administrator. Williams demonstrates it takes more than guns and bullets to win a war as far reaching as WWII.

Williams, Kayla, with Michael E. Staub. *Love My Rifle More Than You: Young and Female in the U.S. Army*. New York: W.W. Norton & Co, 2005. This book is unusual in that it is written from the perspective of an enlisted women in Iraq. One of the first books to be written about women's experiences in the combat zone, Williams provides ample reason to believe that women have few problems performing their duties under wartime conditions. The biggest problem was the behavior of her fellow servicemen.

Wingo, Josette Dermody. *Mother Was a Gunner's Mate: World War II in the WAVES*. Annapolis, MD: Naval Institute Press, 1994. A personal story, told through a series of letters the author sent home while in the Navy. The story focuses on her experiences from boot camp to discharge and includes her outlook, the friendships she made, the work she did, and mischief she and her pals got themselves into. An entertaining look at the historical context of the war through a young woman's eyes.

Wise, James E., Jr., and Scott Baron. *Women at War: Iraq, Afghanistan, and Other Conflicts*. Annapolis, MD: Naval Institute Press, 2006. The biographies of individual women who served in Iraq, Afghanistan, Vietnam, Korea, and WWII.

Edited Sources

Blacksmith, E. A., ed. *Women in the Military*. New York: H.W. Wilson Company, 1992. This is an edited edition of articles about issues, both pro and con, important to military women in the early 1990s. Many of the issues have since been resolved, with the exception of the issue of women in ground combat.

Katzenstein, Mary Fainsod, and Judith Reppy, eds. *Beyond Zero Tolerance: Discrimination in Military Culture*. Lanham, MD: Rowman & Littlefield Publishers, 1999. An anthology of the issues and concerns of women in the military in regards to discrimination and sexual harassment.

Putko, Michele M., and Douglas V. Johnson II, eds. *Women in Combat Compendium*. Carlisle, PA: U.S. Army War College Strategic Studies Institute, 2008. A study of the women-in-combat issue from the perspective of both men and women in the Army War College class of 2006. Results show that ambivalence remains about women's roles in infantry, armor, and special operations, but also that other restrictions should be eliminated.

Seeley, Charlotte Palmer. *American Women and the U.S. Armed Forces: A Guide to the Records of Military Agencies in the National Archives*. Washington, D.C. National Archives and Record Administration. 1992. Compiled by Charlotte Palmer Seeley and revised by Virginia C. Purdy and Robert Gruber. This is a guide for researchers wishing to access records regarding women's military service, primarily federal records, but also those within certain presidential libraries.

Online History

Cathay Williams: Female Buffalo Soldier. http://www.buffalosoldier.net/CathayWilliams FemaleBuffaloSoldierWithDocuments.htm.

Center of Military History, United States Army. *Women in Army History*. http://www. history.army.mil/topics/women/Women-USA.htm.

John W. Listman. *Women in the Army National Guard*. National Guard Educational Foundation. 1998. http://www.ngef.org/tier.asp?bid=3.

Naval Historical Center. *Women in the U.S. Navy*. http://www.history.navy.mil/faqs/ faq48-1.htm.

Stremlow, Colonel Mary V., USMCR (ret.). *Free a Marine to Fight: Women Marines in World War II*. http://www.nps.gov/archive/wapa/indepth/extContent/usmc/ pcn-190-003129-00/index.htm.

U.S. Coast Guard, U.S. Coast Guard Historian's Office, *Women and the U.S. Coast Guard*. http://www.uscg.mil/history/WomenIndex.asp.

WASP on the Web. WASP Resources, http://wingsacrossamerica.us/wasp/resources/ index.htm.

Women in Vietnam. Numerous topics. http://www.illyria.com/vnwomen.html.

Online Bibliographies

Air University, Muir S. Fairchild Research Information Center. Bibliographies. Various bibliographies in alphabetical order, including *Women in Combat* and *Women in the Armed Forces*. http://www.au.af.mil/au/aul/bibs/bib97.htm#W.

Alliance for National Defense, Resources, Reading List,http://www.4militarywomen.org/Reading_List.htm.

All Navy Women's National Alliance, Recommended reading. http://anwna.com/reading.html.

Military Women in Books. http://userpages.aug.com/captbarb/books.html.

Naval History and Heritage Command. *Nurses in the U.S. Navy*. http://www.history.navy.mil/faqs/faq50-1.htm.

Naval History and Heritage Command. *Women in the U.S. Navy*. http://www.history.navy.mil/faqs/faq48-2.htm.

U. S. Coast Guard. *Women and the U.S. Coast Guard, A Historical Bibliography*. http://www.uscg.mil/history/uscghist/womenbib.asp.

Women are Veteran's Too! Recommended Reading, *Books on Military Women for Young Adults*. http://userpages.aug.com/captbarb/booksjuv.html.

Women in Military Service for America Memorial Foundation. History and Collections, Resources, Bibliography. http://www.womensmemorial.org/H&C/Resources/h&cresources.html.

Selected Web Sites for or about Military Women

Air Force Women Officers Association. http://www.afwoa.org/.

All Navy Women's National Alliance. http://anwna.com/.

Alliance for National Defense. http://www.4militarywomen.org/.

Army Nurse Corps Association. http://www.e-anca.org/.

Angell Productions, *Brave Women of Oceana: Women's History of the South Pacific Area*. http://www.angellpro.com.au/women.htm.

Defense Advisory Committee on Women in the Services. http://www.dtic.mil/dacowits/.

Harriet Tubman Historical Society. http://www.harriettubman.com/.

Military Women. http://www.militarywoman.org/.

Military Women Veterans, Yesterday–Today–Tomorrow. http://userpages.aug.com/captbarb/index.html.

The Minerva Center. A nonprofit educational center supporting the study of women in war and in the military. http://www.minervacenter.com/.

National Association of Black Military Women. http://www.nabmw.com/.

National WASP World War II Museum. http://waspmuseum.org/.

Navy Nurse Corps Association. http://www.nnca.org.

North Atlantic Treaty Organization. *Committee on Women in the NATO Forces*. http://www.nato.int/issues/women_nato/index.html.

Office of Navy Women's Policy. http://www.npc.navy.mil/AboutUs/BUPERS/WomensPolicy/.

Retired Army Medical Specialist Corps Association. http://www.ramsco.org.

Sea Service Leadership Association. http://www.sealeader.org/.

Society of Air Force Nurses. http://www.safn.org/.

United Female Veterans of America, Inc. http://www.ufva.us/.

U.S. Army Women's Foundation. http://www.awfdn.org.

U.S. Army Women's Museum. http://www.awm.lee.army.mil/.

U.S. Department of Veterans Affairs, Center for Women Veterans. http://www1.va.gov/womenvet/.

Veterans for America. *Resources for Military Women.* http://www.veteransforamerica.org/woundedwarrior/military-women/.

Vietnam Women's Memorial Project. http://www.vietnamwomensmemorial.org/.

The Virtual Wall: Vietnam Veterans Memorial. *American and Civilian Women Who Died in the Vietnam War (1959–1975).* http://www.virtualwall.org/women.htm.

WAVES National. http://womenofthewaves.com/wavesnational/index.htm.

Women in Military Service for America (WIMSA). http://www.womensmemorial.org/.

Women Marines Association. http://www.womenmarines.org/.

Women Military Aviators, Inc. http://www.womenmilitaryaviators.org

Women Military Reenactor's Homepage. http://www.geocities.com/womansoldier/.

Women Veterans of America. http://www.womenveteransofamerica.com/.

Women's Army Corps Veteran's Association. http://www.armywomen.org.

Women's Overseas Service League. http://www.wosl.org/.

Women's Research and Education Institute (WREI). http://www.wrei.org/.

Selected Oral History Projects

Library of Congress. *Veteran's History Project.* http://www.loc.gov/vets/.

The Rutgers Oral History Archives. World War II, Korea, Vietnam, Cold War. http://oralhistory.rutgers.edu/.

The Vietnam Center and Archive, Texas Tech University. *The Oral History Project of the Vietnam Archive.* http://www.vietnam.ttu.edu/oralhistory/.

Women in Military Service For America Memorial (WIMSA). History and Collections, *Women's Oral Histories.* http://www.womensmemorial.org/H&C/Oral_History/oralhistory.html.

Index

About the Author

DARLENE M. ISKRA completed her doctorate in sociology from the University of Maryland College Park. She is a retired Navy commander and has the distinction of being the first woman in the Navy to command a ship.